Social Justice and Adequate Housing

This book presents a critical analysis of the concept of "adequate housing".

While the concept of adequate housing is used largely as a normative standard in the protection of housing rights and in the implementation of housing policies, its apparent objectivity and universality have never been questioned by political and legal theory. This book analyses and challenges the understanding of this term in law and politics by investigating its relationship with the idea of "home". "It is necessary to provide them with adequate housing!" It is very common to hear this phrase when dealing with housing poverty, especially in relation to migrants, minorities, indigenous and other subaltern groups. But what does "adequate housing" mean? This book tackles this issue by proposing a critical analysis of this concept and of its use in the development of housing policies addressing the subaltern group *par excellence* in Europe, Roma. In so doing, it focuses on the lives of Roma and Sinti in Italy who have been the target of inclusion policies. Highlighting the emotional connection to housing, and dismantling some of the most "common sense" ideas about Roma, it offers a radical revision of how social justice in the housing sector might be refigured.

This book will be invaluable for scholars and students working on relevant themes in socio and critical legal studies, sociology, human rights, urban studies, human geography and Romani studies

Silvia Cittadini is a research fellow at the Department of Political and Social Sciences of the University of Bologna – Alma Mater Studiorum. She holds a PhD in Politics, Human Rights and Sustainability, obtained in 2019 at the Sant'Anna School of Advanced Studies of Pisa, and she has been a post-doctoral research fellow at the Romani Studies Program of the Central European University in Budapest and a research fellow at the European Centre for Minority Issues of Flensburg, Germany.

Social Justice and Adequate Housing

Rights, Roma Inclusion and the Feeling of Home

Silvia Cittadini

Routledge
Taylor & Francis Group
LONDON AND NEW YORK

First published 2021
by Routledge
2 Park Square, Milton Park, Abingdon, Oxon OX14 4RN

and by Routledge
605 Third Avenue, New York, NY 10158

Routledge is an imprint of the Taylor & Francis Group, an informa business

British Library Cataloguing-in-Publication Data
A catalogue record for this book is available from the British Library

Library of Congress Cataloging-in-Publication Data
A catalog record has been requested for this book

ISBN: 978-0-367-62360-9 (hbk)
ISBN: 978-1-032-02671-8 (pbk)
ISBN: 978-1-003-18453-9 (ebk)

DOI: 10.4324/9781003184539

Typeset in Bembo
by Taylor & Francis Books

Contents

Tables

Acknowledgements

This book is the product of years of research and theoretical reflection that brought me to travel extensively, to work in a number of institutions and to meet people whose contribution to this work has been crucial.

The roots of this work ground on my experience working in the nomad camps of Torino. I would like to thank all the persons that I met during that period and that guided me through the difficulties encountered by the inhabitants of the camps. This work is the product of a process that started back then, and I sincerely hope that it will contribute to shed light on the consequences of the deprivation of a home.

This work would not exist without the support and motivation that I have received within the Master in Democracy and Human Rights in South-East Europe (ERMA). In particular, I would like to thank Mersiha Behlulović who served as my academic tutor during the Master with dedication and positivity, motivating me to engage in this research and develop it further within a PhD.

The research here presented has been conducted during the years of my PhD in Politics, Human Rights and Sustainability at the Sant'Anna School of Advanced Studies of Pisa. All my gratitude goes to the colleagues and professors who contributed to this work with their suggestions and assistance. Special thanks go to my thesis's supervisor, Prof. Barbara Henry, for supporting my research project from the beginning and encouraging me also during the difficult moments. I would also like to thank the European Centre for Minority Issues and the Centre for Politics and Gender Studies of the University of Belgrade for hosting me during my research work.

The fieldwork conducted in Pisa, Messina and Trento-Rovereto owns much to the persons who have been involved in the study and who offered their availability and support. In this context, special thanks to Clelia Bargagli and Sultan Dibran of the Association Articolo 34 in Pisa, Alessandro Bezzi of the cooperative Kalediosco and Costanza Righetto of Gruppo 78 in Trento and Rovereto, Stefania La Malfa and the Association Bahtalo Drom in Messina, who took their time to arrange the interviews and to accompany me in the different locations. I would also like to express my most sincere gratitude to all the persons who gave their availability to be interviewed and particularly to those who opened their homes to me and shared personal aspects of their life stories.

The revision of the research work and the preparation of this monograph benefited greatly from the support received within the Romani Studies Program at the Central European University, where I have been granted a one-year post-doc fellowship. I would like therefore to thank the academic board of the Romani Studies Program for their support and trust in my work. Furthermore, I am grateful to Prof. Iulius Rostas and Dr Joanna Kostka for their precious feedbacks, which proved essential to improving my argument and work. I would also like to thank my editor at Routledge, Dr Colin Perrin, for his interest in publishing this monograph, his kindness and professionalism.

Least but not last, I would like to thank my parents for their continuous support through all these years, despite the numerous obligations that often kept me apart from them.

I would like, finally, to dedicate this work to the memory of Prof. Nicolae Gheorghe and Prof. Zdravko Grebo, who I had the honour to meet and whose humanity and activism, along with their academic rigour, greatly motivated my engagement in this field. I hope that their work and commitment will continue to inspire future generations of scholars.

Introduction

Roma inclusion as a starting point for a reflection on social justice and adequate housing

The origins of this book can be traced back in 2011, when, as a young graduate in Political Science, I was working for a small NGO operating in a nomad camp located at the outskirts of Torino, Italy. Here about 500 people lived, all Roma from former Yugoslavia, divided into three main groups along national lines. The camp was located approximately two kilometres away from the outskirts of the city, in an area enclosed between a river and the highway. It could be reached by car or by bus, which was stopping about 500 metres from the camp on the main road. After that, you had to walk the last distance on an unpaved street bringing you to the camp. The conditions of the structures were diverse: some had built a fully equipped wooden house, others had added a veranda to a caravan used as sleeping room, others had modified a shelter poorly built with scrap materials. Bathrooms were almost inexistent, heating was ensured through wood and some electric stoves, garbage was stored outside of the camp and it was not clear who was supposed to collect it and when.

This camp was one of the many created from the end of the 70s by Italian institutions, through regional laws. The idea was to provide local Romani nomads with halting sites where they could stop temporarily with their caravans before moving on with their trip. Their creation was the product of a mix of positive and negative stereotypes that presented Roma, on one side, as free and fascinating nomadic spirits always on the move and, on the other, as dirty Gypsies who leave a garbage dump behind them. The camps seemed to respond perfectly to both stereotypes: they provided a space where nomads could stop temporarily, and, at the same time, they prevented them from stopping in the city centres where the inhabitants would complain about their presence. Other than being evidently based in a deep-rooted anti-gypsysm that treated this group as something both exotic and dangerous, the creation of the nomad camps did not recognise the fact that most of the local Roma were going through a process of sedentarisation.

This was going to be speeded up by the system of the camps where local charity organisations – as the one I was working in – were operating to "help the poor Gypsies" to integrate into mainstream society, by sending their kids to school and by "supporting" them in a process of "de-romanisation". The transformation of the camps from temporary halting sites to permanent Romani

DOI: 10.4324/9781003184539-1

ghettos became irreversible in the 90s when the wars in Yugoslavia brought to Italy, among other refugees, a consistent number of Roma. This group, instead of being received through the usual humanitarian channels, was placed in camps. Since they were Roma, indeed, they were not considered and treated as refugees, but as "nomads who migrated to Italy with the excuse of the war". It did not matter the evident fact that they had never practiced nomadism and were used to live in brick-houses back in their countries. According to Italian authorities, their place was in the nomad camps. (Piasere, 2004; Piasere et al., 2014; Picker, 2011; Sigona, 2003, 2005, 2011; Sigona & Monasta, 2006; Tavani, 2012; Tosi Cambini, 2013)

Since then, Italy has been described as the "country of the camps", as far as Roma are concerned. It is therefore no coincidence that the housing issue is crucial when talking about their marginalisation or inclusion in the Italian context. This was also evident to me while working in the nomad camp of Torino, as this space affected all aspects of the life of its inhabitants, the camp being the main marker of a specific stereotyped idea of the "Roma". For those living in a camp, it was almost impossible to find a job, not only because of the physical difficulties caused by its marginality and precariousness, but especially because of its stigmatisation. For the same reason, kids living in the camp were marginalised most of the time in school by teachers and other children and were growing up with the awareness of inhabiting a space that others were afraid to enter, that was considered a "separate world". The relevance of the camp for their life was evident also in the fact that the house was the main topic of conversation. It could be a complaint about the poor structural conditions, or a display of the quality of the shelter just self-built, or the description of the house that was going to be built in the country of origin, or the hopes for exiting the camp. The house was central and the experience of the camp was showing me its relevance in all aspects of the life of the individual, beyond being a physical repair.

In the same period, Italian newspapers were filled with the latest evictions carried out by Italian municipalities against Roma. It was the period of the "nomad emergency", when the central government had adopted a national decree that presented this group as a "national emergency" and allowed large powers to local authorities to implement anti-Roma policies (*d.c.p.m. Dichiarazione dello stato di emergenza in relazione agli insediamenti di comunita' nomadi nel territorio delle regioni Campania, Lazio e Lombardia*, 2008). In that context, forced evictions and the dismantlement of nomad camps were among the most common and sensationalised initiatives. Almost every day the national news was commenting on the latest evictions, showing images of people dragged out with force from their poorly built shelters, these then destroyed by bulldozers. The recurrent public narrative did not only argue the necessity of getting rid of areas presented as "a danger for public health and security", but also implied a sort of "missionary" message: "those shelters are nothing but a pile of garbage inadequate for living – by evicting Roma living in camps, we are making a favour to them".

This narrative contrasted with my experience of the nomad camps. Almost every family dreamt of leaving the stigmatising and segregating condition of the camps, but, at the same time, made every effort to improve the current shelter where they have been living for years. Also, the desire of leaving the camp did not result in accepting every kind of accommodation. After all, all the investments in improving the quality of life in the camp could not be wasted for an accommodation that did not lead to a substantial improvement. And this meant many different things: four brick walls may have not been perceived as an improvement to a wooden shelter if the house did not have enough space for all the members of the family, or was located in an area away from the social and economic network necessary for survival, or was surrounded by non-Romani families that loudly complained for the arrival of Roma. Back then, I started realising the complexity and significance of the place of living and its emotional relevance, and I felt that this complexity was not displayed, but rather rejected, in the images of the evictions. Here, indeed, places charged with significance were simply divided between proper accommodation and inadequate shacks.

It was back then, therefore, that I started questioning an issue that went beyond the housing conditions of Roma, but concerned the way housing was conceived and protected in general: what is adequate? Who decides what is adequate or not? Imposing a housing solution to a person, while denigrating another as "inadequate", does not represent a form of violence or misrecognition?

Housing has always been treated as an issue regarding essentially redistribution. Its provision is largely ensured by housing markets, following the rules of demand and supply, while national welfare-states address risks of housing poverty with the provision of public housing and the regulation of the market. In this context, housing is considered an economic good meant to respond to basic biological needs, which are supposedly the same for everyone. Accordingly, social justice can be achieved by simply ensuring the access to housing that responds to a series of basic needs. None ever questioned the validity of these needs for everyone and the implications of their use. Namely, none questioned whether the protection and provision of housing designed around a series of basic needs could be really considered neutral in front of the variety of functions (physical, social, emotional, cultural, etc.) that housing ensures for the individual. This topic, therefore, never entered the debate on the politics of recognition that touched many other sectors, education *in primis*, questioning the neutrality of the structures regulating social life.

Nonetheless, this apparent disinterest appears surprising if we consider the fact that the topic of the dialogic relationship between the self-identity and the surrounding constructed space was already tackled by George Herbert Mead (Mead, 1934), whose work inspired one of the most important papers on the politics of recognition (Taylor, 1994). Taylor, nevertheless, did not give importance to the space, while focusing solely on the role of the "significant others" in the development of the self-identity. The work of Mead on identity and space was not forgotten, though, and led to the development of the discipline of environmental psychology, which exactly deals with the implications of their dialogical relationship (Proshansky et al., 1983). Furthermore, this topic has been addressed by numerous other authors from different disciplines in between geography, sociology and philosophy, whose work has been recollected within some recent publications on the matter (Blunt & Dowling, 2006; Richardson, 2019). All these authors reaffirmed the strict relationship between self-identity and the space of the house, highlighting how its design becomes a manifestation of the identity of the individual, which, in turn, is affected by the way the house is constructed and perceived by others.

Departing from these theoretical considerations, in this work I question how the concept of "adequate housing" is defined and used in law and policy discourses and how it affects the implementation of policies especially when racialised and marginalised groups are concerned. The main assumption is that social justice in this sector cannot be achieved through simple redistribution, but it requires also a process of recognition of the diversity that can emerge in the definition of the housing needs. In this context, recognition is not only due in order to prevent discriminatory practices that hinder the equal access to the provision of housing services and benefits, but also to avoid the universalisation of falsely neutral understandings of the house that risk overlooking or denigrating different housing needs and their relevance for the well-being of the individual. Here, the construction of knowledge in the definition and assessment of "adequate" and "inadequate" plays a central role because of its supposed objectivity.

In this reflection, I especially refer to the work of Pierre Bourdieu on the reproduction of relations of power and the concept of symbolic violence. With this term, the French sociologist identifies the construction by the dominant group of a social order based on undisputed structures that naturalise roles and hierarchies in society. In the eyes of the dominated, the order of things and the organisation of time and space that ensure their subjugation are not constructed by the dominant group but correspond to the objective reality. An example of symbolic violence is the gender division, which maintains the oppression of women by defining the "natural" roles of each gender. It also represents a powerful tool of domination in the colonial context: here, the construction of classifications perceived as objective, such as the dichotomies between "rational" and "irrational", or "modern" and "pre-modern", ensure the reproduction of a subjugation beyond the territorial occupation. The strength of symbolic violence lies exactly in its hidden nature, in the impossibility of contesting it without a long process of deconstruction that unveils its bias. Until then, the subaltern will be pushed to internalise a sense of inferiority that will limit their autonomy of choice.

Does the dichotomy between "adequate" and "inadequate" housing contribute to the construction of a social order that reinforces the oppression of subaltern groups? With the aim of answering this question and to analyse how and why the definition and use of "adequate housing" may represent a form of symbolic violence, I take the discourses and policies for the inclusion of Roma as a case study. The choice of focusing on this group, which is here taken not as a defined ethnic/cultural group but rather as a target of a specific public representation and policy framework, is not only moved by my personal experience, but also because of their racialisation and marginalisation in the European context (Cortés Gomez & End, 2019; McGarry, 2017; Vincze, 2014). For this reason, the analysis of the reasons behind the persistence of their subjugation can contribute to deconstructing those structures that reproduce the oppression of certain groups along ethnic and racial lines. Their subjugation has been recently compared to the oppression of the colonial subject and, for this reason, post-colonial studies offer a variety of methodological tools that can be used in the analysis of the case of Roma.

Here, as well, the construction of knowledge plays a crucial role: exactly like the colonial subjects, Roma have been long object of study from non-Romani scholars, who investigated their traditions, customs and way of living. These works have focused mostly on the differences between Roma and non-Roma which have then been interpreted in collective terms, especially cultural. In this way, the characteristics/issues of some persons have been interpreted as representative of the entire group of individuals, whose behaviour was considered a consequence of these characteristics. This way of studying Roma had numerous consequences: it constructed this group as the internal "Other", something different to the rest of society; it represented them as a homogeneous community attached to a backward tradition that prevented them from adapting to contemporary society; it neglected the agency of the Romani individual, whose action would have been exclusively driven by defined socio-cultural characteristics, hindering their autonomy. As a consequence, Roma have been long treated as inferior citizens, outsiders, individuals bearing a fascinating but dangerous culture, never as equal peers, preventing the deconstruction of the structures and of the stereotypes that inform their oppression (Bogdán et al., 2015; Mirga-Kruszelnicka, 2015; Tremlett, 2009).

Because of the similarities between the position of Roma and those of the colonial subject, post-colonial studies have been more and more used in the development of a different paradigm in the production of knowledge on Roma, focusing on the structures that preserve their exclusion rather than on their supposed socio-cultural characteristics (Marushiakova & Popov, 2017; McGarry & Drake, 2013; Trehan & Kóczé, 2009). In this context, the term anti-gypsyism has been increasingly used to identify the racism suffered by various Romani groups in Europe, which is not only manifested in practices of daily discrimination, but is based on structures that systematically exclude these groups within liberal society, which is supposed to be neutral to race. The division between a "us" non-Roma and "them" Roma represents its first manifestation, but anti-gypsyism can be traced in every sector of society where Roma are excluded or remain invisible (Cortés Gomez & End, 2019; Fekete, 2014; Kóczé, 2017; Rostas, 2019).

Housing is one of the sectors that have always been affected by anti-gypsyism and that, therefore, played a major role in the oppression of Roma. The above-mentioned nomad camps are probably the most visible form of anti-gypsyism in Italy, as especially highlighted by Picker (Picker, 2017; Picker & Vivaldi, 2019) and Sigona (Sigona, 2005, 2011). But housing has also played an important role in their marginalisation in other contexts: in the UK, the lack of halting sites and the regulations limiting the possibility to move have greatly affected the well-being of Gypsies and Travellers living in caravans, reinforcing their exclusion (Berlin, 2011; Greenfields & Smith, 2010; Richardson, 2006); in Eastern Europe, under communist regimes as well as during the reign of Maria Theresa Habsburg, the forced sedentarisation of Roma was one of the main measures adopted with the assimilationist attempt to turn them into "good citizens" (Barany, 2002; McGarry, 2017; Mirga & Gheorghe, 1997).

At the same time, housing policies have also played a major role in colonial settings, both at the physical and symbolic level. On one side, displacements, forced sedentarisations and the creation of segregated urban areas had an important impact in the eradication of local practices, dismantling social networks of support and preventing the access to resources and services. On the other side, the home of the coloniser became symbol of the power of the white man, an imaginary border between the danger and chaos of the colony and the safety, hygiene and order of the coloniser (Blunt, 1999; Blunt & Rose, 1994). This series of examples also highlights the implications of the strict link between the identity of the person and the house, which is not only a physical refuge, but deeply affects materially and symbolically all other aspects of the life of a person. Furthermore, its symbolic value and the fact that forced sedentarisations and relocations in these contexts have most of the time been presented not as an act of oppression, but as a due passage to achieve "modernity", bring to light the necessity of carefully analysing the protection of housing nowadays.

Finally, the case of the policies implemented for the inclusion of Roma in the housing sector appears interesting because of the role played in this sector by the European Union. Indeed, the starting point of my analysis, the *EU Framework for National Roma Integration Strategies*, has been one of the first and most ambitious EU initiatives in the social sector. Its implementation represented a test of the capacity of the European Institutions to act as social actors towards the achievement of a sustainable and inclusive Europe – as foreseen within the broader strategy Europe2020. Nevertheless, despite the undeniable engagement of the EU Commission and the significant investments, scholars and activists largely agree upon the lack of substantial results that, in some cases, even worsened the situation of Roma (Matache, 2017; Rostas, 2019; Zentai, 2018). For this reason, the analysis of the causes of this failure has the potential to inform a change of approach of the EU institutions towards the achievement of social goals and in their action for the creation of an inclusive society. In this context, with this work I also aim to contribute to the debate for a revision of the EU action in this sector.

With these objectives, the first part of this work presents a critical analysis of the EU discourses on the inclusion of Roma and on the provision of "adequate housing". Specifically, the analysis focuses on the discursive constructions that reinforce the subordinate position of Roma and of their relationship with a specific way of conceiving and assessing housing adequacy. The first chapter then moves to analyse how adequate housing is defined and protected in International and European law. This study is conducted in order to find out whether the origins of a certain idea of "adequate housing", and of its use, can be traced in International legislation, where this concept first appeared. Here, the analysis takes into consideration the protection of the Right to Adequate Housing and the Right to Home and investigates the implications of the definitions and obligations enshrined in the legal documents and of their relationship. This work highlights the ambivalences emerging especially in regard to the protection of informal housing and of diversity in this sector. Finally, in light of the fallacies of an approach to housing that adopts exclusively physical standards in the assessment of adequacy and is unable to properly recognise the subjectivity and agency of the individual, the first chapter presents the methodology adopted in the fieldwork. The aim is to challenge the approach so far adopted both in the assessment of housing adequacy and in the development of inclusion policies for Roma by reversing it and grounding the reflection on a qualitative work that brings the subjectivity of the individual at the centre of the analysis.

Accordingly, the second, third and fourth chapters present the fieldwork conducted in three Italian local contexts where the local authorities have implemented initiatives aimed at providing Roma living in nomad camps with an adequate alternative solution. The analysis of the measures implemented aims to highlight the practical consequences of practices still based on anti-gypsyism and of their relationship with a certain idea of housing adequacy. The analysis of these initiatives is then supported with the presentation of a series of interviews conducted with Roma and Sinti living in the area considered. The main objective of this work is to challenge the persistent prejudices on this group and to emphasise the numerous factors and variables intervening in the definition of the individual well-being in housing.

In light of the findings of the empirical work, the last chapter elaborates on the main fallacies emerged in the implementation of inclusion policies towards Roma in the housing sector, with the aim to inform a new approach in this field. It furthermore proposes a reflection on the contradictions emerged between a certain idea of adequate housing promoted at the legal and policy level and the results of the qualitative work conducted in this study. It consequently offers some insights for a revision of the definition of housing rights and policies towards a recognition of the subjectivity and agency of the individual in this sector.

References

Barany, Z. D. (2002). *The East European Gypsies: Regime Change, Marginality, Ethnopolitics*. Cambridge: Cambridge University Press.

Berlin, J. (2011). Housing – Related problems of Roma in Finland and Gypsies and Travellers in England. In *Proceedings of the Salford Postgraduate Annual Research Conference* (pp. 278–288). Salford: Salford University.

Blunt, A. (1999). Imperial geographies of home: British domesticity in India, 1886–1925. *Transactions of the Institute of British Geographers, 24(4)*, 421–440.

Blunt, A., & Dowling, R. (2006). *Home*. Abingdon: Routledge.

Blunt, A., & Rose, G. (1994). *Writing Women and Space. Colonial and Postcolonial Geographies*. New York: The Guilford Press.

Bogdán, M., Ryder, A., & Taba, M. (2015). The Roma spring: Knowledge production and the search for a new humanity. *Roma Rights, 2* (Special Issue: Nothing About Us Without Us).

Cortés Gomez, I., & End, M. (2019). *Dimensions of Antigypsyism in Europe*. Brussels: European Network Against Racism and Central Council of German Sinti and Roma.

d.c.p.m. Dichiarazione dello stato di emergenza in relazione agli insediamenti di comunita' nomadi nel territorio delle regioni Campania, Lazio e Lombardia (2008).

Fekete, L. (2014). *Europe against the Roma*. Race & Class, *55(3)*, 60–70. https://doi.org/10.1177/0306396813509196.

Greenfields, M., & Smith, D. (2010). A question of identity: The social exclusion of housed Gypsies and Travellers. *Research, Policy and Planning, 28(3)*.

Kóczé, A. (2017). Race, migration and neoliberalism: Distorted notions of Romani migration in European public discourses. *Social Identities*, 1–15. https://doi.org/10.1080/13504630.2017.1335827.

Marushiakova, E., & Popov, V. (2017). Orientalism in Romani Studies: The case of Eastern Europe. In H. Kyuchukov, & W. New, eds, *Languages of Resistance: Ian Hancock's Contribution to Romani Studies*. Lincom Europa.

Matache, M. (2017). Biased elites, unfit policies: reflections on the lacunae of Roma integration strategies. *European Review, 25(4)*, 588–607.

McGarry, A. (2017). *Romaphobia. The Last Acceptable Form of Racism*. London: Zed Books.

McGarry, A., & Drake, H. (2013). The politicization of Roma as an ethnic «Other»: Security discourse in France and the politics of belonging. In U. Korkut, G. Buckem-Knapp, A. Mcgarry, J. Hinnfors, & H. Drake, eds, *The Discourses and Politics of Migration in Europe* (pp. 73–91). Palgrave MacMillan. https://doi.org/10.1057/9781137310903_5.

Mead, G. H. (1934). *Mind, Self and Society*. Chicago: University of Chicago Press.

Mirga, A., & Gheorghe, N. (1997). *The Roma in the Twenty-First Century: A Policy Paper*. Project on Ethnic Relations.

Mirga-Kruszelnicka, A. (2015). Romani Studies and emerging Romani scholarship. *Roma Rights, 2* (Special Issue: Nothing About Us Without Us? Roma Participation in Policy Making and Knowledge Production), 39–46.

Piasere, L. (2004). *I rom d'Europa. Una storia moderna*. Roma, Bari: Laterza.

Piasere, L., Solimano, N., & Tosi Cambini, S. (A c. Di). (2014). *Wor(l)ds which Exclude. The Housing Issue of Roma, Gypsies and Travellers in the Language of the Acts and the Administrative Documents in Europe*. Fiesole: Fondazione Michelucci Press.

Picker, G. (2011). Welcome in. Left-wing Tuscany and Romani migrants (1987–2007). *Journal of Modern Italian Studies, 16(5)*, 607–620. https://doi.org/10.1080/1354571X.2011.622469.

Picker, G. (2017). *Racial Cities: Governance and the Segregation of Romani People in Urban Europe*. London: Routledge.

Picker, G., & Vivaldi, E. (2019). Racial segregation: Camps for Roma and slums in Italy. In I. Cortés Gomez, & M. End, eds, *Dimensions of Antigypsyism in Europe* (pp. 180–197). Brussels: ENAR.

Proshansky, H. M., Fabian, A. K., & Kaminoff, R. (1983). Place-identity: Physical world socialization of the self. *Journal of Environmental Psychology, 3*(*1*), 57–83. https://doi.org/10.1016/S0272-4944(83)80021–80028.

Richardson, J. (2006). Talking about Gypsies: The notion of discourse as control. *Housing Studies, 21*(*1*), 77–96. https://doi.org/10.1080/02673030500391171.

Richardson, J. (2019). *Place and Identity. The Performance of Home.* Abingdon: Routledge. https://doi.org/10.4324/9781315816852.

Rostas, I. (2019). *A Task for Sisyphus. Why Europe's Roma Policies Fail.* Budapest: CEU Press.

Sigona, N. (2003). How can a "nomad" be a "refugee"?: Kosovo Roma and labelling policy in Italy. *Sociology, 37*(*1*), 69–79. https://doi.org/10.1177/0038038503037001445.

Sigona, N. (2005). Locating "the gypsy problem". The Roma in Italy: Stereotyping, labelling and "nomad camps". *Journal of Ethnic and Migration Studies, 31*(*4*), 741–756. https://doi.org/10.1080/13691830500109969.

Sigona, N. (2011). The governance of Romani people in Italy: Discourse, policy and practice. *Journal of Modern Italian Studies, 16*(*5*), 590–606. https://doi.org/10.1080/1354571x.2011.622468.

Sigona, N., & Monasta, L. (2006). *Imperfect Citizenship. Research into Patterns of Racial Discrimination against Roma and Sinti in Italy.* osservAzione – Centre for Action Research Against Roma and Sinti Discrimination.

Tavani, C. (2012). *Collective Rights and the Cultural Identity of the Roma, A Case Study of Italy.* Leiden, Boston: Martinus Nijhoff Publishers.

Taylor, C. (1994). The politics of recognition. In C. Taylor & A. Gutmann, eds, *Multiculturalism: Examining the Politics of Recognition* (pp. 25–73). Princeton: Princeton University Press. https://doi.org/10.1037/a0020654.

Tosi Cambini, S. (2013). Accesso all'abitazione e problemi di salute delle popolazioni rom e sinti. In C. Saraceno, N. Sartor, & G. Sciortino, eds, *Stranieri e disuguali Le disuguaglianze nei diritti e nelle condizioni di vita degli immigrati* (pp. 225–250). Bologna: Il Mulino.

Trehan, N., & Kóczé, A. (2009). Racism, (neo-)colonialism and social justice: The struggle for the soul of the Romani movement in post-socialist Europe. In G. Huggan, & I. Law, eds, *Racism Postcolonialism Europe* (pp. 50–74). Liverpool: Liverpool University Press. https://doi.org/10.5949/liverpool/9781846312199.003.0004.

Tremlett, A. (2009). Bringing hybridity to heterogeneity in Romani Studies. *Romani Studies, 19*(*2*), 147–168.

Vincze, E. (2014). The racialization of Roma in the "new" Europe and the political potential of Romani women. *European Journal of Women's Studies, 21*(*4*), 435–442. https://doi.org/10.1177/1350506814548963.

Zentai, V. (2018). National Roma Inclusion Policies in Central and Eastern Europe: Diverging Learning Paths with Residual Outcomes. In A. Batory, A. Cartwright, & D. Stone, eds, *Policy Experiments, Failures and Innovations: Beyond Accession in Central and Eastern Europe* (pp. 88–108). Cheltenham, Northampton: Edward Elgar Publishing.

1 "Adequate housing" in policy and law

limits and ways forward

A path towards housing inclusion? The EU Framework for National Roma Integration Strategies

One of the main criticisms moved to the EU action for the inclusion of Roma concerns its incapacity to fully recognise and tackle the roots of the marginalisation of Roma in Europe: Anti-Gypsyims. As mentioned, this term does not refer exclusively to act of direct discrimination but to a whole series of structures and practices that keep Roma in a subjugated position. In this context, a major role is played by the construction and representation of this group in public discourse, which can be critically analysed through the concept of symbolic violence. This form of oppression is based on the construction of a reality that defines the position and the role of each element composing the social picture and that is perceived as natural and objective. Here, classification and dichotomies are crucial as they divide society in sections, forming a hierarchy that *de facto* neglects the principle of "equality" – individuals are divided between those "belonging" and "non-belonging", "civilised" and "uncivilised", "deserving" and "undeserving", and this divisions define the position and the rights of each person. The construction and representation of Roma in public discourses reflects this model: they have always been presented as something "other" from the rest of European society, and, therefore, "non-belonging"; their agency and subjectivity was hidden by a series of stereotypes that depicted them as "exotic" and "dangerous", attached to a backward culture that prevented them to adapt to contemporary society. As a consequence, they have been excluded from knowledge production and decision-making as they have been considered not ready to be treated as peers in the modern world, and this prevented the eradication of the prejudices that maintained their subordinate position.

According to some of the main scholars who analysed the implementation of the EU Framework for National Roma Integration Strategies 2011–2020, the EU institutions did not only fail to tackle this issue, but also reproduced some of the most common stereotypes that informed this model (Fekete, 2014; Iusmen, 2018; Kavrakova, 2013; Matache, 2017; Rostas, 2019). Great hopes were place on the new phase of the EU engagement for the inclusion of

DOI: 10.4324/9781003184539-2

Roma, whose start can be found in the Roma Summit held in 2008 in Brussels, when the first guidelines of the new approach were established. Before that, the EU action in this field was limited to Eastern European countries, which were required to enforce anti-discriminatory legislation before being accepted as Member States. Nevertheless, the failure of such measures in improving the conditions of Roma within these areas, the growth of Romani migrants towards West and the rise of anti-Roma policies moved EU institutions to strengthen their engagement in this field and to change the approach. This led to the adoption of the *EU Framework for National Roma Integration Strategies* in 2011, a document requiring all Member States to adopt and implement National Strategies for the integration of Roma in four sectors: education, employment, health and housing. Along with the establishment of the Framework, EU institutions and agencies commissioned a series of studies in this field and regularly published recommendations on the measures to be taken and monitoring reports. For this reason, the authority and influence of EU Institutions in directing strategies for the inclusion of Roma in Member States increased significantly, attracting the attention of social scientists.

The poor outcomes of the Strategy and the persistent rise of anti-Roma sentiments all over Europe sparked a debate on the reasons of such failure, which surely lie also in the lack of engagement by Member States that have implemented local policies discontinuously. Nevertheless, the socio-economic approach adopted by EU institutions for tackling the issue has been criticised for overlooking the structural barriers to inclusion based on anti-gypsyism and for promoting a narrative that reinforces stereotypes and informs a paternalistic approach, which, in turn, feeds anti-Roma sentiments. In this context, the narrative on the inclusion of Roma plays a primary role because it naturalises a certain construction of Roma that, as above explained, prevents their emersion and empowerment. This is especially true when such narrative is reproduced by public institutions perceived as authoritative and objective (Kóczé, 2017; Kostka, 2015; Marushiakova & Popov, 2015; Richardson, 2006). For this reason, a critical discourse analysis of the EU documents investigating the presence of narrative constructions based on anti-gypsyism can reveal some of the aspects behind the failure of the EU action in this sector and inform a change of approach.

This criticism of EU institutions has already been moved before the adoption of the EU Framework (McGarry & Drake, 2013; Rövid, 2011; Simhandl, 2009). As a consequence, the documents released after 2008 pay major attention to some issues that were raised on the representation of Roma. The first one regarded the construction of the subject "Roma", which did not recognise diversity within the group, reifying the constructed division between "non-Roma" and "Roma" and supporting the "otherness" of the latter. This criticism moved the EU institutions to clarify that "Roma" is used as an umbrella term to refer to a series of different groups. Nevertheless, a critical discourse analysis of the documents released between 2008 and 2017 highlights how terms such as "Roma community", "Roma minority" and "the Roma" remain largely used, alluding to the presence of a well-defined "Minority". This narrative construction is also confirmed by the reference to Roma as "Europe's largest ethnic minority", present in many documents. Moreover, the use of "Roma" as umbrella term continues to be justified by the argument that Roma would share "similar cultural characteristics" (European Commission, 2008a, 2010a), overlooking the fact that most of the Romani groups have more characteristics in common with the fellow citizens than with other Romani groups.

Another narrative construction largely used and that irremediably reifies this group as a well-defined and distinct community is the use of "Roma" as an adjective in the identification of other terms, such as "Roma issues", "Roma needs" and "Roma culture". A significative example, in this sense, is the use of "Roma culture" in the EC's document *Vademecum – The 10 Common Basic Principles of Roma Inclusion*. Within the section addressing intercultural approach, it states: "through this approach, the majority population is provided with tools and competencies to help them understand the Roma culture, and the Roma are provided with tools and competencies to understand mainstream culture" (European Commission, 2010c). The resulting narrative, instead of breaking the constructed boundaries, reinforces the idea of the existence of two identifiable and distinct groups with their own specific cultures.

This process of identification and division is then backed by the association between Roma and a series of social issues, such as poverty, unemployment, social exclusion, etc. The cultural homogenisation that presents Roma as a group distinguished by a series of cultural characteristics is, therefore, followed by a form of social homogenisation. Indeed, the documents here considered indiscriminately describe Roma as: "particularly exposed to high rates of poverty, unemployment", "excluded", "young population with disadvantages" (European Commission, 2008a), "particularly vulnerable to social exclusion, poverty and discrimination" (European Commission, 2008c). They are associated with "disadvantaged groups", "vulnerable groups", "socio-economic/social exclusion", "marginalised communities" (European Commission, 2012a, 2012c, 2016). Furthermore, according to these documents, they would "lack the education needed to find a job" (European Commission, 2011a), "live in deep poverty lacking access to healthcare and decent housing" (European Commission, 2012a), and are "vulnerable to exploitation" (Council of the European Union, 2013).

Marushiakova and Popov (2015) rightly point out that the apparently contradictory representations of Roma as an ethnic group with specific cultural characteristics, on one hand, and as a social group marked by poverty and marginality, on the other, are actually two sides of the same coin. The resulting ethnicization of poverty blames the victims and their "culture" for the poor conditions in which they live and the role of racism and structural discrimination is completely neglected. In this picture, the agency of the Romani individual disappears – they are seen as trapped into a vicious circle made of poverty and backwardness, which prevents them to improve their conditions without the support of someone from the outside. This narrative, along with reproducing a series of dangerous stereotypes, informs a specific policy-making, raising two main issues.

The first one is the perception of "Roma" as something "Other", feeding an approach that considers them as something that does not belong in European society. They are indeed treated like immigrants who need to be "integrated" into the host society, forgetting their presence since the Middle Ages and their role in the European history and society. Furthermore, the constructed "otherness" of Roma moves political institutions to develop "special policies" for their inclusion. This approach, as highlighted by Joanna Kostka (2015), leads to the realisation of policies detached from the broader social policies and that consequently fail to address the institutional barriers to inclusion. The resulting outcomes, other than missing the goal of improving their conditions, risk increasing anti-Roma sentiments as other disadvantaged groups see public funds spent on Roma in vain (Vermeersch, 2012). They also risk nourishing the idea that Roma are the problem and that they do not want to "integrate", since investments in this sector did not bring change (Piasere et al., 2014)

The second issue concerns their representation as indiscriminately poor and marginal, because it leads to a paternalistic approach that treats them either as children, who need to be educated before becoming real citizens, or as objects that can be moved according to the will of the policy-maker (Boschetti & Vitale, 2011; Gay y Blasco, 2003; Marushiakova & Popov, 2017; Rodriguez Maeso, 2014; van Baar, 2017). In their analysis of the European approach to Roma, Angela Kóczé and Nidhi Trehan (2009) refers to the post-colonial term *infantilization*, coined by Frantz Fanon (1963) to identify the tendency to treat colonial subjects as immature beings. Exactly like in their case, policies towards Roma are designed around the idea that the members of this group have to go through a process of training and change before being able to exit the circle of poverty and backwardness that keeps them at the margins. In this context, Roma are kept out of decision-making, their participation remains tokenistic and often linked to a supposed process of "training". They are simply supposed to follow the rules and accept what others decide for them. This typically colonial approach prevents Roma from emerging as equal peers in decision making, keeping them in a subordinate position.

"Roma integration" and "adequate housing"

What has "adequate housing" to do with this? As mentioned, housing is one of the main sectors addressed by the EU Framework and, for this reason, part of the analyses conducted by EU institutions and policy recommendations concern the housing situation of Roma. Here, the argument is largely constructed around two main divides which often go hand in hand: segregated vs. integrated housing and inadequate vs. adequate housing. The studies conducted in this field by EU Agencies generally present the housing conditions of Roma as inadequate and segregated and, therefore, call for policies aimed at tackling the issue, mostly with the relocation of Romani families living in such settings to integrated and adequate accommodation.

If we look at the documents supporting the EU Framework, it is possible to notice that the representation of the housing conditions of Roma is in line with, and contributes to, the depiction of Roma as intrinsically poor and disadvantaged. Indeed, in all the documents taken into consideration, the houses inhabited by Roma are described as "to be developed", "poor", "low/sub-standard", "inadequate", "segregated", "problematic". Furthermore, they are associated with: "disadvantaged neighbourhoods/areas", "overcrowding", "unauthorised settlements", "underdeveloped city areas", "slums", "low quality", "lack of urban planning or chaotic expansion", "squatting/illegal dumping". The description of the housing conditions of Roma is then opposed to what is meant to be the objective of inclusion in this sector, namely the inclusion within accommodation deemed: "standard", "mainstream", "adequate", "decent", and in "integrated settings" (see Table 1.1 for references). Along with fostering the narrative presenting Roma as intrinsically characterised by poverty and illegality, the description of housing feeds the opposition between Roma and a "majority" that conducts a "normal life".

Table 1.1 Predication of "Roma housing" vs. "mainstream housing" in EU documents: references

Terms	*References*
To be developed	European Commission, 2008a
Poor	European Commission, 2008a, 2011a, 2011c
Low- sub-standard	Committee on Civil Liberties Justice and Home Affairs of the European Parliament, 2010; Eurofound, 2012; European Commission, 2010a; European Union Agency for Fundamental Rights, 2009c, 2009d, 2010b
Inadequate	Eurofound, 2012; European Commission, 2012c; European Union Agency for Fundamental Rights, 2009a, 2010b, 2012
Segregated	Council of the European Union, 2013; European Commission, 2010c, 2010f, 2011c, 2012a, 2012c; European Union Agency for Fundamental Rights, 2009c, 2010b
Problematic	European Commission, 2008a; European Union Agency for Fundamental Rights, 2009a
Disadvantaged neighbourhoods/areas	European Commission, 2010c, 2010f
Overcrowding	Eurofound, 2012; European Commission, 2012c; European Union Agency for Fundamental Rights, 2010b, 2016b
Unauthorised settlements	European Commission, 2008a, 2012c; European Union Agency for Fundamental Rights, 2010b
Under-developed city areas	European Union Agency for Fundamental Rights, 2010b
Slums	Eurofound, 2012; European Commission, 2012c, 2016; European Union Agency for Fundamental Rights, 2009c

(*Continued*)

Table 1.1 (Cont.)

Terms	*References*
Lack of urban planning or chaotic expansion	European Commission, 2012c
Low quality	European Commission, 2012c; European Union Agency for Fundamental Rights, 2010b
Squatting/illegal dumping	European Commission, 2011c, 2016
Standard	European Union Agency for Fundamental Rights, 2009c
Mainstream	European Commission, 2010c
Adequate	European Commission, 2016; European Union Agency for Fundamental Rights, 2009c, 2010b, 2016b
Decent	European Commission, 2011c, 2012a; European Union Agency for Fundamental Rights, 2012
Integrated settings	European Commission, 2016

Another side effect of this narrative is the inevitable association between Roma as a group and "inadequate housing". This is evident in the FRA report *The State of Roma and Traveller Housing in the European Union*, where the argument on inadequate housing is developed around a new term, "Roma and Traveller housing". The adoption itself of such term conveys the idea that exists such a thing as a "Roma and Traveller housing", clearly identifiable and distinct from a supposed "mainstream housing". Furthermore, this term is explicitly associated with "inadequate housing", when it states that "there is ample evidence that the quality and location of Roma and Traveller housing fails to conform to these requirements [adequacy requirements]" and identifies "low quality and lack of infrastructures" as "two of the characteristics of Roma and Traveller accommodation" (European Union Agency for Fundamental Rights, 2010b, pp. 6, 14).

In addition, the way of living and the housing conditions are often used as the main features to distinguish between different Romani groups and to mark their level of integration. Particularly significant in this sense is the working document of the European Commission *What Works for Roma Inclusion in the EU,* published in 2012 and meant to provide policy recommendations to national authorities in the implementation of the integration strategies (European Commission, 2012c). After stating that Roma are not a homogeneous group, it recalls a subdivision already presented in a communication of 2010 (European Commission, 2010f), mainly based on the location and way of living. Roma are divided into five groups: "Roma communities living in segregated urban and suburban neighbourhoods"; "Roma communities living in segregated rural settlements"; "Roma migrants and Roma EU nationals moving within the EU-15 Member States"; "Roma Travellers and (semi-)mobile lifestyle"; "Roma communities living in integrated urban and suburban neighbourhood".

According to this document, Roma included within the first two categories (Roma living in segregated and disadvantaged conditions, either urban or rural) are exclusively characterised by poverty, social exclusion, segregation, social dependency, delinquency and violence. The living conditions are marked by segregation, which is here presented as one of the main issues: "one village or some village neighbourhoods are ghettoised with the risk of becoming a Roma territory with dramatic consequences in terms of segregation, discrimination and socio-economic exclusion" (p. 12). The segregated houses and settlements are described as "self-made", "inadequately built", "badly maintained", "makeshift shacks made of cardboard, metal scraps and mud bricks frequently devoid of windows, doors and walls". Such situation is presented as the result of discriminatory policies, but as well of practices such as early marriages and high birth rates, associated with Roma as a group.

The description of migrant Roma, besides stressing the conditions of poverty and social exclusion, highlights two other aspects: the dichotomy between the sedentary and mobile way of living and the relation with the majority population. Regarding the first one, the document describes migrant Roma as aiming to a sedentary life, but:

> remain to some extent nomadic in spirit and are consistent with the traditional way of life of Roma, not only surprise citizens but also provoke a generalised confusion in administrations which perceive Roma to exploit, if not plunder welfare states without demonstrating any further commitment to the host country.
>
> (P. 14)

Likewise, nomadism is perceived as a primary characteristic of "Roma way of life", which is considered, on the one hand, as fading away and, on the other hand, as a challenge to local administrations. Roma are further presented as the problem when discussing the impact of migration on hosting countries: indeed, "Roma migration … has contributed to worsen public perceptions of Roma. Roma migration has also repeatedly led to diplomatic tensions between governments" (p. 14).

What Works for Roma Inclusion is particularly representative of an approach that overlooks the differences between and within Romani groups, both in cultural and social terms, presenting them as trapped in a socio-cultural vicious circle that prevents them to escape the conditions of poverty. Culture is explicitly blamed for this situation, which is also presented as a burden and a problem for the local administrations. Not surprisingly, the only Roma who are considered on the way to integration (but not completely independent yet) are the ones who have abandoned the "Roma habits" and live with others.

This narrative has crucial repercussions in the development of a policy approach for the improvement of the housing conditions and inclusion of this group. Here particular attention is paid to the issue of segregation, which is presented as one of the main problems affecting the housing conditions of

Roma and it is often connected to issues of inadequacy in a causal relationship. As a consequence, the "concentration" of Roma in certain neighbourhoods is seen as an adequacy risk in itself, while it is not recognised the fact that segregation and inadequacies are most of the time both consequences of structural policies that exclude and marginalise Roma (Claps & Vitale, 2010; Picker, 2017). Following this narrative, the majority of the documents recommends the implementation of policies directed to the relocation of Roma in desegregated locations. One of the main problems in the development of these policies is the fact that the participation of concerned individuals remains at the mere rhetoric level, already within the policy recommendations.

One example is the report *Improving Roma Housing and Eliminating Slums* by the EU Agency for Fundamental Rights (European Union Agency for Fundamental Rights, 2009c). This document presents as "success stories" two projects implemented in Spain for the inclusion and desegregation of Roma. They are praised as positive policy examples, despite the fact that Roma have been involved only formally and always with the mediation of non-Romani NGOs in the whole process, as explicitly admitted by the report. This lack of participation appears highly problematic not only because it reproduces a model that excludes Roma from decision-making, but it also affects the outcomes of the relocations. It indeed prevents the recognition of all the intangible housing needs – affective or social – that do not emerge in the statistics. This is already evident in the presentation of one of the projects above mentioned: because the relocation of the Romani beneficiaries planned by the project required the respect of a series of standards in the selection of the new flats – size, price, and location – the housing choice was limited, and many families had to move to more isolated areas. For this reason, the beneficiaries complained that the relocation obliged them to abandon the supportive context of their families, which could be essential also for the economic livelihood.

The lack of participation is also produced by the recurring idea that Roma are themselves the cause of their condition and that they therefore need to be helped from the outside. In the housing sectors, this idea is translated in the prejudice that Roma tend to segregate themselves from the rest of society. In *What Works for Roma Inclusion in the EU* (European Commission, 2012c), this prejudice is evident in the recommendation of adopting appropriate rules for the relocation of Romani families as "practices such as permitting the free selection of the flat, housing together the biggest families, etc. will tend towards Roma concentration" (p. 23). Another consequence of blaming Roma for their situation is the tendency to condition the provision of a house with the respect of behavioural rules, such as the fulfilment of "certain obligations, for example attending relevant employment training, sending children to school and looking after their health" (European Union Agency for Fundamental Rights, 2009c, p. 11) or even the adoption of an undefined "adequate behaviour" (European Commission, 2012c, p. 44). For instance, *Inadequate Housing in Europe* (Eurofound, 2016) praises a project implemented in a small town in Slovakia for tackling a series of problems supposedly connected to the inadequate housing conditions of the local Romani community: "bad hygiene", "non-working habits" and "financial illiteracy". It reports how the project tackled the issues mentioned above with the organisation of training aimed at involving the Romani beneficiaries in the construction of new accommodation with the supervision of NGOs' professionals. It finally emphasises how Roma demonstrated to be collaborative and to "obey the rules" (pp. 82–84) conveying the implicit message that Roma usually do not do so.

The rationality of "adequate housing" in EU policy documents and the subordination of Roma

Bearing in mind what just said, what is meant with adequate housing and how is it assessed? If we look at the documents released by EU institutions and agencies between 2008 and 2017 on housing in general, it appears difficult to find a common definition. For instance, the European Commission's report *Discrimination in Housing* presents an interpretation of housing adequacy grounded on a human rights narrative. It lists a series of physical parameters to be considered in its assessment and highlights the importance of recognising the cultural aspects implied with the place of living: "housing currently available on the market may also prove to be unsuitable for certain populations for cultural reasons" (European Commission, 2013b, p. 6). Here, it specifically addresses the difficulties of the Traveller communities to find proper halting sites to place their caravans. This interpretation, therefore, seems to promote an understanding of adequacy open to diversity. Nevertheless, this is not the case of other documents here analysed. Two of them – *Confronting Homelessness in the European Union* and *Inadequate Housing in Europe* – make references to the definition of housing adequacy provided by the European Federation of National Organisations Working with the Homeless (FEANTSA) in the *European Typology on Homelessness and Housing Exclusion (ETHOS)* (FEANTSA, 2006). This text, rather than giving a series of parameters intended to assess housing adequacy, lists different typologies of housing inadequacy – *roofless, houseless, insecure, inadequate* – with the correspondent description.

The most striking aspect of this division is the explicit inclusion of "mobile home/caravan", "non-standard building" and "temporary structure" – all defined as "temporary/non-standard structures" – within the "inadequate" category. *Confronting Homelessness in the European Union* specifies that are considered inadequate "caravans without access to public utilities such as water, electricity or gas" (European Commission, 2013a, p. 4). Nevertheless, the direct inclusion of caravans and non-standard buildings within this category forcibly conveys the message that these housing typologies represent themselves an adequacy risk and are less fit for habitation than other "standard" accommodation. This interpretation, therefore, enters into conflict with the one provided by *Discrimination in Housing* and its intention to recognise the housing needs of minorities as equally worthy of attention.

In addition, these documents prefer an economic-oriented discourse to the human rights narrative presented in *Discrimination in Housing*. *Inadequate Housing in Europe* builds its argumentation on a calculation of the benefits and costs of tackling housing inadequacies. These are understood as "social and economic" and mostly related to the health risks due to the physical insecurities of inadequate dwellings. With the aim of reducing the costs due to housing inadequacy, this document develops a model based on "standards" and "metrics" and provides a strictly quantitative analysis of inadequacies (Eurofound, 2016). The other documents here analysed (Directorate-General for Internal Policies European Parliament, 2013; Eurostat, 2011; PES Group Committee of the Regions, 2012) follow a similar narrative using terms derived from the economic/financial language and treating housing as mostly an economic asset.

What is meant with the term "adequate housing", or "decent housing", as often called within the EU documents, can also be traced by the standards identified in the assessment of housing adequacy. In this framework, *Inadequate Housing in Europe* and *Housing Conditions in Europe in 2009* refer mainly to the standards identified by the EU-SILC (Statistics on Income and Living Conditions, Table 1.2), while another kind of measurement is identified in the *European Quality of Life Survey*, adopted also by *Inadequate Housing in Europe*. Despite small differences, all these measurements mostly consider the physical quality of the dwelling and label as "inadequate" accommodation with more than one of the listed features. Furthermore, they exclusively adopt a quantitative approach to the analysis. Particularly significant in this sense is the methodological part in *Inadequate Housing in Europe*, because it explicitly states that the selection of the academic works has identified solely the ones that adopted a quantitative approach in the assessment of adequate housing.

These parameters are also used in the analysis of the housing conditions of Roma. During the last ten years, indeed, EU Agencies such as the EU Agency for Fundamental Rights and Eurofound have published a series of studies on the housing conditions of Roma, often comparing them with data regarding non-Roma. The approach is always strictly quantitative, looking exclusively at

Table 1.2 Inadequacy features identified by EU-SILC and the European Quality of Life Survey (EQLS)

Features of severe housing deprivation by EU-SILC	*Features of housing inadequacy by EQLS*
Overcrowding	Lack of indoor flushing toilet
	Lack of bath or shower
Leaking roof	Rent or mortgage arrears
	Utility arrears
Neither a bath, nor a shower, nor an indoor flushing toilet	Damps or leak
	Rot
	Can't keep home adequately warm
Dwelling considered too dark	Lack of space to sit outside
	Shortage of space

the identified parameters and, consequently, overlooking the general context and the subjective opinion of the individuals living in the accommodation considered. All the analyses highlight the "considerable differences between Roma and non-Roma" in terms of housing adequacy. In none of the studies presented, and in none of the countries considered, Roma score better or equal to the majority of the population. Although such surveys aim to highlight the undeniable difficulties that Roma encounter in accessing housing and housing-related services, the resulting image is the one of a population at the mercy of the poverty circle and housing inadequacy:

> EU-MIDIS II shows that 80% of Roma continue to live below the at-risk-of-poverty threshold of their country; that every third Roma lives in housing without tap water; one in 10 in housing without electricity; and that every fourth Roma (27%) and every third Roma child (30%) live in a household that faced hunger at least once in the previous month.
>
> (European Union Agency for Fundamental Rights, 2016b, P. 9)

This way of defining and assessing housing adequacy appears problematic because it does not take into account a whole series of aspects and factors that affect housing choices and overlook the subjectivity and agency of the individual. Although the physical quality of the house and the access to basic services have a crucial role in the well-being of the individual, numerous studies have already highlighted the broader implications of the dwelling, which go beyond its mere physical quality. For instance, studies conducted in the field of environmental psychology have shown how housing needs and preferences are influenced by a series of social, economic and emotional factors that may move the individual to opt for housing solutions that apparently are less "adequate" than others (Anton & Lawrence, 2014; Bernardo & Palma-Oliveira, 2016; Manzo, 2003; Proshansky et al., 1983). These studies have also focused on the strict relationship between the living environment and the identity of the person, highlighting how this relationship deeply affects the individual perception of the house and the surrounding neighbourhood. On the other hand, the link between housing and identity has important repercussion also for the external image of the person as it can already be noticed in the analysis of the representation of Roma in the EU policy documents here considered. The place of living is indeed taken as one of the main features to distinguish Roma and their level of integration.

In his analysis of the consequences of the relationship between places and identity, David Sibley (1995) focuses on what he calls "geographies of exclusion". This author, among others who developed his work (Hepworth, 2012; Strange & Bashford, 2003), argues that practices such as isolating marginal groups in specific neighbourhoods do not only have the immediate effect of deteriorating their living conditions but also deeply affect their external image, decreasing consistently the possibilities of exiting the condition of marginality on the long term. The policy of the nomad camps and its consequences on the representation of Roma is particularly telling, in this sense. Leonardo Piasere (1991), not by chance, talks of Roma in Italy as the "people of the garbage dumps", to identify the consequence of the policy practice of placing nomad camps on lands of poor value, with not proper waste collection, and often close to a garbage dump. The abjection deriving from living in these areas is indeed reflected in the wide-spread prejudice that Roma are "dirty", "chaotic", a "mobile garbage dump". Although the Italian case is particularly representative, the link between housing and Romani identities can be traced also in other contexts. Gail Kligman (2001), in her study among Roma in Romania, highlights how living in "real houses" is perceived by Roma themselves as a marker of "civilisation" and "gadjeness".[1] For this reason, the external perception changes also the attitude towards the place of living. Both Andrea Racles (2014) and Catherine Hepworth (2012), for instance, show how the persistent prejudice that Roma are "dirty" and "backward" brings Romani housekeepers, living in conditions of marginality, to pay particular attention to the tidiness of the house and to invest in furniture perceived as "fashionable" and "modern".

The house, in this context, is a space where the identity of the person is reflected in the material world. Identity is a changing and fluid concept and it is deeply influenced by the external context and by the relationship with the others – the way they see us, the way they treat us. The house can be a place where the person feels represented and welcome, or an alienating space that does not satisfy the emotional needs, or even leads to a conflictual relationship with the place of living and its surroundings. This can explain why housing choices are often perceived as "irrational". Amos Rapoport (1998) in this regards talks of the importance of what he calls housing *wants*, which, compared to housing *needs*, are more connected to emotions and socio-cultural practices but often are the one directing housing choice. It is also important to remember that the house plays a crucial role in the reproduction of cultural practices, and, for this reason, it is not culturally neutral. Also Pierre Bourdieu (1977) highlights this aspect in his reflection on *habitus*. According to the French sociologist, the house is the space where socio-cultural practices, conscious and unconscious, are most objectified. Through the contact with the spaces of the house, its objects and its design, children socialise with the values of their society or group, such as the gender division, the sense of privacy, sexual behaviours, consumption habits, etc. For this reason, the house plays a crucial role also for the reproduction of values and behaviours that define everyone's life.

The reflection of Bourdieu is particularly important because, unlike Rapoport who develops the reflection exclusively on the cultural implications of housing, he highlights the role of the agency of the individual and of the personal experiences. Habitus, manifested in the house, is not only the product of the socio-cultural context, but also of the experiences of the individual and of their subjectivity. The analyses of the relationship between the house and the identity and the house and culture have indeed often overlooked the agency of the individual and the fluidity of these concepts. As Blunt and Dowling (2006) later argue, social, economic and cultural factors surely play a role in defining housing choices and preferences, and for this reason cannot be considered culturally neutral, but the personal experiences of the person play a role that cannot be neglected.

The broader and crucial implications of the house for the well-being of the person highlight three aspects that should be taken in account in the definition and assessment of adequacy: to label as "inadequate" the house of an individual or a group can represent a form of misrecognition of the identity of its inhabitants and, therefore, a form of symbolic violence; the physical quality of the house does not determine alone the well-being of the individual as other social, cultural, economic and emotional factors may intervene; the subjectivity of the person is essential in defining housing needs. It is clear that a model defining and assessing housing adequacy through apparently "rational" physical standards and solely quantitative analyses completely disregards the variety of housing needs emerging and the subjectivity of the individual. It simplifies such complexity with a division between "adequate" and "inadequate" housing that overlooks the broader context and the personal considerations. In this way, it is unable to recognise the structural obstacles that prevent the individual to satisfy all their personal housing needs. Furthermore, with the implementation of relocations based on this model, it even risks hindering the practices that inhabitants carry out in order to recreate a welcoming and familiar domestic space.

Covered by the veil of apparent objectivity and rationality, this understanding of housing adequacy and the consequent use of its standards support a model that reproduces the oppression of subaltern groups, such as Roma, through classifications that justify their exclusion from decision-making and knowledge production. Instead of ensuring the equal access to material and intangible resources, it further naturalises unquestioned dichotomies that maintain certain groups in a subjugated position.

"Adequate housing" in International and European law

In light of these considerations, the question that here arises is: is this approach to housing adequacy specific of the EU action in this field of does it have its origins somewhere else?

The term "adequate housing" has been defined and used for the first time in international human rights law in protection to the Right to Housing and from there it has been adopted as a widespread normative concept and policy goal. This section, therefore, analyses how international and European legislation define "adequate housing" and what are the State obligations. The objective is to investigate whether the definitions and obligations foreseen by these legal documents in protection to housing rights support different understandings of the house, with its broader implications, or rather endorses a model that reproduces forms of symbolic violence. The analysis, indeed, is conducted departing from the assumption that human rights discourses are not immune to the reproduction of forms of symbolic violence. This is the case, for instance, of discourses that present human rights as an ideal to be achieved through civilisation, as the salvific mission of the white man, rather than a protective shield for the subalterns against the physical and symbolic oppression of the dominant group (Henry & Certomà, 2013). In the housing sectors, does "adequate housing" ensure the equal access to legal protections, services and resources necessary to enjoy the house with its multiple functions, or rather prioritise a certain idea of the house as the "norm" to be achieved, neglecting the others as "irrational", "exceptions", or "inadequate"?

In order to answer these questions, I analyse both the Right to Housing and the Right to Home, commonly identified as housing rights (J. Hohmann, 2013). The decision of including in the analysis the right to home is moved by the fact that this right is protected as a Civil and Political Right, enshrining, therefore, different obligations for the State. It, furthermore, has the potential to better acknowledge the emotional and identity-related aspects connected to the idea of "home", compared to the right to housing. Their analysis, therefore, considers also their relationship and investigates potential complementarities and conflicts between the two rights. This is done through an analysis of both International and European legislation in protection to Human Rights, with the aim of seeking a possible evolution in the understanding of the normative concepts enshrined in these legal documents.

The definition of "adequate housing" in International and European legislation

The concept of "adequate housing" first appeared in the International Covenant on Economic Social and Cultural Rights (ICESCR), adopted in 1966, which included the protection of the right to housing in Art. 11, together with the right to food and clothing:

> The States Parties to the present Covenant recognize the right of everyone to an adequate standard of living for himself and his family, including adequate food, clothing and housing, and to the continuous improvement of living conditions. The States Parties will take appropriate steps to ensure the realization of this right, recognizing to this effect the essential importance of international cooperation based on free consent.
>
> (International Covenant on Economic, Social and Cultural Rights, 1966, n. Art. 11 P. 1)

Although this right is present in several other international treaties[2], the ICESCR remains the primary reference for its protection and interpretation. This because it is part of the Bill of Rights together with the Universal Declaration of Human Rights (UDHR) and the International Covenant on Civil and Political Rights (ICCPR), it has been ratified by almost all members of the United Nations[3] and it is supported by a series of General Comments.

Interestingly, at the beginning, one of the main aspects that attracted the attention of the legal scholars was the meaning of "adequate". As Herman von Hebel highlighted in his analysis of the *travaux préparatoires* of the Covenant (von Hebel, 1987), the text was not completely clear regarding the obligations of the State concerning the implementation of the right to housing and no specific indication of how the right had to be interpreted was given. This lack of clarity has been criticised because the term "adequate" left too much freedom for interpretation and could be understood as covering exclusively the "basic needs". Nevertheless, it is interesting to notice that, as von Hebel specified, the term "adequate" was preferred over the term "decent" because the latter was interpreted to carry a moral bearing that the drafters wanted to avoid. Furthermore, the Covenant's preparatory text already emphasised the necessity of considering the house as something more than a roof over the head.

Nevertheless, the implementation of the right required a more detailed interpretation of the term "adequate" to set a list of indicators for the assessment of the adequacy of the accommodation. This necessity led the Committee to adopt in 1991 the General Comment No. 4 to the Right to Adequate Housing (UN Committee on Economic Social and Cultural Rights, 1991). The text, although not binding, is considered as the most authoritative source in interpreting this right and it became quite influential in the development of other international legal documents (J. Hohmann, 2013). The two main issues tackled by the General Comment are the definition of adequate housing and the obligations deriving from the right. Regarding the first point, the Committee specifies that "adequate housing" should not be interpreted in a narrow sense as to cover only basic needs, but it should consider the many implications that housing has on the life of a person. The broad significance of the house is underlined in par. 7 of the Comment, where the Committee specifies that the right to housing must be interpreted as "the right to live somewhere in security, peace and dignity". It, furthermore, specifies that the term "adequate" refers to a set of standards that has "to be taken into account in determining whether particular forms of shelter can be considered to constitute "adequate housing" for the purposes of the Covenant" (par. 8).

In its main part, the General Comment n.4 invites the State parties to consider a list of minimum standards that, according to the Committee, are significant for all contexts and have to be adopted in the protection and provision of "adequate housing":

a. *Legal security of tenure* – referring to the legal protection against forced evictions that can be ensured through a series of contractual forms: "rental (public and private) accommodation, cooperative housing, lease, owner-occupation, emergency housing and informal settlements, including occupation of land or property" (par. 8(a)).
b. *Availability of services, materials, facilities and infrastructures* – concerning the access to "natural and common resources, safe drinking water, energy for cooking, heating and lighting, sanitation and washing facilities, means of food storage, refuse disposal, site drainage and emergency services" (par. 8(b)).
c. *Affordability* – based on the idea that housing costs should not be too high to threaten the satisfaction of other basic needs, it calls for measures aimed at controlling housing costs, both in private and public sector.
d. *Habitability* – connected with the physical security and safety of the house also in relation to health-related risks, it specifies that the house shall provide adequate space and protect the individual from "cold, damp, heat,

rain, wind or other threats to health, structural hazards, and disease vectors" (par. 8(d)).

e. *Accessibility* – referring to the necessity of ensuring equal access to housing to all groups of society, it requires giving priority to those disadvantaged groups that may encounter more difficulties in accessing housing of adequate standards (disables, victims of natural disasters, HIV-positive individuals, etc.) in the provision of land and housing.
f. *Location* – concerning the necessity for the house to be located in an area accessible to "employment options, health-care services, schools, childcare centres and other social facilities" (par. 8(f)), and away from polluted areas.
g. *Cultural adequacy* – based on the assumption that the house "must appropriately enable the expression of cultural identity and diversity of housing" (par. 8(g)), it requires consideration for the cultural dimension of housing in the development and modernisation of housing structures.

This list of requirements is particularly relevant as it became one of the main instruments in defining and assessing housing adequacy also within other frameworks and contexts[4]. For this reason, it is important to pay attention to their meaning and to potential issues that may arise. Despite the intentions to avoid interpretations that neglect diversity in this sector and justify the excessive intervention of the State, the provision of a list of standards may prioritise certain housing needs over others, overlooking the needs of minority and subaltern groups. In other words, the risk is to exclusively mark as "adequate" a housing model reflecting the needs and desires of a dominant group, penalising marginal sectors of the society.

In this context, one of the most problematic criteria is the *habitability* of the shelter, because it regards the structure of the house directly. Matthew Craven (1998) notices that, while the habitability parameters are appropriate in regulating the work of construction firms, they may represent an obstacle for the self-build of a house by private individuals or groups. The issue is particularly relevant as the inadequacy of housing structures informally built is often interpreted and used as a justification for eviction. Furthermore, strict regulations on the physical conditions of the house may hinder the access to housing-related services by those who have self-built their house. Consequently, rigid rules in this sense may increment homelessness, rather than promoting adequacy. Even though the Committee explicitly supports the informal housing sector and emphasises that private individuals or groups should have the possibility to construct houses for themselves without excessive conditions, a strict interpretation of the habitability criteria surely represents an obstacle to self-building.

In addition, this criterion may enter in conflict with the aim, as also highlighted by Scott Leckie (2001), of protecting the right of individuals "to build their own dwellings and order their living environments in a manner which most effectively suits their culture, skills, needs and wishes" (p. 156). Indeed, the brick house can be perceived by the policy maker as a better option to protect from "cold, damp, heat, rain, wind, [etc.]" and be imposed over other solutions that may be designed to respond to other needs that are not considered in this list. It, namely, may justify actions of forced relocation of indigenous or minority groups to housing solutions considered more "adequate" by the majority.[5] Beyond the cultural issue of recognising different designs of the house as valuable choices, the habitability standard fails to acknowledge other health-related risks, such as the mental well-being. Jessie Hohmann (2013) brings the example of the family relations and of the domestic violence, which deeply affect the well-being of women within the house, but are not properly considered as "habitability issues". Furthermore, structural adequacy is not sufficient in determining the well-being of the individual: anonymous buildings can lead to alienation; structures that do not meet the emotional and social needs can be perceived as prisons; and bad relations with the neighbourhood can affect the subjective perception of the house more than its physical quality (Proshansky et al., 1983).

Similar issues arise from the standard of *location*, because, as in the case of the habitability, it is mainly interpreted to meet a number of specific needs, overlooking other aspects that may influence the housing choice. The standard indeed requires the house to be accessible to "employment options, health-care services, schools, childcare centres and other social facilities", but does not consider other spiritual or social needs. It, namely, reflects the housing needs of an industrial society organised around specific structures and rhythms, while individuals may prefer different locations because of religious reasons or because they want to live closer to family and friends. Here too, the "rationality" of the standard may collide with the immateriality of other needs, but to ignore those needs as "secondary" or as "irrational" may threaten the well-being of the person. It, furthermore, reinforces the symbolic violence intrinsic in the divide between the "rationality" of what is considered to be "the norm" and the supposed "irrationality" of the "exception".

The last standard, *cultural adequacy*, represents a deviation compared to the previous ones, as it deals with an intangible factor such as culture, and it aims to acknowledge cultural diversity within the housing sector. Both Hohmann and Craven recognise the importance of this standard because of the role of culture in influencing the design and composition of the house. Particularly, they stress the potential consequences, in terms of cultural loss or denial of the right itself, of housing policies that do not recognise cultural diversity. Nevertheless, they both emphasise how this standard does not attract much attention both by the work of the Committee and in the academic analysis. Cultural adequacy, indeed, significantly remains the last of the standards, it is undoubtedly vaguer in its formulation, and the Committee has never further developed it. Also, despite the commendable attention of the Committee towards cultural diversity, the use of this standard may result in communitarian interpretations. Specifically, it raises the issue of who is in charge of deciding what is "culturally adequate" – the State, the community, the individual? The risk, here, is to bound the individual into fixed and stereotyped ideas of culture that overlook their actual needs and desires.

Furthermore, it may lead to interpret as "culturally driven" all housing needs that deviate from the "norm" of the other standards, informing a narrative that divides society between a majority that lives according to the norms of the contemporary world and a series of minorities still attached to cultural traditions. It, namely, would feed the tendency of referring to cultural norms only when minorities are concerned, reinforcing the dichotomy between a supposed West, liberated from the "obscurantism of culture", and the "others", still attached to traditions that do not fit into modernity. Interpreting culture as a coherent lens of analysis, as a specific set of practices and norms enclosed by defined group's borders, continues to inform this model. This because it fails to recognise the dynamicity of culture and the absence of any defined border between the "Us" and the "Them". It, furthermore, neglects the agency of the individuals belonging to minorities and all other aspects, such as gender and class, that affect their self-identity, as it tends to interpret all their practices and behaviours as "culturally driven" (Benhabib, 2002; Geertz, 1973; Phillips, 2007).

In the housing sector, the consequences of using culture as a coherent category in the interpretation of different housing needs can be seen in the creation of the nomad camps in Italy. Here the association between Roma and nomadism resulted in the creation of camps that, from halting sites for nomads, turned into permanent Romani ghettos where all Roma, sedentary or not, were placed to live. This example shows how interpreting different housing needs exclusively as culturally driven has serious repercussions. Nevertheless, the rejection of the use of culture as a coherent lens of analysis should not lead to rejecting diversity itself. As mentioned, housing cannot be interpreted as culturally neutral and it is, therefore, necessary to recognise that housing needs may vary also for cultural reasons.

If in this analysis we move to investigate how these standards are translated at the European level, we find the right to housing protected under the Revised European Social Charter, adopted by the Council of Europe in 1996 in replacement to the previous Charter of 1961. This legal document is the most authoritative source in the protection of social-economic rights at the European level, although it is perceived as a second-class document compared to its sister in protection of civil and political rights, the European Convention on Human Rights. This because the Social Charter is not supported by the same enforcement mechanism as the European Convention: instead of benefitting from a Court with the authority to rule on individual cases, the Charter can only receive collective complaints through the Social Committee, which releases recommendations and engages in a dialogue with the parties concerned. (J. Hohmann, 2013)

Within this legal document, the Right to Housing is protected under Art. 31, which engages the Parties to "take measures designed to promote access to housing of adequate standard" (European Social Charter, 1996, par. 1). Here, the meaning of "housing of adequate standard" is not specified officially. Nevertheless, Pedraic Kenna (Kenna, 2005) argues that through an analysis of its recommendations it is possible to conclude that with this term the Social Committee means a dwelling that respects a series of physical standards, such as the possession of essential amenities (water, heating, waste disposal, sanitation facilities, electricity) and the absence of potentially dangerous construction materials (lead or asbestos). Furthermore, the shelter should not be over-crowded, meaning that enough space needs to be ensured according to the number of inhabitants, and national legislation should provide protection from forced evictions. Kenna stresses that States should ensure the application of standards by the owners, also when they are the ones inhabiting the concerned structures and, consequently, also in cases of self-building. State parties are requested to ensure that housing is adequate by providing access to essential services such as water, electricity and telephone and through injunctions to those that do not respect the rules.

The Social Committee gives an interpretation of adequate housing even more focused on the physical structure of the house compared to the General Comment no. 4 to ICESCR. Indeed, it does not mention standards such as location and cultural adequacy. Although this interpretation is the product of the recommendations delivered by the Committee following country reports and it does not have the same authority as the General Comment no. 4, the exclusive focus on physical parameters proves to be problematic. It may, indeed, inform an approach to housing that further overlooks the importance of intangible factors for the well-being of the person in the dwelling and justifies the excessive intervention of the State. This concern is reinforced by the explicit requirement of ensuring the application of the adequacy standards also in cases of self-building. As already highlighted in the case of the habitability standard of the General Comment no. 4 to ICESCR, over-regulations in this sector may increase homelessness instead of ensuring the right to adequate accommodation.

"Adequate housing" between the positive Right to Housing and the negative Right to Home: a misleading division?

The second important aspect to be considered in the analysis of the Right to Adequate Housing are the obligations enshrined by its protection: what are the States required to do to protect the right to housing? The answer to this question is still affected nowadays by the division of human rights into two sets – civil and political rights and social, economic and cultural rights – which rose during the negotiations for the translation of the principles contained in the Universal Declaration of Human Rights into legally-binding obligations. For a long time this division was justified by the argument that the two sets of rights were different in nature and enshrined different obligations. In particular, it was suggested that, while civil and political rights required the non-interference of the State and, therefore, could be applied immediately and evoked in front of a Court, ESC rights needed the intervention of the State, were costly and could be achieved only through a progressive realisation. This interpretation led the international community to consider socio-economic rights as mere "programmatic goals", rather than real rights. Nowadays, this argument is largely rejected by legal scholars, as it is recognised that civil and political rights require public investments in order to be ensured and that the protection of social and economic rights also foresee the non-interference of the State (Eide, 2001; Ssenyonjo, 2009).

In light of these considerations, it has then been recognised that the division of human rights is exclusively the product of the Cold War and that the two sets are indivisible.[6] Furthermore, legal scholars agree that socio-economic rights, as all human rights, entail three different levels of obligations: *to respect, to protect* and *to fulfil*. While the first two can be considered "negative" obligations as they require the non-interference of the State and the protection against external interferences, the obligation to fulfil represents the "positive" side of the protection of human rights and entails the intervention of the State to ensure the full realisation of the rights. In the housing sectors, this means that the right to adequate housing does not only imply the adoption of measures aimed at ensuring the provision of affordable and adequate accommodation, but also the protections from external actions that may hinder the capacity of the individual to use the resources necessary to satisfy housing-related needs.

Nevertheless, the recurrent narrative dividing human rights in different categories or generations continues feeding the idea that socio-economic rights are different and "inferior" to civil and political rights. This narrative is supported by the language used in the Covenants: while in the ICCPR the States are required "to respect and to ensure to all individuals the rights recognised in the Covenant" (Art. 2, Par. 1), the ICESCR engages the States "to take steps, to the maximum of its resources, with a view to achieving progressively the full realisation of the rights recognised in the Covenant" (Art. 2, Par. 1). Although the Committee on Economic, Social and Cultural Rights has specified that "progressive realisation" does not release the State from moving towards it (UN Committee on Economic Social and Cultural Rights, 1990), such phraseology may justify failures in the protection of socio-economic rights. It, furthermore, feeds the idea that the protection of these rights requires mostly the intervention of the State, and not the protection against excessive interferences in the private life of the individual. The same issue can be found at the European level in the case of the Right to Housing, as the European Social Charter uses a similar narrative requiring the States "to take measures designed to promote" in Art. 31, although it has affirmed that this does not release the Parties from demonstrating "sufficient progress" in their realisation (European Social Committee, 2006).

This issue is particularly important as the protection of the right to housing does not only imply the provision of services and infrastructures necessary for its enjoyment, but also the protection from actions that may hinder their access and use. The most evident example, in this sense, is the protection against forced evictions, included in the standard of the *security of tenure*. The International Committee on ESC Rights has released the General Comment no. 7 (UN Committee on Economic Social and Cultural Rights, 1997) in order to clarify its limitations and the procedures that have to be followed in case of legitimate eviction. This protection appears particularly relevant for those individuals living in conditions of marginality and vulnerability, because often deprived of the legal entitlement to occupy a structure and of the means to resist an eviction. Nevertheless, the protection against forced eviction may collide with other rights, as the right to property, and, for this reason, it was necessary to set its limitations.

In this document, the Committee acknowledges that forced evictions may be legitimate under certain circumstances such as the persistent non-payment of the rent, or of damages to the rented property, but it affirms that the State has to refrain from "arbitrary and unlawful interference with one's home" (UN Committee on Economic Social and Cultural Rights, 1997, par. 8). The document does not clarify what is meant with "home", but it refers to the protection of the Right to Home, included within the International Covenant on Civil and Political Rights, and its definition of this term. Here, the Committee just specifies that the States must adopt and enforce legislative measures to ensure the security of tenure and identify precisely when a forced eviction is justified. It, furthermore, lists a series of procedures that authorities have to follow during an eviction in order to protect the rights of the individuals concerned.

This General Comment surely has also the role to reaffirm the "negative" side of the right to housing and the fact that its protection must be ensured also through non-interference and legislative measures. It remains partly unclear whether the protection of this right may be understood also in reference to other actions that may hinder the individual's enjoyment of the house, as in the case of legislation or regulations that limit the use of land or the access to resources, or that pose a serious obstacle to self-building. These obstacles affect especially those individuals who do not have access to the regular housing market because of financial reasons or because the accommodation offered does not satisfy their housing needs. Then, regulations inhibiting self-building or the use of public or private land for housing purposes risk worsening the situation of individuals already living at the margins. Is it possible to identify a violation of the right to housing in these cases?

This question regards also the above mentioned Right to Home, enshrined in Article 17 of the ICCPR and in Article 8 of the European Convention on Human Rights. This right, indeed, protects the individual's home against external interferences, which can be found also in the excessive intervention of the State. This is most of the time translated in a protection against forced evictions, which can be evoked also in cases of illegal occupations when the intervention is deemed as an "unreasonable violation of one's home"[7]. For this reason, and because of the advanced protection mechanisms supporting civil and political rights, this right appears particularly interesting also for the protection of the right to housing, as also affirmed by other authors (J. M. Hohmann, 2013; Kenna, 2005; Remiche, 2012). Nevertheless, it presents a number of issues that question its capacity to protect the rights of the most vulnerable and that surely limit its potential. The first issue rises from the definition of the "home", which is crucial to identify when an eviction is legitimate or not. Because of its emotional and intangible nature, to define home appears a task far from simple. It is, indeed, not a coincidence that the question "What is home?" has since long attracted the attention of many scholars from different disciplines.

From the beginning, this reflection focused particularly on the dialogical relationship between the home and the self-identity, which greatly influenced its definition. The home was interpreted as the material reflection of the identity, the most significant place for the person, the point of departure for interpreting the world (Bachelard, 1969; Relph, 1976; Sack, 1997; Tuan, 2001). As a consequence, the reflection on the meaning of home followed the one on the identity of the person. For instance, the bounded and atomistic understandings of the identity, blind to diversity, typical of the classic liberalism, was associated with the idealisation and naturalisation of an idea of home constructed around the values of the white man. In this context, the home was seen as the refuge where the man could rest from the chaos and alienation of the public space and where he could find and develop his true self. This idea of home was based on a sense of stability (in time and place) and on a strict division between public and private sphere, perceived as natural. It was therefore representative of a social model that justified the subordination of a series of groups. On one side, the idealisation of the home as a heaven against the chaos of the outside veiled the subordination of women in the domestic space. On the other side, it fed a constructed division between the "barbarism" of the colonies and the peace and comfort of the home of the coloniser – symbol of the values and principles of the white man. (Donald, 1999; Goldsack, 1999; Rose, 1993)

The oppressive consequences of this interpretation led some feminist authors, such as Biddy Martin and Chaldra Talpade Mohanty (1986), Luce Irigaray (1992) and Bonnie Honig (1994) to call for a rejection of the home, together with the post-modern rejection of identity and identity politics. Nevertheless, this total rejection of the home has been criticised because it reinforced the naturalisation of a certain idea of the home-place, failing to recognise that it may have different meanings for different groups. Exactly like identity, its denial risked bringing back a model blind to diversity, instead of deconstructing unbalanced relations of power. This criticism, first moved by bell hooks (1990) and then further developed by Iris Marion Young (2005), highlighted that the oppression and violence – symbolic and physical – reproduced within the four walls of the domestic space was not a consequence of the concept of home itself but of its epistemological construction as the stable and static nest of the white man. Namely, it was the result of the specific values, not the manifestation of a universal paradigm. Furthermore, a static and stable idea of home irremediably supported a static and stable idea of identity, attached to traditional values and constructed in opposition to the "others", which is nowadays largely rejected in favour of a fluid and negotiable identity continuously constructed in dialogue with the external context (Benhabib, 2002; Fraser & Honneth, 2003; Hall, 2000; Phillips, 2007). As a consequence, like the self-identity, also home is now understood as a fluid and negotiable concept. Being in continuous transformation, home cannot be understood as a fixed reflection of cultural features, neither it can be seen as the idealised nest of an "authentic identity" (Massey, 1995).

This new interpretation of home, on one side, opened the doors to diversity in the housing sector. Indeed, the naturalisation of a certain idea of home, constructed around the values of the dominant group, irremediably resulted in the denigration of different housing choices. For instance, caravans have always been considered as "second-choice homes" or, even, as not "real homes", because of their mobility and territorial detachment. Accordingly, people living in mobile homes were regarded as "quasi-homeless". The recognition that home is in constant transformation and can take different shapes has the potential to avoid these forms of denigration. On the other hand, the rejection of reified ideas of home makes even more difficult to answer to the question "what is home?". The latest works on this topic define it as the changing product of a continuous process of negotiation between the individual and the external world, highlighting both the aspects that influence the personal idea of the home and the agency of the individual. In this context, it gains central importance the concept of home-making, which refers to the process of home construction – both material and emotional (Boccagni, 2013; Brun, 2015; Cancellieri, 2017).

It is evident from these reflections the importance of the concept of home for the individual, but at the same time, the difficulty to handle its meaning. How is then interpreted home in international and European legislation and how is it protected? The Human Rights Committee, in the General Comment no. 16, specifies that "home" is understood as "the place where a person resides or carries out his usual occupation". It, then, invites States to "indicate in their reports the meaning given in their society to the terms "family" and "home"" (Human Rights Committee, 1988, par. 5). The main criterion to identify home is therefore the residence in a specific place, implying a sense of stability. This idea seems to reproduce the classic understanding of home as something intrinsically connected to a territory and built through time. This despite the apparent attempt to open to diversity asking States to indicate what is meant with "home" within their society. Like in the case of cultural adequacy, this request does not specify who is supposed to decide what home means, overlooking the possibility that States may not be able to fully grasp differences within their territories.

The European Court of Human Rights does not provide any specific rule for the interpretation of the concepts enshrined in the Convention as it intends to deal with it on a case-by-case basis. This is justified by the purpose of keeping their definition open and flexible, in consideration of the social, legal and technological developments that may arise over time (Koch, 2006). The Court has therefore the authority to interpret the meaning of the concepts included in the Convention. Regarding home, the main criterion so far used for its identification is the existence of "sufficient continuous links" with the place where the individual lives (Remiche, 2012; Roagna, 2012). Also in this case, therefore, the idea of home as something stable and durable seems to prevail, despite the intention of the Court to avoid culturally biased definitions, as highlighted by Ivana Roagna. Indeed, with "home" the Court intends to refer to a long series of shelters, among which "non-traditional residences such as caravans and other non-fixed abodes" (Roagna, 2012). Nevertheless, if we look at cases that concerned individuals living in caravans, it can be noted that the presence "sufficient continuous links" is used as the main criterion to identify "home", failing to protect individuals living in shelters that do not demonstrate a stable connection with a place.

The issue appears particularly relevant in the UK where the lack of proper halting sites has always posed a serious barrier to the right to housing and home of people living in caravans, who mostly belong to the local Gypsy and Traveller communities. For this reason, the European Court of Human Rights has been called to rule on a number of cases that concerned the eviction by British authorities of Traveller and Gypsy individuals who placed their caravan on lands without the proper permissions. In the cases of *Buckley vs the UK* (European Court of Human Rights, 1996) and *Chapman vs the UK* (European Court of Human Rights, 2001) the evictions concerned two women who placed their caravans on lands that they owned, because they could not find proper halting sites. Nevertheless, the Court ruled in favour of the local authorities, arguing that the evictions were legitimate under local planning regulations and did not represent an unreasonable violation of home. In its argumentation, the Court did not consider the argument of the lack of halting sites, affirming that the provision of this kind of structures is not implied in the right to home, which cannot be interpreted as a right to be provided with a home (Donders, 2016).

These two cases attracted the criticisms of many legal scholars for overlooking the broader context and the difficulties for Gypsy and Travellers to find spaces to place their caravans (Donders, 2016; Henrard, 2004; Ringelheim, 2011). This disapproval has also been shared by seven judges of the Court who released a dissenting opinion (Joint dissenting opinion of Judges Pastor Ridruejo, Bonello, Tulkens, Straznicka, Lorenzen, Fischbach and Casadevall in Chapman v. The United Kingdom, 2001) after the decision on Chapman vs. the UK. Particularly, the judges criticised the argument that Article 8 does not imply the right to be provided with a home and concluded that it actually contains "a positive obligation on the authorities to ensure that Gypsies has a practical and effective opportunity to enjoy their rights to home, private and family life, in accordance with a traditional lifestyle" (par. 8–10). This document was, therefore, welcomed by the scholars who criticised the decisions of the Court as an important step towards the protection of the "traditional ways of life" of minorities and of their "special needs".

The obligation of the State to protect "the gypsy way of life" was then reaffirmed in the case *Connors vs the UK* (European Court of Human Rights, 2004), in which the Court condemned the UK authorities for evicting a Gypsy family from a halting site where they lived for 13 years. Here the Court explicitly affirmed the positive obligation of the State "to facilitate the gypsy way of life" (par. 84) enshrined by Article 8. Nevertheless, it is dubious whether the decision of the Court in favour of the applicant was really based on this argument or, rather, on the fact that the family concerned lived in that area for 13 years, demonstrating the existence of a "continuous link" with the land (Donders, 2016). In addition, this decision can be criticised for feeding stereotypes. Indeed, the reference to the protection of a "gypsy way of life" irremediably reifies a group and its culture, reinforcing their "otherness". This aspect has already been noted by Doris Farget who criticises those who welcomed the decisions of the Court for overlooking the risks of such narrative. Referring to a sort of mythological "gypsy way of life", other than feeding prejudices, poses a series of ambivalences. Indeed, if living and travelling in a caravan is protected as a fundamental aspect of this "gypsy way of life", what about Gypsies who are sedentary, like the Connors? The Court in this case has argued that there has been a "shift in habit in the Gypsy population which remains nomadic in spirit if not in actual and constant practice". So, why to protect a practice that is disappearing, after all?

The evident weaknesses of the argument based on traditions can also be traced in the fact that, at the end, the "stability on a determinate place" remains the main criterion used to recognise "home" and living in caravans is considered a mere "cultural exception". As a consequence, the first is the norm and the second something that deviates from it. Significant, in this sense, is the argument of the Court on the request of Chapman to place the caravan on her land for the absence of halting sites: "she claimed, in effect, special exemption from the rules applying to everyone else" (*Connors vs the UK*, par. 86). Although many scholars and judges recognise that the lack of halting sites represents itself a violation, they fail to acknowledge that it is the reproduction of an idea of home based on place stability that hinders the protection of mobile shelters. By developing the narrative on the "cultural specificities" of Gypsies and Travellers, they actually support this idea: if living in a caravan is a cultural exception, then the stable home is not the expression of the values of a dominant group, but a universal norm. The division between universal norms and cultural exceptions endorses, in turn, the symbolic violence produced by the dichotomy between "the modern western man" and the "subaltern attached to backward traditions".

This narrative is also supported by the recurring argument that the right to home does not imply the right to be provided with a home, affirmed both by the International Committee on Civil and Political Rights (J. Hohmann, 2013) and by the European Court of Human Rights in several occasions, as in the decision on *Chapman vs the UK*. This argument fails to acknowledge the structural barriers that prevent minorities from creating a home in a society where the housing market and the social services provide housing structures designed around the needs and values of the majority. It, namely, fails to recognise that legal and material obstacles to the enjoyment of home constitute themselves a violation of the right to home as they actually prevent home-making. Actually, the European Court of Human Rights has already moved towards a recognition of these positive obligations in other cases (European Court of Human Rights, 1998, 2011), but it did not apply this emerging principle in the case of Chapman. Here, the Court stated that the lack of halting sites did not justify the violation of domestic planning and that "Article 8 does not go so far as to allow individual's preferences as to their place of residence to override the general interest" (par. 81–82). The result is that living in a caravan remains considered something in between a "cultural exception" and a mere "housing preference".

From the statistics to the individual: a reflexive approach to housing adequacy and Roma inclusion

This analysis has shown some of the consequences of an approach to housing adequacy that does not take into account the broader implications of the dwelling, its importance for the identity of the individual, and the subjectivity of the person. Furthermore, the use of solely physical standards and quantitative analyses, with their supposed objectivity and rationality, supports a model that presents Roma as indiscriminately poor and disadvantaged, informing a paternalistic approach to policy that overlooks the agency of the Romani individual and the role of anti-gypsyism. For this reason, it is my intention to propose here a new approach to the assessment of policies addressing the inclusion of this group and of their housing conditions. With this aim, I present a fieldwork conducted in three Italian local contexts where the local authorities have implemented initiatives aimed at offering the local Roma and Sinti population a housing alternative to the nomad camp. The three cases – Pisa, Messina, and the autonomous province of Trento-Rovereto – have been selected because they concern measures that have been considered innovative and that have adopted different approaches to the housing issue. This work has a double aim: to analyse the impact at the local level of policies designed for the housing inclusion of Roma and to challenge the rationality of the adequacy standards with a qualitative study that brings the individual at the centre of the study.

I present these three initiatives by analysing their initial objectives, implementation and results, also through a series of interviews with the policy-makers and stakeholders involved in their realisation. This is done to propose a critical analysis of measures that are considered "success-stories", by highlighting the difficulties and shortcomings emerged during their implementation and the possible insights for future improvements. The cases here analysed have indeed been presented as "positive examples", both at the Italian and European level for different reasons, and have been praised for their objective to achieve the complete closure of all nomad camps. The case of Pisa concerns one of the most ambitious projects realised in Italy in this sector, because of the number of beneficiaries and because of the variety of measures and solutions foreseen. Messina is considered a positive example for its use of public funds in the implementation of a project aimed at involving the local Romani community in the renovation of public building for their reconversion into housing units. The autonomous province of Trento-Rovereto has been selected because it is the first local authority to adopt a law for the creation and regulation of "micro-areas" as an alternative to the nomad camps. As will be explained, the issue of the "micro-areas" is debated also in other contexts, and legislations for their regulation have been subsequently adopted in other areas. The analysis of these cases highlights the impact of initiatives based on a certain interpretation of housing adequacy and on assumptions influenced by anti-gypsyism. At the same time, they provide interesting insights for a reflection on possible evolutions in the development of other policies in this sector.

This analysis is then supported with a series of interviews with Roma and Sinti living in the area considered. Here, the group of interviewees does not include only those who have been addressed by the local policies of housing inclusion, but also those who remained out for different reasons or found a housing alternative autonomously. This choice is moved by the intention of presenting different housing stories and to highlight the variety of possible solutions, along with supporting the analysis of the policies. Indeed, another objective of this study is to challenge generalisations on the "Roma way of living", still object of debate. While the creation of the nomad camps was based on an essentialised and stereotypical association between Roma and nomadism, the debate on alternatives risks being developed around similar prejudices. Namely, it risks building the reflection around the homogenising question "what is the best solution for Roma?", without considering differences within the group and without involving the persons concerned.

Furthermore, the choice of presenting different cases is also moved by the intention of breaking other "common senses" on this group. As highlighted by Sigona (2002), the public perception of Roma in Italy tends to overestimate the percentage of those living in camps, which actually represents only one quarter or less of the entire Romani population in the country. For this reason, I intend to bring here different stories and points of view, often overlooked in statistics and public representations. This does not mean that this study aims to be representative of a specific population, whose definition, as I already specified, remains highly questionable. It, rather, aims to question possible generalisations on a group that is perceived as homogeneous but actually includes a universe of different situations. With the same intention, I include in the empirical work all individuals who are targeted by the EU Framework and the Italian Strategy for Roma Integration and I do not focus on a specific group (e.g., Sinti, Italian Roma, migrant Roma, etc). Namely, I consider in this book all persons identified as Roma or Sinti, not as members of the same ethno-cultural group, but as recipients of a specific policy framework.

With these aims, the interviews with Roma and Sinti tackle different aspects connected with the well-being of the person within the house, including their emotional attachment to the place of living, their memories and projects for the future. The design of the interviews owes much to previous sociological and ethnographical studies conducted on the impact of the relationship between the person and the dwelling within processes of social inclusion. I refer especially to the works of Catherine Brun (2015) among displaced persons in Georgia and Adriano Cancellieri (2017) in a multicultural and stigmatised condominium in

Italy. These two works, indeed, highlight the strong relationship between the place of living, the identity of the person and processes of inclusion and empowerment and they do so through a qualitative work that focuses on the person. The work of Brun, especially, analyses the impact of different housing policies on the level of inclusion of the beneficiaries. Furthermore, she highlights the importance and implications of creating a sense of "home" within the house, and the role that memories and projects for the future play in this sense. For this reason, I adopt a similar technique, by asking the interviewees to present their housing story from childhood, the current satisfaction with the place of living and the dreams for the future. An important aspect that is tackled is also the relationship with the surrounding context, intended both as the city and the national level.

Nevertheless, the aspect that most influenced the development of my methodological approach is a reflection on the potential implications of conducting this kind of research, especially with a group that has long been a passive object of research by non-Romani scholars. As already highlighted in the introduction to this book, anti-gypsyism has also been fed by academic works that, claiming a supposed objectivity for social sciences, treated Roma as exotic objects of study rather than individuals provided with agency. Much of the knowledge production on Roma, indeed, still focuses on their "cultural characteristics", on the differences from the majority, and on their "origin", reproducing the idea that Roma are a well-defined group external to the European context (Bogdán et al., 2015; Mirga-Kruszelnicka, 2015; Tremlett, 2009). Furthermore, anti-gypsyism remains a wide-spread and well-rooted phenomenon that requires a long process of deconstruction to be fully addressed. For this reason, the non-Romani researcher, despite good intentions, can never be sure of conducting research on Roma without applying prejudices and analytical frameworks derived from anti-gypsyism.

In addition to this, the aim of challenging forms of symbolic violence through fieldwork research risks producing other forms of symbolic violence. It namely risks replacing a biased representation of reality with another that falls into the same mistake of supposed "objectivity". Social sciences have long acknowledged the impossibility of achieving "objectivity" in research, as well as the "neutrality of the researcher", which were the main objectives of the positivist approach. It is now recognised that the subjectivity of both the researcher and the researched always influences the collection and elaboration of data. This cannot be avoided but can become an added value in the research work, if the subjectivity is recognised and empowered. The reflexive approach exactly has the aim to acknowledge and highlight the position and subjectivity of all individuals involved in the research process (Attia & Edge, 2017; Sherman Heyl, 2001). According to Bourdieu, this can be achieved by analysing the position of the researcher with the same attention used in the analysis of the object of research. Always according to this author, the recognition of the need of applying a reflexive approach has not been followed by a factual change of the way fieldwork is done, because of the "pride" of the "Westerner" researcher, who believes to be untouched by the external context (Bourdieu & Wacquant, 1992). Since then, reflexivity has surely made some progresses within social research, but if we look at the literature on Roma, it can be argued that the claim of Bourdieu is still valid.

Only recently, indeed, the need to adopt a reflexive approach and its implications have entered the debate on research on Roma (Brooks, 2015; Dunajeva, 2018; Fremlova, 2018; Silverman, 2018; Tremlett, 2014). These authors, along with outlining the consequences of fieldworks that do not acknowledge the position of the researcher and its normative baggage, highlight the possibilities of applying a feminist and intersectional approach in the development of a reflexive methodology. Feminist scholars have been the first to develop an approach to social research that is not based on the "invisibility" and "neutrality" of the researcher, but on a dialogue that balances the relations of power by giving the space to the researched subjects to shape the interview and raise their voices. This method appears useful not only to tackle the risks of a false "objectivity", but also to highlight the subjectivity and emotions of the person that can reveal new aspects, otherwise invisible (Sherman Heyl, 2001).

Furthermore, the recognition of the fluid and dialogical nature of the identity of the person and of its relationship with the others highlights the variety of aspects that intervene in determining the position of the researcher and the outcomes of the research. Lucie Fremlova particularly analyses this aspect within her work on LGBTIQ Roma (2018). Being a non-Romani LGBTIQ scholar and activist, Fremlova reflects on her position, highlighting how this influences the results of her work, but also how it is influenced by the context and the mutual perception. She can be considered an external, since she is not Roma, but also an internal, being an openly lesbian activist. Furthermore, these perceptions also change according to the social status, the nationality, the relation created with the researcher, the goals of the research work. In her reflection, Fremlova identifies what I consider a key point: the research work conducted by non-Roma on Roma is surely affected by anti-gypsyism – because of the prejudices of the researcher, the possible reticence of the researched to speak openly, etc. – but also by other identifying features and related norms (gender, sexuality, social status, etc.). This means that the attention to the relations of power affecting the fieldwork conducted by a non-Romani researcher on Roma must be supported by the recognition of all other aspects influencing their position. Otherwise, the aim of reversing a model based on anti-gypsyism may reproduce its same bases: the division between two well-defined groups – Roma and non-Roma – whose characteristics prevail on others.

My research work, with its objective of reversing a model based on the rejection of the subjective understanding of housing and on the invisibility of Romani voices, would have not been possible without involving directly the persons concerned by the analysed policies. Nevertheless, the results of this work were threatened by two main risks: interpreting the finding through analytical lenses distorted by anti-gypsyism, and/or falling into what Gayatri

Chakravorty Spivak (1992) calls an excessive "celebration of Third-Worldism". The first risk is often translated in the persistent tendency of interpreting empirical finding on Roma in collective terms, either cultural or social or both. As Annabel Tremlett (2009) highlights, empirical studies on this group too often tend to explain behaviours, practices and answers as culturally or socially-driven, falling into a determinist approach that overlooks the agency of the research subject. Furthermore, within this approach, differences between "Roma" and "non-Roma" become the main object of the analysis, and a certain idea of the Roma – segregated, poor, deviant – results in the invisibility of the individuals that do not reflect this stereotype. The second risk, the one of a celebration of Third-Worldism, is somehow related to the first and, in this context, is associated to a form of "well-intentioned" anti-gypsyism. With "celebration of Third-Worldism", Spivak refers to the practice of moving from an empirical model that veils the agency of the marginal subject to one that excessively celebrates "the voice of the marginal". This model may overlook the impact of the conditions of marginality and consequently reinforce the division between the "centre" and the "margins" (Gandhi, 1998; Spivak, 1992). Furthermore, it may, as well, focus too much on those individuals that live in conditions that are interpreted as far from the "centre".

From the beginning of my fieldwork, I was partly aware of these risks and their repercussions, not only because of the existing literature on the topic, but also because of my previous experience working within a nomad camp in Italy as a social worker. There, I already had the opportunity to face the impact of my position as a well-educated middle-class non-Romani woman in my relationships with the Romani inhabitants of the camp. At the same time, the following academic studies and confrontations allowed me to reflect on some of the prejudices that affected my work back then. For this reason, acknowledging some of the factors that could affect my research work, I opted for a methodological approach aimed at limiting the impact of my prejudices in the interview process and in the analysis. Furthermore, it was my intention to create a space of comfort where interviewees could feel safe and empowered to express their opinions. The objective was of giving space for talking and of carefully listening. I, therefore, designed an open-ended interview model to provide a direction and a reminder of the main macro-topics touched by the study. The interview was constructed as an informal conversation – interviewees had the space to shape the interview and to touch or not some points they deemed important. For this reason, the interviews could take different directions, and all of them resulted different in content, length and number of persons involved.

In the development of the methodology, the second aim was to avoid the risk of overlooking some cases and of giving too much weight to the "most visible Roma", then interpreted as representative of the entire group. With this aim, I looked for the support of different gate-keepers, namely individuals who would put me in contact with persons to interview. I asked all policy-makers and social workers involved in the first part of the fieldwork to introduce me to

Roma and Sinti, beneficiaries or not of policies, that could contribute to my study. I then asked for the support of the same Romani interviewees to reach other cases. This was done especially when the interviewees, both Roma and social workers, mentioned cases that in their opinion were "different". The main objective was, indeed, to interview Roma and Sinti living in different accommodation and expressing different housing needs and preferences. For obvious reasons, it was not always possible to reach all cases identified, through the difficulties of contacting them or them not being willing to take part in the study. At the same time, Roma living in nomad camps, or that lived in nomad camps, remain over-represented in this study, partly because they were the beneficiaries of the initiatives here analysed. Nevertheless, this approach allowed me to reach Romani people who were not usually considered in policy-planning and academic works. Their stories and perspectives appear, therefore, particularly interesting and significant as they display life experiences that are still largely invisible.

Finally, the adoption of this methodology was also justified by the intimate and personal nature of the topics treated. While the interviews with social workers and policy-makers tackled the realisation of policy measures and they were addressed as representatives of an organisation or institution – and asked to sign a consent form to appear in the study as such, the interviews with Roma touched also personal and, in some case, delicate aspects of their lives – housing story, attachment with the current house, desires for the future, feelings of belonging. For this reason, this part of the empirical work required further attention and respect. All interviewees, after being identified, were first contacted by the gate-keepers who informed them of the aim and content of the study. Where the person agreed, an appointment was fixed to conduct the interview, which, in most of the cases, was done in the house of the interviewee. Before proceeding, I further explained the object of my study, asked for their consent to conduct and to record the interview and specified that the interviews would remain completely anonymous. For this reason, in my analysis I refer to the interviewees with fake names and I omit aspects that may reveal their identity. This approach also aimed at creating a space of comfort and safety necessary to open the way for a conversation as much as possible informal. This kind of interview, indeed, offered also the opportunity to better highlight emotions associated with the house and different perspectives emerging in the confrontations between interviewees.

All the interviews were conducted in Italian, which was, for most of the interviewees, their second or third language. Nevertheless, all interviewees were able to express themselves in Italian, although sometimes with the help of a Romani fellow and with some grammatical mistakes. All the interviews have been transcribed and translated by me and I tried to remain as much as possible faithful to the words and style of the interviewees. Nevertheless, this was not always possible because of some specificities of the Italian language. The main one, in this case, is the absence of two different words translating "house" and "home" that are both translated as "casa", also true when it refers to the symbolic level. For this reason, it was not possible to ask: "Do you feel this house is your home?". The answer to this question could be achieved by asking other questions regarding their satisfaction and feeling of belonging in the place of living. In the transcription, I therefore translated the word "casa" as "home" when I had the impression that it was used at the symbolic level – when, for instance, it referred to an intangible space. Nevertheless, this lack of two different words may have brought me to misinterpret some expressions.

Although one of my initial goals was to challenge generalisations on "the Romani way of living" or "the best solution for Roma", the outcomes of the empirical work exceeded expectations. It also dismantled some of the assumptions that, consciously or unconsciously, were driving my research work. For instance, I realised how I was also falling into the mistake of looking for differences in terms of housing needs and desires between Roma and non-Roma, and of interpreting such differences exclusively in cultural terms. The interviews conducted not only rejected this assumption, but also displayed a variety that made any attempt of interpreting them in collective terms impossible. Nevertheless, this initial result moved me to engage with further reflection on my position and on the ways to interpret and present the findings of my research work. I further realised the risk, on one hand, of interpreting some outcomes through the lenses of my prejudices and, on the other hand, of disregarding the conditions that influenced them. Indeed, the risk of falling in an excessive celebration of the marginal laid behind each corner. Finally, the variety emerged during the fieldwork represented the core of my research findings and, therefore, required an analysis that highlighted as much as possible the individuality of each interviewee.

For this reason, I decided to select a number of interviews that displayed the variety of stories and points of view emerged during the work and that touched the most important issues and topics addressed in the analysis of the policy initiatives. These interviews are fully presented in Chapters 2, 3, 4, after the analysis of the measures implemented in each local context, using the transcription of the interviews and exposing my impressions to narrate the conversation. In this way, the reader can get acquainted with the complexity, fluidity and dynamicity of the relationship between the house, the person and the rest of society, in an intimate way. Furthermore, some of the consequences of the policy measures implemented in the past towards Roma, invisible to statistics – such as the repercussions for the identity of the person and their emotional well-being – can here emerge in all their gravity. This analysis, therefore, provides important insights for a reflection on a revision of the approach adopted both in the inclusion of Roma and in the protection of housing rights; namely, it supports the analysis of the policy measures, in light of the interviews with stakeholders and Roma, and of their potential alternatives.

Notes

1 Gadjo is the word used in Romani language to refer to non-Roma. Since Gadjo is used in opposition to "Roma", "gadjeness" refers to a certain idea of the "way of living of non-Roma".

2 International Convention on the Elimination of All Forms of Racial Discrimination; Convention on the Elimination of All Forms of Discrimination Against Women; Convention on the Rights of the Child; International Convention on the Protection of the Rights of All Migrant Workers and Members of Their Families.

3 166 out of 197 members of the United Nations have ratified the ICESCR, while the ICCPR has been ratified by 169 countries. Important to notice the missinng ratification of the ICESCR by the United States. (United Nations Human Rights Office of the High Commissioner, n.d.).

4 Some of the texts that have been used and analysed in this work and that tackle the housing conditions in Europe and among Roma refer explicitly to this list of adequacy parameters. (Eurofound, 2016; European Commission, 2013b, 2013a; European Roma Rights Centre, 2010)

5 On this matter, there are some interesting studies on the consequences of forced relocation policies on the life of indigenous groups living in structures considered inadequate by the white coloniser. See Chokor, 2005; Collignon, 2001.

6 The indivisibility of the two sets of rights has been officially established by the Vienna Declaration (*Vienna Declaration and Programme of Action*, 1993), which states that both sets of rights are "universal, indivisible and interdependent and interrelated" and for this reason shall be treated in a "fair and equal manner, on the same footing, and with the same emphasis".

7 This principle is affirmed within the General Comment n.16 to Art. 17 of the ICCPR (Human Rights Committee, 1988) and embraced in a number of sentences by the European Court of Human Rights (e.g. Connors vs the UK, 2004; Yordanova and Others vs Bulgaria, 2012)

References

Anton, C. E., & Lawrence, C. (2014). Home is where the heart is: The effect of place of residence on place attachment and community participation. *Journal of Environmental Psychology, 40*, 451–461. https://doi.org/10.1016/j.jenvp.2014.10.007.

Attia, M., & Edge, J. (2017). Be(com)ing a reflexive researcher: A developmental approach to research methodology. *Open Review of Educational Research, 4(1)*, 33–45. https://doi.org/10.1080/23265507.2017.1300068.

Bachelard, G. (1969). *The Poetics of Space*. Boston: Beacon Press.

Benhabib, S. (2002). *The Claims of Culture. Equality and Diversity in the Global Era*. Princeton: Princeton University Press.

Bernardo, F., & Palma-Oliveira, J. M. (2016). Urban neighbourhoods and intergroup relations: The importance of place identity. *Journal of Environmental Psychology, 45* (April), 239–251. https://doi.org/10.1016/j.jenvp.2016.01.010.

Blunt, A., & Dowling, R. (2006). *Home*. Abingdon: Routledge.

Boccagni, P. (2013). What's in a (migrant) house? Changing domestic spaces, the negotiation of belonging and home-making in Ecuadorian migration. *Housing, Theory and Society, 31(3)*, 277–293. https://doi.org/10.1080/14036096.2013.867280.

Bogdán, M., Ryder, A., & Taba, M. (2015). The Roma spring: Knowledge production and the search for a new humanity. *Roma Rights, 2* (Special Issue: Nothing About Us Without Us).

Boschetti, L., & Vitale, T. (2011). Les Roms ne sont pas encore prêts à se représenter eux-mêmes! Asymétries et tensions entre groupes Roms et associations "Gadjé" à Milan. In M. Berger, D. Cefai, & C. Gayet-Viaud, eds, *Du civil au politique. Ethnographies du vivre-ensemble* (pp. 403–429). Peter Lang.

Bourdieu, P. (1977). *Outline of a Theory of Practice*. Cambridge: Cambridge University Press.

Bourdieu, P., & Wacquant, L. J. D. (1992). *An Invitation to Reflexive Sociology*. Polity Press. https://doi.org/10.2307/2168398.

Brooks, E. C. (2015). The importance of feminists and "halfies" in Romani studies: New epistemological possibilities. *Roma Rights 2: Nothing About Us Without Us? Roma Participation in Policy Making and Knowledge Production*, ERRC.

Brun, C. (2015). Home as a critical value: From shelter to home in Georgia. *Refuge, 31* (*1*), 43–54.

Cancellieri, A. (2017). Towards a progressive home-making: The ambivalence of migrants' experience in a multicultural condominium. *Journal of Housing and the Built Environment, 32*(*1*), 49–61. https://doi.org/10.1007/s10901-015-9489-7.

Chokor, B. a. (2005). Changing urban housing form and organization in Nigeria: Lessons for community planning. *Planning Perspectives, 20*(January), 69–96. https://doi.org/10.1080/0266543042000300546.

Claps, E., & Vitale, T. (2010). Not always the same old story: Spatial segregation and feelings of dislike against Roma and Sinti in large cities and medium-size towns in Italy. In M. Stewart, & M. Rovid, eds, *Multi-Disciplinary Approaches to Romani Studies* (pp. 228–253). Budapest: CEU Press.

Collignon, B. (2001). Esprit des lieux et modéles culturels. *La mutation des espaces domestiques en arctique inuit. Annales de Geographie, 110*(*620*), 383–404. https://doi.org/10.3406/geo.2001.1731.

Committee on Civil Liberties Justice and Home Affairs of the European Parliament (2010). *Draft Report on the EU strategy on Roma Inclusion* (2276).

Council of the European Union (2013). Council Recommendation on effective Roma integration measures in the Member States. *In* Recommendations, 2013/C 378/01.

Craven, M. (1998). *The International Covenant on Economic, Social, and Cultural Rights: A Perspective on Its Development*. Oxford: Clarendon Press.

Directorate-General for Internal Policies European Parliament (2013). *Social Housing in the EU*.

Donald, M. (1999). Tranquil Havens? Critiquing the idea of home as the middle-class sanctuary. In I. Bryden & J. Floyd, eds, *Domestic Space. Reading the Nineteenth-Century Space*. Manchester University Press.

Donders, Y. (2016). Protecting the home and adequate housing. Living in caravan or trailer as a human right. *International Human Rights Law Review, 5*(*1*), 1–25. https://doi.org/10.1163/22131035-00501002.

Dunajeva, J. (2018). Power hierarchies between the researcher and informants: Critical observations during fieldwork in a Roma settlement. *Critical Romani Studies, 1*(*2*), 124–143. https://doi.org/10.29098/crs.v1i2.3.

Eide, A. (2001). Economic, social and cultural rights as human rights. In A. Eide, C. Krause, & A. Rosas, eds, *Economic Social and Cultural Rights. A Textbook*. Boston, London: Martinus Nijhoff Publishers.

Eurofound (2012). *Living Conditions of the Roma: Substandard Housing and Health*. Office of the European Union.

Eurofound (2016). *Inadequate Housing in Europe: Costs and Consequences*. Office of the European Union.

European Commission (2008a). *Community Instruments and Policies for Roma Inclusion*. Commission Staff Working Document accompanying the Communication from the Commission to the European Parliament, the Council, the European Economic and

Social Committee and the Committee of the Regions, 31/ 01/2008(COMM(2008) 420).

European Commission (2008c). *Press Release: Summit promotes joint commitment to improve inclusion for millions of Roma.* IP/08/1326.

European Commission (2010a). *Improving the Tools for the Social Inclusion and Non-Discrimination of Roma in the EU.*

European Commission (2010c). *The 10 Common Basic Principles on Roma Inclusion.* Vademecum.

European Commission (2010f). The Social and Economic Integration of the Roma in Europe. *Communication from the Commission to the Council, the European Parliament, the European Economic and Social Committee and the Committee of Regions,* COM(2010)133 final, Article COM (2010) 133 final.

European Commissionn (2011a). An EU Framework for National Roma Integration Strategies up to 2020. *Communication from the Commission to the European Parliament, the Council, the European Economic and Social Committee of Regions,* COM(2011) 173 final, Article COM (2011) 173 final.

European Commissionn (2011c). *Working together for Roma inclusion. The EU Framework explained.*

European Commission (2012a). *A First Step in the Implementation of the EU Framework.* Communication from the Commission to the European Parliament, the Council, the European Economic and Social Committee of the Regions. National Roma Integration Strategies, COM (2012) 226, Article COM(2012) 226 Final.

European Commission (2012c). *What Works for Roma Inclusion in the EU – Policies and Model Approaches.*

European Commission (2013a). *Confronting Homelessness in the European Union.* Commission Staff Working Document, SWD(2013) 42 Final, Article SWD(2013) 42 Final.

European Commission (2013b). *Discrimination in Housing.*

European Commission (2016). *Assessing the Implementation of the EU Framework for National Roma Integration Strategies and the Council Recommendation on effective Roma Integration Measures in the Member States.* Communication from the Commission to the European Parliament, the Council, the European Economic and Social Committee of the Region, COM (2016) 424, Article COM (2016) 424.

European Court of Human Rights (1996). *Buckley vs. The United Kingdom. 20348/92.*

European Court of Human Rights (1998). *Botta vs Italy. 21439/93.*

European Court of Human Rights (2001). *Chapman vs the United Kingdom. 27238/95.*

European Court of Human Rights (2004). *Connors v United Kingdom. 66746/01.*

European Court of Human Rights (2011). *Dubetska and Others vs. Ukraine. 30499/03.*

European Roma Rights Centre (2010, December). *Standards Do Not Apply: A Report by the European Roma Rights Centre Inadequate Housing in Romani Communities.*

European Social Charter *(Revised)* (1996).

European Social Committee (2006). *European Federation of National Organisations Working with the Homeless (FEANTSA) v. France. 39/2006.*

European Union Agency for Fundamental Rights (2009a). *Housing conditions of Roma and Travellers in the European Union. Comparative Report.*

European Union Agency for Fundamental Rights (2009c). *Improving Roma Housing and Eliminating Slums. Case Study Spain.*

European Union Agency for Fundamental Rights (2009d). *The Situation of Roma EU Citizens Moving to and Settling in Other EU Member States.*

European Union Agency for Fundamental Rights (2010b). *The State of Roma and Traveller Housing in the European Union. Steps towards Equality.*

European Union Agency for Fundamental Rights (2012). *Fundamental Rights: Challenges and Achievements in 2012.*

European Union Agency for Fundamental Rights (2016b). *Second European Union Minorities and Discrimination Survey. Roma – Selected Findings (EU-MIDIS II).*

Eurostat (2011). Housing conditions in Europe in 2009. *Statistics in Focus, 4.*

Fanon, F. (1963). *The Wretched of the Earth.* Grove Press. https://doi.org/10.1002/9780470755679.ch3.

FEANTSA (2006). *ETHOS European Typology on Homelessness and Housing Exclusion – Taking Stock.*

Fekete, L. (2014). *Europe against the Roma.* Race & Class, *55(3)*, 60–70. https://doi.org/10.1177/0306396813509196.

Fraser, N., & Honneth, A. (2003). *Redistribution or Recognition? A Political-Philosophical Exchange.* London, New York: Verso.

Fremlova, L. (2018). Non-Romani researcher positionality and reflexivity: Queer(y)ing one's own privilege. *Critical Romani Studies, 1(2)*, 98–123. https://doi.org/10.29098/crs.v1i2.25.

Gandhi, L. (1998). *Postcolonial Theory. A Critical Introduction.* Crows Nest, NSW: Allen & Unwin. https://doi.org/10.1002/9781118958933.ch21.

Gay y Blasco, P. (2003). "This is not a place for civilised people". In C. Strange & A. Bashford, eds, *Isolation. Places and Practices of Exclusion* (pp. 208–221). Taylor & Francis. https://doi.org/10.4324/9780203405222_chapter_13.

Geertz, C. (1973). *The Interpretation of Cultures.* New York: Basic Books.

Goldsack, L. (1999). A haven in a heartless home? Women and domestic violence. In T. Chapman & J. Hockey, eds, *Ideal Homes : Social Change and Domestic Life.* Routledge.

Hall, S. (2000). Old and new identities, old and new ethnicities. In L. Back & J. Solomos, eds, *Theories of Race and Racism* (pp. 144–153). Abingdon: Routledge.

Henrard, K. (2004). The European Convention on Human Rights and the Protection of the Roma as a controversial case of cultural diversity. *European Diversity and Autonomy Papers – EDAP, 5.*

Henry, B., & Certomà, C. (2013). Social Sciences as Sciences and "Hermeneutics". "Matteo Ricci's Legacy". In A. Loretoni, J. Pauchard, & A. Pirni, eds, *Questioning Universalism. Western and New Confucian Conceptions* (pp. 149–163). Pisa: Edizioni ETS.

Hepworth, K. (2012). Abjecting geographies: Imagining and inhabiting the "nomad camp" in Italy. In C. Certomà, N. Clewer, & D. Elsey, eds, *The Politics of Space and Place* (pp. 16–44). Newcastle Upon Tyne: Cambridge Scholars Publishing.

Hohmann, J. (2013). *Right to Housing: Law, Concepts, Possibilities.* Oxford and Portland: Hart Publishing. https://doi.org/10.5040/9781472566416.0004.

Hohmann, J. M. (2013). The true radicalism of the right to housing. *British Academy Review, 21*, 22–25.

Honig, B. (1994). Difference, dilemmas, and the politics of home. *Social Research, 61(3)*, 563–597. https://doi.org/10.1057/9780230305076.

hooks, b. (1990). *Yearning. Race, Gender, and Cultural Politics.* New York: Routledge. https://doi.org/10.4324/9781315743110.

Human Rights Committee (1988). *General Comment No. 16: Article 17 (Right to Privacy) The Right to Respect of Privacy, Family, Home and Correspondence, and Protection of Honour and Reputation.*

Irigaray, L. (1992). *Ethics and Sexual Difference*. Ithaca: Cornell University Press.

Iusmen, I. (2018). "Non multa, sed multum": EU Roma policy and the challenges of Roma inclusion. *Journal of European Integration, 6337*, 1–15. https://doi.org/10.1080/07036337.2018.1462803.

Joint dissenting opinion of Judges Pastor Ridruejo, Bonello, Tulkens, Straznicka, Lorenzen, Fischbach and Casadevall in Chapman v. The United Kingdom, (2001).

Kavrakova, Y. (2013). The Roma issue in the European multilevel system: Ideas, interests and institutions behind the failure of inclusion policies. *European Yearbook of Minority Issues*, 359–380. https://doi.org/10.1163/22116117–01001015.

Kenna, P. (2005). *Housing Rights and Human Rights*. Brussels: FEANTSA (European Federation of National Organisations working with the Homeless).

Kligman, G. (2001). On the social construction of "otherness" identifying "the Roma" in post-socialist communities. *Review of Sociology*, 7(*2*), 61–78. https://doi.org/10.1556/RevSoc.7.2001.2.4.

Koch, I. E. (2006). Economic, social and cultural rights as components in civil and political rights: A hermeneutic perspective. *The International Journal of Human Rights, 10*(*4*), 405–430. https://doi.org/10.1080/13642980601019730.

Kóczé, A. (2017). Race, migration and neoliberalism: Distorted notions of Romani migration in European public discourses. *Social Identities*, 1–15. https://doi.org/10.1080/13504630.2017.1335827.

Kostka, J. (2015). Implementation of Roma inclusion policies: Why defining the problem matters. *Social Inclusion, 3*(*5*), 78–89. https://doi.org/10.17645/si.v3i5.231.

Leckie, S. (2001). The human right to adequate housing. In A. Eide, C. Krause, & A. Rosas, eds, *Economic Social and Cultural Rights. A Textbook* (pp. 149–168). Boston, London: Martinus Nijhoff Publishers.

Manzo, L. C. (2003). Beyond house and haven: Toward a revisioning of emotional relationships with places. Journal of Environmental Psychology, *23*(*1*), 47–61. https://doi.org/10.1016/S0272-4944(02)00074–00079.

Martin, B., & Mohanty, C. T. (1986). Feminist politics: What's home got to do with it? In T. de Lauretis, ed., *Feminist Studies/Cultural Studies* (pp. 191–212). Bloomington: Indiana University Press. https://doi.org/10.1007/978–1-349–18997-7_12.

Marushiakova, E., & Popov, V. (2015). European policies for social inclusion of Roma: Catch 22? *Social Inclusion, 3*(*5*), 2183–2803. https://doi.org/10.17645/si.v3i5.241.

Marushiakova, E., & Popov, V. (2017). Orientalism in Romani studies: The case of Eastern Europe. In H. Kyuchukov & W. New, eds, *Languages of Resistance: Ian Hancock's Contribution to Romani Studies*. Lincom Europa.

Massey, D. ed. (1995). *A Place in the World: Places, Cultures and Globalisation*. Oxford: Oxford University Press.

Matache, M. (2017). *Biased elites, unfit policies: Reflections on the lacunae of Roma integration strategies. European Review, 25*(*4*), 588–607.

McGarry, A., & Drake, H. (2013). The politicization of Roma as an ethnic "other": Security discourse in France and the politics of belonging. In U. Korkut, G. Buckem-Knapp, A. Mcgarry, J. Hinnfors, & H. Drake, eds, *The Discourses and Politics of Migration in Europe* (pp. 73–91). Palgrave MacMillan. https://doi.org/10.1057/9781137310903_5.

Mirga-Kruszelnicka, A. (2015). Romani studies and emerging Romani scholarship. *Roma Rights, 2* (Special Issue: Nothing About Us Without Us? Roma Participation in Policy Making and Knowledge Production), 39–46.

PES Group Committee of the Regions (2012). *A European Agenda for Social Housing*.

Phillips, A. (2007). *Multiculturalism without Culture*. Princeton: Princeton University Press.

Piasere, L. (1991). *Popoli delle Discariche. Saggi di antropologia zingara*. Roma: CISU Edizioni.

Piasere, L., Solimano, N., & Tosi Cambini, S. (A c. Di). (2014). *Wor(l)ds which Exclude*. Fiesole: Fondazione Michelucci Press.

Picker, G. (2017). *Racial Cities: Governance and the Segregation of Romani People in Urban Europe*. London: Routledge.

Proshansky, H. M., Fabian, A. K., & Kaminoff, R. (1983). Place-identity: Physical world socialization of the self. *Journal of Environmental Psychology*, *3*(*1*), 57–83. https://doi.org/10.1016/S0272-4944(83)80021–80028.

Racles, A. (2014). Stories with and about wall carpets. An anthropological account on the inhabitation of Ursari Romanian Roma. *Journal of Comparative Research in Anthropology and Sociology*, *5*(*2*), 107–132.

Rapoport, A. (1998). Using "culture" in housing design. *Housing and Society*, *25*(*1–2*), 1–20.

Relph, E. (1976). *Place and Placelessness*. London: Pion Limited.

Remiche, A. (2012). Yordanova and Others v Bulgaria: The influence of the social right to adequate housing on the interpretation of the civil right to respect for one's home. *Human Rights Law Review*, *12*(*4*), 787–800. https://doi.org/10.1093/hrlr/ngs033.

Richardson, J. (2006). Talking about Gypsies: The notion of discourse as control. *Housing Studies*, *21*(*1*), 77–96. https://doi.org/10.1080/02673030500391171.

Ringelheim, J. (2011). Chapman redux. The European Court of Human Rights and Roma traditional lifestyle. *Mainstreaming Diversity – Rewriting Judgments of the European Court of Human Rights*. https://doi.org/10.1017/cbo9781139208130.026.

Roagna, I. (2012). *Protecting the Right to Respect for Private and Family Life under the European Convention on Human Rights*. Strasbourg: Council of Europe.

Rodriguez Maeso, S. (2014). "Civilising" the Roma? The depoliticisation of (anti-) racism within the politics of integration. *Identities: Global Studies in Culture and Power*, *22*(*1*), 53–70. https://doi.org/10.1080/1070289X.2014.931234.

Rose, G. (1993). *Feminism and Geography. The Limits of Geographical Knowledge*. Cambridge: Polity Press.

Rostas, I. (2019). *A Task for Sisyphus. Why Europe's Roma Policies Fail*. Budapest: CEU Press.

Rövid, M. (2011). *One-size-fits-all Roma? On the normative dilemmas of the emerging European Roma policy*. Romani Studies, *21*(*1*), 1–22. https://doi.org/10.3828/rs.2011.1.

Sack, R. D. (1997). *Homo Geographicus*. The Johns Hopkins University Press.

Sherman Heyl, B. (2001). Ethnographic interviewing. In P. Atkinson, A. Coffey, S. Delamont, J. Lofland, & L. Lofland, eds, *Handbook of Ethnography* (pp. 369–383). London: Sage Publications.

Sibley, D. (1995). *Geographies of Exclusion*. London and New York: Routledge.

Sigona, N. (2002). *Figli del ghetto. Gli italiani, i campi nomadi e l'invenzione degli zingari*. Civezzano: Nonluoghi Libere Edizioni.

Silverman, C. (2018). From reflexivity to collaboration: Changing roles of a non-Romani scholar, activist, and performer. *Critical Romani Studies*, *1*(*2*), 76–97. https://doi.org/10.29098/crs.v1i2.16.

Simhandl, K. (2009). Beyond boundaries? Comparing the construction of the political categories "Gypsies" and "Roma" before and after EU enlargement. In N. Sigona & N. Trehan, eds, *Romani Politics in Contemporary Europe* (pp. 72–93). Basingstoke: Palgrave MacMillan. https://doi.org/10.1057/9780230281165_4.

Spivak, G. C. (1992). *Outside in the Teaching Machine*. London and New York: Routledge.

Ssenyonjo, M. (2009). *Economic, Social and Cultural Rights in International Law*. Oxford and Portland: Hart Publishing.

Strange, C., & Bashford, A. eds (2003). *Isolation: Places and Practices of Exclusion*. London and New York: Routledge.

Trehan, N., & Kóczé, A. (2009). Racism, (neo-)colonialism and social justice: The struggle for the soul of the Romani movement in post-socialist Europe. In G. Huggan & I. Law, eds, *Racism Postcolonialism Europe* (pp. 50–74). Liverpool: Liverpool University Press. https://doi.org/10.5949/liverpool/9781846312199.003.0004.

Tremlett, A. (2009). Bringing hybridity to heterogeneity in Romani Studies. *Romani Studies, 19(2)*, 147–168.

Tremlett, A. (2014). Making a difference without creating a difference: Super-diversity as a new direction for research on Roma minorities. *Ethnicities, 14(6)*, 830–848. https://doi.org/10.1177/1468796814542183.

Tuan, Y.-F. (2001). Cosmos versus hearth. In P. C. Adams, S. Hoelscher, & K. E. Till, eds, *Texture of Places. Exploring Humanist Geographies* (pp. 319–325). Minneapolis and London: Minnesota University Press.

UN Committee on Economic Social and Cultural Rights (1990). *General Comment No. 3: The Nature of States Parties' Obligations (Art. 2, Par. 1, of the Covenant). E/1991/23.*

UN Committee on Economic Social and Cultural Rights (1991). *General Comment No. 4: The Right to Adequate Housing (Art. 11). 11(E/1992/23), 1–7.*

UN Committee on Economic Social and Cultural Rights (1997). *General Comment No. 7. The right to Adequate Housing (Art. 11 (1) of the Covenant): Forced evictions.*

International Covenant on Economic, Social and Cultural Rights (1966).

United Nations Human Rights Office of the High Commissioner (n.d.). *Status of Ratification Interactive Dashboard*. http://indicators.ohchr.org/.

van Baar, H. (2017). Contained mobility and the racialization of poverty in Europe: The Roma at the development–security nexus. *Social Identities*, 1–17. https://doi.org/10.1080/13504630.2017.1335826.

Vermeersch, P. (2012). Reframing the Roma: EU initiatives and the politics of reinterpretation. *Journal of Ethnic and Migration Studies, 38(8)*, 1195–1212. https://doi.org/10.1080/1369183X.2012.689175.

Vienna Declaration and Programme of Action (1993).

von Hebel, H. (1987). The implementation of the Right to Housing in Article 11 of the U.N. Covenant on Economic, Social and Cultural Rights. *SIM Newsletter, 20*, 24–41.

Young, I. M. (2005). *On Female Body Experience: "Throwing like a Girl" and Other Essays*. Oxford: Oxford University Press. https://doi.org/10.1093/0195161920.001.0001.

2 Pisa, the project "Città Sottili" ("Thin Cities")

Towards a sustainable alternative to the nomad camps?

Pisa is a middle-size town located in the region of Tuscany. Especially known for its touristic attractions, as the Piazza dei Miracoli and the Leaning Tower, Pisa is also one of the main university centres in Italy, hosting three universities. Despite its rather small size – it has about 90,000 inhabitants – and the absence of significant productive activities, Pisa is considered an important historical and cultural site, and this ensures its inhabitants a fairly wealthy quality of life. Its urban structure consists of an historical city centre, mostly occupied by commercial activities, museums and students' residences, a series of residential neighbourhoods and an industrial area. The limited urban structure is immediately followed by a country-side landscape, characterised by small villages, and the seaside coast. Furthermore, although economic and social differences can be traced in urban structure and despite the presence of neighbourhoods slightly more exposed to criminal activities, Pisa does not include areas that can be considered particularly marginal or abject as in other bigger Italian towns.

The presence of Roma and Sinti in Pisa is relatively higher compared to other Italian towns of similar size and higher than the number of Roma and Sinti present in the areas of the other two cases considered in this study. Their presence is composed of three main groups: the Sinti, historically present on the territory; the Roma from ex-Yugoslavia, arrived since the beginning of the 80s and then in the 90s, during the wars; and the Roma from Romania, who started arriving after the year 2000.[1] Over the years, the approach of the local municipality towards these groups has been in line with the rest of Italy, combining the creation of nomad camps (from the 80s) with a series of other securitarian measures, such as evictions and expulsions. In that period, the registered presence of Roma and Sinti amounted to a number between 300 and 600, varying according to the number of evictions and to the consequent movements. In 1991, the municipality approved the construction of a new nomad camp, replacing the old one that was closed, to be constructed near the local village of Coltano. The structure was finally inaugurated in 1996 and became the main nomad camp in Pisa (Bontempelli, 2006a).

Nevertheless, the situation started changing during the end of the 90s, when a series of xenophobic attacks against Romani children in the region of

DOI: 10.4324/9781003184539-3

Tuscany mobilised protests against the segregation of this group in nomad camps and raised the attention of the local media. Consequently, local regional administrations started considering the necessity of closing these segregating structures in order to offer housing alternatives and to foster social inclusion. This debate, in the year 2000, brought the adoption of the first regional law for the inclusion of Roma and Sinti (Interventi per i popoli rom e sinti, 2000) that planned the dismantling of the system of the nomad camps. With this main objective, the law proposed a series of solutions that could be offered by the local municipality according to the available resources and the housing needs of the population concerned. The possible alternatives included: access to public housing[2], subsidized rents, reconstruction and recovering of abandoned buildings, construction of small "villages" hosting enlarged families and integrated within the urban fabric and upgrading of the accommodation found independently by Roma and Sinti (Bontempelli, 2006a; Furlan, 2011; Tosi Cambini & Solimano, 2014).

In this context, the municipality of Pisa developed the project "Città Sottili", implemented between 2002 and 2010. This project represented one of the first and most ambitious initiatives implemented in Italy, with the intention of closing all local nomad camps. For this reason, it has often been presented as a positive example of public policies towards Roma both by EU documents (European Commission, 2010; European Union Agency for Fundamental Rights, 2009) and in academic works (Tosi, 2009). Along with its ambitious objective (closing all nomad camps hosting around 500 individuals), the project was praised for addressing a series of other social issues (education, first of all) in what was then called an "integrated approach". Nevertheless, the project also attracted some criticisms before its closure (Bontempelli, 2006a, 2006b) and, as it is going to be shown, the final outcomes did not match the expected results. For this reason, this initiative represents an ideal case in analysing the difficulties and obstacles that can emerge in the implementation of similar projects. The analysis has been conducted by considering the policy documents released before and during its implementation, the previous studies conducted on its results and the outcomes of my fieldwork. This included interviews with five persons involved, in different capacities, in the development, implementation and monitoring of the project[3] and 16 Romani individuals living in the area.[4] All the interviews were conducted between November and December 2016.

The pioneering project of "Città Sottili": objectives and results

The main objective of the project was to achieve the closure of all local nomad camps (authorised and unauthorised[5]) with the provision of a series of alternative housing solutions, to be realised progressively. Along with this main goal, the initiative aimed also at supporting Roma in a process of "empowerment", understood as the acquisition of autonomy and the full participant in the social life, through the access to the education and job system (Società della Salute Zona Pisana, 2007). The initiative, indeed, intended to move beyond the emergency approach, so far adopted in dealing with these groups, and to offer sustainable solutions. Consequently, the provision of housing alternatives was supported by two other initiatives: *Anglunipé*, focusing on the mediation between Roma and social services, and *Amen bask dza*, dealing with the inclusion of Romani children in the school system. Another important aspect touched by the project was the support to the acquisition of documents for those who were *de facto* stateless or did not have regular residence permit (Azienda USL 5, 2004; Società della Salute Zona Pisana, 2007).

The first action undertaken in 2002 was a census of all Roma living in two camps (the authorised one of Coltano and the unauthorised one of Oratoio) and in three other smaller areas/occupied buildings. The total number of individuals counted by the census and therefore entering the project was about 500, all Roma of Yugoslav origin, with a high majority of Macedonians[6]. Following the census, the municipality, together with other public entities/social services (Tuscany region; ASL 5; Società della Salute) and local organisations (three social cooperatives: Elleuno, il Simbolo, Il Progetto; Fondazione Michelucci) started identifying a range of housing solutions and planning the progressive transfer of the families. The housing solutions identified were several: apartments found in the housing market, whose rent was initially covered by the project, inclusion within the waiting lists of public housing, acquisition of public buildings and their reconversion into flats, the self-build construction of a "Romani village" (Azienda USL 5, 2004). The project foresaw, as well, the active participation of Romani families both in the identification of the housing solutions and in the renovation and construction of new housing structures (Bontempelli, 2006a; Manca, 2013).

Despite the intentions of the project, which all individuals interviewed during the study defined as innovative and courageous, from the very beginning a series of difficulties hindered its full and progressive realisation. The first issue that emerged was the increasing number of Roma on the territory of the municipality, because of the arrival of Romani migrants from Romania. According to Sergio Bontempelli, researcher and activist interviewed in the study, local media started over-emphasising these arrivals, triggering public protests and insinuating the idea that the project would have produced a sort of "call effect", moving other Roma to Pisa. This, together with the already existing idea that "too many Roma are not sustainable", led local authorities to exclude from the project all the Romani families that were not included in the initial census and to affirm that this initiative was "exceptional". This exclusion resulted in a division between the "included" and the "excluded", provoking important and lasting conflicts within the communities.

The second problem was the sudden eviction of the families living in two minor occupied areas, ordered by the local legal authorities. This pushed the organisations in charge of the project to abandon the initial plan and to find immediate housing solutions for those evicted. According to Antonio Minghi and Elisa Mennucci, coordinators of the project for the organisation La Città della Salute and the cooperative Il Simbolo, this urgency obliged the organisations to find "quick" solutions and the families to accept them, also when they did not respond to their needs or their location was far away from Pisa. Indeed, the accommodation consisted of flats whose rent was initially covered by the project, often located in small towns far from Pisa. This posed a problem for those who did not have means of transportation. Although the idea was to place them somewhere safe temporarily waiting for permanent solutions fitting their needs and possibilities, the relocation into new housing units for most of the cases was never realised.

The situation of urgency did not allow the officers working on the implementation of the project to consider entirely the individual situations. As a result, some of the beneficiaries relocated to flats did not have the economic means to contribute to the payment of the housing bills and of the rent, and the distance with Pisa decreased their chances to find a job. Furthermore, according to Minghi, a number of families caused severe damage to the housing units, while others abandoned them, supposedly because they were not used to living in these kinds of structures, and they saw them as something "transitory". This aspect was partially confirmed also by Sergio Bontempelli and Sultan Dibran and by some of the Romani persons interviewed in the village of Coltano. Here, indeed, a number of Romani families were pointed to by others as the ones who "do not want to live in houses". Unfortunately, these families refused to be interviewed and it was, therefore, not possible to collect their account. These differences in "perceiving and living the house" were, nevertheless, not interpreted in cultural terms – as was done with the Sinti in Trento (see Chapter 4) – or associated to the level of integration. Indeed, Minghi and Mennucci themselves highlighted that differences could be traced within the same family or the same group, and they did not depend on the level of integration of the person.

The damages provoked to the structures, together with the common tendency of the owners to benefit from the situation and to declare higher damages that the effective ones, consistently raised the costs of the project. In addition, this problem resulted in a further delay in its implementation, already hampered by the slowness of the bureaucratic procedures for the acquisition of the residence permits necessary to obtain a house. This provoked an important extension of the time considered necessary for the complete realisation of the project (initially planned for three years). Such extension exasperated the families still waiting for accommodation and temporarily placed in containers, rising further conflicts within the community.

Because of this, the participatory mechanisms foresaw by the project in order to involve the Romani community in decision-making also failed their objective. Initially, the appointment of three representatives and the organisation of collective meetings was planned. Elisa Mennucci remembered this experience as positive because it created a relation between the community and the administration. Nevertheless, she also admitted that these initiatives missed their main goal, namely of providing solutions that responded as much as possible to the necessities of the families. This was because of the appointment of representatives, the division between "included" and "excluded" and the frustration due to the delays in the realisation of the project raised conflicts that hampered the possibility of taking decisions in a collective manner. The Romani mediator Sultan Dibran considered the failure of the participatory systems and the conflicts that emerged as one of the main reasons for the shortcomings of the project.

The last of the measures planned by the project entered its implementing phase in 2007– the construction of the "Romani village" to be located in the same area of the nomad camp, near the municipality of Coltano. This village was meant to represent an innovative housing solution for Romani families: constructed in cooperation with its inhabitants, it was supposed to unite the necessity to find economically sustainable solutions with the provision of good quality accommodation. Nevertheless, retrospectively, most of the stakeholders who took part in the implementation of "Città Sottili" did not consider the solution a successful one. Indeed, even though the buildings, constructed with a technique in between the brick house and the prefabricated structure, presented a condition certainly improved compared to the dwellings in the camps, in all other characteristics it did not differ much from the situation of the camp. It still consisted of a monoethnic village, isolated from the rest of society, and very badly connected to the city. Furthermore, in this case the intention of involving the community in the construction of the village was abandoned because of the delays and the technical challenges that self-build presented.

Also the interviews conducted with the inhabitants of the Romani village highlighted the numerous and serious challenges posed by living in this structure. None of the inhabitants interviewed (nine persons) expressed full satisfaction with the housing solution: although some recognised the improved conditions compared to the "nomad camp", the problems remained many, and the majority expressed the strong desire to leave the village. One of the main issues was its isolated position, kilometres away from any urban structure, and the fact that public transportation did not reach it. Consequently, for most of the people without a car, the village had become a segregating prison, preventing also the possibility of finding a job outside. Another issue often raised was the fact that only Roma lived there, resulting in its stigmatisation as a "nomad camp", with all the negative consequences. Furthermore, many complained about the proximity of other Romani families. Indeed, despite the fact that each family had its own plot, the absence of proper public spaces and their vicinity resulted in a *de facto* forced cohabitation. Finally, the poor quality of the housing structures and of the sewing system – surely improved compared to the camp but not comparable to a regular brick house – was reason for discontent.

Nevertheless, the Romani village was the only outcome of the project "Città Sottili" that lasted any amount of time. The end of its construction, 2010, marked, as well, the end of the project. In 2008, the new administration had already declared the closure of the project and the adoption of a rather securitarian approach, following a violent conflict between two Romani families in the camp of Coltano (Manca, 2013). Its closure determined the lack of the funds necessary to cover the expenses resulting from the payments of the rents that the families could not afford. Bontempelli, in 2006, warned of the risk that the families allocated in apartments would not be able to pay the rent without financial support because of the persistent and increasing difficulties of finding an occupation (Bontempelli, 2006b). And this is what effectively happened after the closure of the project, with the result that the families allocated in flats were again evicted. Since very few could be allocated in public housing and the reconversion of public buildings into housing units was not realised because of bureaucratic challenges, a consistent number of beneficiaries suffered a new eviction and returned to live in precarious conditions.

As a result, the objective of dismantling all local nomad camps was not achieved. In 2016, when I conducted the interviews, many Romani families had returned to live in the unauthorised camp of Oratorio, located close to the industrial area of Pisa. Others were accommodated among relatives living in the Romani village or had built a self-built shelter in its proximity. The failure of the other solutions, therefore, moved to a reconsideration of the solution of the "village". Elisa Mennucci, for instance, noticed how the security of a "house" ensured in the village improved the social inclusion of its inhabitants, especially of the younger generations that attended the local schools more regularly. Nevertheless, the segregation suffered by its inhabitants still represented the major obstacle to their inclusion. This was the opinion expressed by the majority of the interviewees, especially by Sergio Bontempelli and Sultan Dibran, who reflected on the psychological consequences of living in a segregated village. This, indeed, continued marking a sort of physical border between what was considered "Roma" and what "Gadje", preventing the exchange necessary to deconstruct the mutual prejudices that reproduce the exclusion of Roma.

Life in and beyond the Romani village of Coltano

The fieldwork in Pisa brought me to interview 16 Roma living in the town and its surroundings. Most of them lived, at the time, in the Romani village of Coltano, but not all lived there as a result of the project. Some, indeed, such as Carlotta and Pietro, were hosted by relatives after being evicted from the apartment that was provided to them by "Città Sottili"; others, like the Marta's family, had built their own shelter in the same land after losing the concession of their house. Here, I also interviewed Caterina, a middle-age woman living in the village with her family, Giovanni, an older inhabitant of the village, Chiara and Daniela, two teenagers, Monica, around 30 years' old living with her extended family, and Debora and Paola, daughter and mother sharing the same house. The other interviews were conducted in different locations. One involved a mother and daughter, Dora and Rosa, living in a nomad camp after losing the accommodation provided by the project; another interview was conducted with Emma, a woman living with the family in a flat found in the housing market with the support of local volunteers and social services; another involved a couple, Agnese and Luigi, living in a private land/micro-area acquired independently; and the last an homeless man, Vincenzo, who had been evicted from a private land, and was moving with his family on a caravan.

I visited the Romani village of Coltano three times. The first time, mid-November 2016, was to interview Giovanni, whose contact was provided to me by a local volunteer familiar with the Romani community in Pisa. Giovanni was one of the oldest inhabitants of Coltano and, according to the gate-keeper, one of the most respected. Nevertheless, despite the efforts to ask the availability of other inhabitants of the village to take part in the study, during this first visit it was not possible to interview any other apart from him. The second and third visits, mid-December, were possible thanks to the support of the Romani mediator who took part in the research and whose family lived in the village. Thanks to the help of the gate-keeper and of his family, it was possible in two days to conduct all the other interviews. Nevertheless, not all people who were asked to take part in the study accepted. Here, in the village of Coltano, I could not interview a group of Romani families from Bosnia-Herzegovina, who lived marginalised within the village and were pointed to as the ones "who do not know how to live in a brick house" and "do not want to live in an apartment", both by social workers and the other inhabitants of the village. Despite some efforts, they never gave their consent for an interview.

The Romani village was located in a very isolated area beside the rural town of Coltano, at the outskirts of Pisa, accessible almost exclusively by car. It was very difficult for me to find the way to the village: no signal indicated the direction and also the names of the streets were missing; the road was very badly maintained, and it looked like it would have brought me to cultivated fields, not to an inhabited village. Moreover, the village was located beside the highway and kilometres away from any form of commercial activity or social service. All these characteristics forcibly reminded the classical nomad camp, located on lands of poor value and away from the rest of urban fabric. When the study was conducted, also the external aspect of the village did not differ much from the one of the camp: the street in front was poorly maintained and there were small trucks and caravans parked all around. On the other hand, the interior looked more like a residential area with terraced houses facing each a small private garden. Most of the houses differed for level of maintenance and personalisation: while some maintained a minimal structure and presented some damages, others were very well equipped and decorated with plants and flowers. Beside these houses, there were other shelters and containers placed by families who remained out of the project. Nevertheless, the division between the "houses" and the "shelters" was not that evident at first sight.

All the interviews conducted in Coltano differed between each other in terms of the background of the persons interviewed and in terms of needs and desires. Nevertheless, there were some common issues expressed by everyone. The first one, already mentioned above, was the general discontent with the solution of the Romani village. While some did not complain particularly about their life in the village, none expressed the desire to remain there also in the future. Another similarity concerned the trauma of moving from a "house", where they lived in their country of origin, to the nomad camp in Italy. Indeed, those who experienced this passage with the migration remembered it as deeply traumatic. Furthermore, they all emphasised that, before living in a camp, they were living in a "house as all the others" and that, for this reason, they wanted to live in "a house as all the others". This claim sometimes resulted in anger after the question: "In which kind of housing solution would you like to live?" or "In which kind of accommodation did you live before the camp?" as it was probably interpreted as the intention to raise a difference between "them" and "the others". For instance, Giovanni, in answering to the question as to what kind of accommodation he used to live in the country of origin, replied, visibly annoyed: "No, as a house, as your house, do you know what is it?!".

In other cases, as in the one of Monica, the desire to live in "a house as all other" was associated to the will not to be associated with Roma in general, highlighting the strong perceived link between identity and place of living:

> The ideal for me would be, I tell you, a house, outside of Romani community. I don't want to live with Roma because I lived from 95 to 2016 everyone with Roma, I don't want to live with Roma, I want to change life and I want to change style. Rightly I have my family where I live with my relatives, and I want to live outside, I don't want to live with them anymore. Because I don't want any longer to hear that I am one of them. We are not all the same.

The following sections present three interviews conducted in the village. They have been selected because they differ from each other significantly, in terms of their background and for answers given. Indeed, despite the common issues emerging during all the interviews, other aspects touched during the conversations diverged, especially in relation to the wishes connected to the house and to their experience living in the camp and village.

Caterina

I met Caterina in the Romani village of Coltano where she lived with her family thanks to the Romani mediator who personally knew her. At the time of the interview, she was about 40 years old and she had lived in Italy for 19 years. Her house, where the interview was conducted, appeared simple, with few pieces of furniture, but well maintained and clean. Caterina lived there with her husband, a Romani man from Macedonia who was not present during the interview, and three of her sons and daughters, all over 15 years' old. She immediately appeared willing to take part in the study and open in telling her story. For this reason, the interview with her was one of the longest and one of the most intimate. Nevertheless, at the beginning, I had the feeling that she was not being completely honest in expressing her opinion regarding her life in Italy and she did not want to be too critical towards Italian and local policies. She started opening herself up more and shared with me moving memories of her pasts and dreams about the future in a later stage, after the first questions. Her knowledge of Italian language was not perfect, and, for this reason, she sometimes asked the help of the mediator for the translation of some words. For the same reason, some passages were not completely clear, and some words could not be understood during the transcription of the conversation.

Her story started in Kosovo, where she was born and where she grew up with her mother, grandparents, uncles and aunts. Once she got married, she moved to Macedonia and after some years to Pisa, where she always lived in a nomad camp before receiving a house in the Romani village of Coltano by the project "Città Sottili". Despite the very poor living conditions, she and her husband managed to ensure an education for their sons and daughters, who attended schools regularly, in some cases reaching higher levels of education. One of the first topics that she touched during the interview was the realisation of the project "Città Sottili" and the provision of an accommodation in Coltano. Although she did not appear completely critical towards the project itself, she highlighted some critical aspects of living in the village, especially in connection to the persistent stereotype associating Roma to nomadism:

> They have developed a program for Roma, they have built the houses, it lasted a while, we received the houses, and yes, we are fine, but we have some difficulties because we are in the countryside. We don't have the bus, it is not easy for the children to go to school without the bus, when there is some emergencies the doctors have no trust in coming here in Romani houses. Because they say "Romani camp", but it is not any more a Romani camp, here we have the houses, terraced-houses. Because they say "nomads", and for this reason I am a bit worried and against them, and they say "nomads". And what "nomads" means? That today they are here and tomorrow we don't know where they are. We are not nomads, we are Roma! [emphasised]

Notably, the rejection of the stereotype went hand in hand with a proud claim of her Romani identity. This aspect was recurrent in the conversation with her and it was reaffirmed in the passage that followed, where integration was not presented as a threat to or in contrast with "Romani culture", but as a legitimate evolution that did not have to lead to the rejection of the origin.

> We look for rights as everyone, with the school, with the work, with the house … and our children. … As for our parents, before they wanted their children close, but now it is another culture, the school, the children are growing, and they will see another culture. I, as a mother, I am happy also if the children are not with me, they have to open their own path. Not to

forget me … they know that they have a family behind, a mother, brothers and sisters. … I wanted to say that they have a family behind their shoulders, I wanted to say that for me, I am happy if they study, if they go their own path, they work. If they don't want to get married, who cares! It is not obligatory to have a wife or a husband, this does not mean anything. Before our old people, they married the daughter, 12–13 years old, also the poverty … but not to be ashamed of our Romani culture.

When asked to describe the houses where she lived during her life, from childhood until the present day, the one that she remembered with more details and that raised in her evident emotions was the one of her childhood in Kosovo. As she told during the interview, she used to live in a house built by her grandparents and uncles, in an urban area. Here, some passages of her description:

Did you like it? Do you have good memories? [of the childhood house]

Yes, yes, yes. I remember the garden … my grandfather used to plant. Eh, my grandfather planted fruits and vegetables. Because we did not have difficulties for the food, my grandfather only used to buy the meat, clothes and what was needed for the house, then for the rest, for the food, we had everything. The wood we had, because my grandfather had a forest.

And did you live where there were other Romani families?

Where I was with the house, we are Turkish Roma on the side of my mother, and we were there all close to Turkish people, in a place like this four Turkish families and four Albanian families

But Albanian Roma?

No no, Albanian Albanian, also Turkish, but our nationality is Turkish Roma, but we don't speak Romani, but Turkish.

The memories of the childhood contrasted with the one of the initial life in Italy, living within an unauthorised camp:

What memories do you have of the camp? How did you like it there?

Difficulties, sad, I did not know people there, I was always inside the house, I was afraid for my kids, with unknown people, understand? I was like this … fear, sadness, I did not leave my kids to go out. My mother-in-law used to say: "leave them to play a bit with other kids". But I: "No, no, no, I am afraid, because I don't know people, I don't want arguments". We did not stay in a clean place … sand, without water, with these power generators, always.

But how did you end up there?

Eh, at first my husband was there, they found this place, there were 5–6 people or more: "Yes, yes, we found this place, we stay there, we see as a try for 3 or 4 days, if police leaves us, then ok, otherwise we look for other places". This is why they tell us "nomads", because we are not nomads, we are Roma! For instance, if you leave me in this place, I don't leave it and go to bother in another place, if I bother it is only because there is no other place where to go.

Just after this question, I turned to ask her about the village of Coltano. Interestingly, she did not give much information on this regard, but rather turned to speak of what she would have preferred instead:

Now how do you like to live here in the village of Coltano?

In the village of Coltano we are fine but I here … I mean, I don't like staying here. … I always had an idea … I also always told people within the municipality, to the social workers: I want a house in Pisa or outside of Pisa, I wanted to stay in the city, I wanted to meet people, I wanted to know [not clear], I wanted to know culture.

But in a flat?

A flat, yes, like everyone, a bit … like everyone, right? Also us. Instead here, when people will hear where we are, they will be afraid … job, then we always need to go to town to buy, to do, while we are here in the countryside without a bus. Thanks to them I am still fine, I am not outside, I am not in danger, I am not [not clear]. I mean, where my children are, I also wanted to have a life with them, outside, not always close in the house on a mountain, I mean here we are like on a mountain.

This desire of living outside of the village, in town, is reaffirmed in a second passage, in which this desire was presented as a dream, rather than a concrete possibility:

Are there some positive aspects of living here? [in the Romani village]

I think yes, yes. I also dream, I always dream, I think … but I don't know if it is true or, I don't know how to say it to you, as a game, I don't know, I think that if my children will have a happy life, if they continue with school, it depends which school they do, which job they find, I hope that thanks to them I will manage to get out, I don't know …

To get out from the village?

Yes, yes, yes, I want to change a bit, everything, I don't forget my past, but I want to change a bit.

This passage impressed me particularly, because the understandable hope of having a better life, outside of the village, thanks to the children who were completing education, was presented by Caterina rather as a "childish dream". Namely, what could be perceived as a concrete possibility (considering the level of integration of her kids) was rather seen as a hopeless dream. Indeed, along with presenting this dream "as a game", while talking about it, Caterina appeared almost embarrassed for what she was saying, although she smiled in a dreamy expression. This left me the impression that the possibility that she could realise this desire was so remote, in her opinion, to be almost seen as an embarrassing dream.

The last part focused on her Romani identity and on whether she felt as part or not of the Italian society. Also in this part, Caterina highlighted some interesting aspects: despite the fact that she lived in Italy for almost 20 years, she evidently did not feel integrated in Italian society. Furthermore, she did not feel anymore a concrete attachment (desire to go back) to her country of origin:

> *Are you proud?* [of being Roma]
>
> I am proud because my parents are Roma, they are not really Turkish, but Roma, but also I don't forget the Turkish nationality, I don't offend it. That is what we are: Turkish Roma! [emphasised] Neither we say that we are Turkish and not Roma. … Can I?! A person with nationality, for instance, Albanian Roma, Serbian Roma, Croatian Roma, Romanian Roma … this does not mean … . The important thing is not to hide of being Roma, he is Roma! I am proud, thanks to my parents, I am proud. To lie, with lies and hiding things, this is not good.
>
> *Do you feel like at home here?*
>
> Ehhh … mmm … I feel like a guest.
>
> *In Italy?*
>
> In Italy I feel like a guest, because here is not my home, it is not my town. I am foreigner, but thanks to you [plural] that my children are born and grown here. I don't feel like Italian, I feel like a foreigner, but I am happy, thanks to you. Yes yes, I am happy, my children are a bit free … I don't know how to say it to you, entertainment … friends … they have acquaintances, they go to school, the older one to University, high school. I am happy.
>
> *But would you like to go back to Kosovo when for instance your children will be adults and autonomous?*
>
> I tell you the truth. In Kosovo I go back, it is not that I don't want, I want to see my family, my neighbours, but also to come back here in Italy, because it is almost 20 years that I am here in Italy, I have your habits … how to say …

You got used to it?

> I got used with you here, I like the language, and I want to speak well, but I did not learn well. Thanks to television I started to learn the language with people outside. And like this, always inside speaking your own language, you will never learn.

Of the whole interview with Caterina, two aspects particularly impressed me: the fact that her open-minded attitude towards the children did not clash with her claim of Romani identity and culture, and the impression that she had been living for many years in a sort of limbo between a faraway past and a dreamy future. The first aspect was not so predictable as it may appear. As it will be highlighted in other interviews, integration and the exposition of younger generations to different cultures are often perceived as threats to Romani identity and culture. This last approach, after all, is in line with the still predominant idea of culture as something monolithic and fixed, threatened by modern times and cultural mixture. In opposition, Caterina seemed to present a completely different picture, probably also in the light of her own experience: her family was Turkish Roma, but she was born and raised in Kosovo, she then married a Macedonian Roma and with him moved to Italy, where her children grew up. Despite all of this, she did not forget and strongly claimed her Turkish Romani identity. Exactly like her, her children may always claim to be Roma, despite living an independent life and reaching higher level of education among non-Roma.

The second aspect is more recurrent, especially among those who have been obliged to live in nomad camps for years or went through a series of evictions: the home seems to either belong to a past that cannot come back or to dreams for a better future, although seen as unreachable. The condition of the present is comparable to a limbo in which you are lucky if you have a place to stay, but that does not create an attachment to the place of living. In the case of Caterina, this was seen in the fact that she spent little time in talking about life in a camp or in the current house, while she was much keener to speak about her childhood habitation and her dreams. Furthermore, what seemed to be an understandable and also feasible desire of leaving the experience of segregation, considering the achievements of the sons, became in her words an almost "childish dream". Her only concrete hope was that her children would actually have this possibility.

Marta

I met Marta, a Romani woman less than 40 years old, thanks to Caterina, who introduced us. At the time of the interview, she lived with her family in the village of Coltano. Nevertheless, she did not occupy one of the houses built by the project "Città Sottili", but an informal shelter built independently. Indeed, after receiving one of the houses in the Romani village, she had been evicted with all her family by the local authorities for an apparent criminal act, of which she was later acquitted. Her children went to school but had not yet reached higher levels of education. The interview with Marta was conducted sitting in front of her house. Although she almost immediately accepted taking part in the study, initially Marta appeared a bit more reserved and less willing to talk than Caterina. Nevertheless, as the interview continued, she became more relaxed and talkative. The house where she lived was composed of a container surrounded by a wooden structure. Although very simple and built of poor materials, it appeared very well kept and clean.

As she told at the beginning of the interview, Marta was born and raised in Kosovo, where she got married at young age and lived until the age of 17. At the beginning of the war in Kosovo, she moved to Italy and, after a period in Pescara, she went to live in Pisa in a camp. In describing her house from childhood, she did not go into details, but highlighted how before the war she lived in a brick house in a Romani neighbourhood and had an independent life with her family:

> *Can you describe your house where you were living in Kosovo?*
>
> I was living in a two-floors house, in a neighbourhood with all Roma.
>
> *A brick-house?*
>
> A brick-house, yes, a two floors house, with 5, 6 rooms, because we were 7, 8. And 6 children I think.
>
> *And nearby, was all your family?*
>
> Yes, my family and relatives in the neighbourhood. All ours. Then on the other side of the house we also had a neighbour. We were at the edge of the road where cars were passing and from there the neighbourhoods were starting and we were exactly at the edge of the road. We were all together, Serbians, Albanians. We never had problems until the war started, so we came to Italy. Otherwise, there was no life there, they were killing each other.
>
> *But did you like it there in Kosovo?*
>
> Yes, I was born there, raised there, then my father had a job. He was a mechanic. He had all his things working. We were independent.

The conversation continued with the description of the life in camps in Italy. Particularly, she described the initial trauma of passing from a house to a caravan, but she also highlighted some good memories of a second camp where she had lived and where general conditions were better compared to the previous (in the same area where now is the village). The impression was that she somehow got used to the life in a camp and considered as a satisfactory improvement the access to basic services:

And how did you like it in the camp?

As everyone, also us. I tell you the truth, I was not very happy because I was born and raised in a house. From a house to start living in a caravan, everything changes. Then there, we were without water, without electricity, sand, like in a beach.

While here how do you like it?

Since we came here, it is better.

In the village?

No, I was on that other side, it is short time that we live in the village. We lived many years on the other side, where there is that stone wall. I had a self-made shelter.

Ah ok, when there was the camp here.

Yes, yes. I had a shelter, I had electricity, I had water, everything.

Were you fine there?

Yes.

What were the positive sides of that house?

Everything, because we were relaxed, there were no problems with the neighbours, or between us, none. We were, we were fine. Then they gave us the house. That house there is mine. Then a problem happened [here she refers to the supposed criminal act that led the administration to evict her] and they took it from me and they evicted me. I stayed three months outside in a field, here, in a field, without anything, like this exactly, outside, with 6 children. Then after three months they gave me this house, this container. I then extended it and built this shelter.

When asked how she liked living in the village of Coltano, she replied "Well". Nevertheless, when asked whether she would have continued living there or going somewhere else, her reply was in line with the ones of the others. The difference with the reply of many others regarded the kind of accommodation she would have preferred instead:

For instance, if you had the possibility to go living somewhere else, would you go or would you prefer to stay here?

[I would prefer] to have a house … yes, I prefer to go out from the camp, in order to have a house, to have the residence, to find a job. In order to live as all other people, also us.

> *Namely, would you also like an apartment away from the family?*
>
> No, I cannot make it in apartment, I tell you the truth, because now we are twelve people. I have six children, a daughter-in-law and nephews. I would have preferred a house, also abandoned, that I could repair little by little, you know … houses that are old, I would have been happier.

The desire to live in a big house with all members of her extended family was also expressed in another passage:

> *And for your children, would you prefer that they live with you or rather that they go out?*
>
> I would have preferred to live all together in a big house. If it is not possible to find a big house I am not against them becoming independent. Two of them are adult. For me it is ok, I have nothing against it.

Another aspect in the interview with Marta that differed from the one with Caterina was her perspective on the village of Coltano. Indeed, despite the fact that, as she said, she would have preferred to have a house and to live outside of the "camp", she did not complain about life in there. Also when asked whether she felt at home there, she replied:

> Yes, I feel like my home. I tell you the truth, this space that I have, I keep it all clean, I feel like at home. But here I am unauthorised. After being evicted, the municipality took the property of my house and I am out of the project. Someday the police can come and throw me out.

Also her feelings in regard to her presence in Italy were different:

> *And would you like to continue living here in Italy?*
>
> Yes, yes, I don't think at all to go back to Kosovo. I tell you the truth, there is no house, there is too much poverty, there on one side there are Albanians, on the other Serbian, there is no job … no.
>
> *But do you feel a bit Italian now?*
>
> I don't know. Because it is many years that I am here. I spent more years here that in my country. When I came here I was 17, 16 and half, now I am 39 … I spent more years here
>
> *And do you like it in italy?*
>
> Yes, yes. Apart that we cannot have our documents.

The account provided by Marta is especially interesting for two aspects: unlike Caterina and others who expressed the desire to live in apartments in the city with non-Roma, she manifested the preference to stay with her extended family by rebuilding a big abandoned house; despite this, she did not appear to be less attached to Italian society, and she did not perceive her housing preference as a potential obstacle for her integration. Indeed, despite the risk of reproducing forms of physical segregation and ethnic concentration, a house as the one she desired would have allowed her to escape the stigmatisation of living in a camp and would have given her the possibility to have the residence, simplifying the search for a job and the acquisition of the documents. In this regard, this interview highlighted once more the perceived consequences of living in a segregated village stigmatised as a "camp". Indeed, when talking about her desires, she explicitly referred to Coltano as a "camp", with all the negative aspects connected to it. Finally, she highlighted another recurrent aspect: the continuous fear of being evicted, because of the precarious situation of the current accommodation. As is going to be highlighted in the analysis of other interviews, this is one of the main obstacles to home-making.

Chiara and Daniela

When I conducted the fieldwork, Chiara and Daniela were two teenagers living in the village of Coltano. I interviewed them together in the house where Daniela lived, in the presence of her mother. It was not the first time that I met them, as they took part a couple of times in an after-school activity that I ran as a volunteer in a local school in Pisa. Nevertheless, I did not know them well. I just knew that both of them had completed the primary school circle and had started high school, although I learned during the interview that Chiara had dropped out. During the interview, the Romani mediator who knew personally the girls was also present, although he intervened only once, asking them to explain better what they were talking about. The interview with them was particularly interesting because they had always lived either in a nomad camp or in the village of Coltano. Probably because of that, their answers differed substantially from those of their elders and revealed even more the consequences of growing up in such a context. Furthermore, it was interesting to notice how their perspectives on life in a camp slightly differed, despite being friends with very similar backgrounds.

As they explained, they were both born in Italy and, before entering the village, they always lived in a camp, apart a small experience outside when they were too small to remember. For this reason, the only childhood memories they had were the ones of life in a camp. Despite Chiara recognising the difficulties of living in such conditions, they both highlighted the good memories and seemed to look at the camp as their "childhood home", also rejecting the stigma associated to it:

And what memories do you have of the life in the camp of Coltano?

CHIARA: A lot! Especially with the school, I remember, and with my friends … and so on.

But did you like it there? Why?

CHIARA: Because when you are a child you don't think to the problems with the house, or with the parents. You only think to play and so I liked it a lot. Although we had some problems, I did not pay attention to them. Instead now, yes, I do. But as a child I did not. I was just thinking to play, to watch the TV, to eat and so on …

And you? [to Daniela]

DANIELA: No, not even when I was a child I had these thoughts of a Romani camp like: "you live here and there". We were living here and I have memories as playing around – what a child does, I was also going to kindergarten and everything. But now that I grew up … . A bit the thoughts have changed, but not much. I mean, I live here, it is like. … No, exactly, I always lived here! Therefore, also if they tell me "do you want a flat in town?" or similar, I am not very interested. Actually, I would immediately say no, because at this point it is that.

Although Daniela's opinion regarding the life in a camp appeared to me a bit confusing, she gave the impression of rejecting the idea that the camp is not a real home, by claiming that they always lived there and that they had a normal childhood – playing, going to kindergarten – as all other children. This claim brought her to affirm that she would have not accepted living in town with non-Roma, probably because she considered the village her home. Chiara was more critical towards life in a camp, recognising the difficulties connected to it, but, in the end, she also declared that she would have not liked to abandon it:

And you? [to Chiara] *Do you like it here?*

CHIARA: Sometimes, when I am nervous with people here that make me angry, I say: "Better to have the apartment, so I don't have to see these people". This when I am nervous, but then when I think well about it, I say to myself: "At this point, I am used to stay here".

When asked about the negative aspects of living in the village of Coltano, the issue of stigmatisation emerged immediately, although it appeared to be an impression/perception rather than something that had been experienced directly:

And what are the difficulties? [of living in Coltano]

DANIELA: The difficulties here are that, for instance, when someone sees you and asks you where you live, then he makes fun of you. Apart that it never happened.

It never happened?

DANIELA: No

Then why do you feel this way?

DANIELA: eh, I don't know

Do you feel ashamed?

DANIELA: No, it is not that I feel ashamed, but a Romani camp is always considered in a bad way, stigma "they just steal", stigma "who cares of them".

CHIARA: It does not bother me. To me sometimes they ask where I live, "Do you live here in Coltano?" Why? If they want me, they have to want me for what I am, otherwise, I don't oblige them to.

The stigmatisation of living in a nomad camp is related to the stigmatisation of being Roma. Consequently, just after, I asked them whether they used to hide their identity at school:

When you go to school, do you say that you are Roma or do you hide it?

DANIELA: I don't try to hide it because anyway then it comes out. I say that I am Macedonian, but then, by knowing the people, I come out. But before I don't come out because they immediately think bad. Therefore, I am always myself, but I don't say that I am Roma. Then sometimes, while joking, joking, I throw out that I am Roma

CHIARA: I say that I am Roma from the first moment, I don't mind.

Finally, one of the last points touched during the interview and that revealed a surprising aspect regarded their feeling at home in Coltano and in Italy. Surprising because, although the two girls were born in Italy, always lived in Italy, went to school and listened to Italian music, they declared they did not feel "Italian":

And here [Romani village of Coltano] *do you feel at home?*

DANIELA: Yes. Here it is like our bubble and we are inside of it.

BOTH: "I am in my bubble, I am in my bubble" [singing a song of an Italian contemporary rap singer]

Meaning you feel protected from the outside? What do you mean by bubble?

DANIELA: No, it is like a game, joking. But I feel at home here.

CHIARA: Me too

Do you mean that you don't feel at home outside?

DANIELA: No. Like I am an immigrant in Italy even if I am born here.

Don't you feel Italian?

DANIELA: Not at all

CHIARA: Sometimes when guys from our country come and they cannot speak Italian, then I feel Italian [she laughs].

DANIELA: Not me. Because my professors and my classmates know that I am Macedonian. And they tell me: "And where are you born?" and I say: "In Italy" they reply: "But then you are Italian!" but I am not Italian, I am Macedonian.

But, for instance, would you go back to Macedonia?

DANIELA: I would go back to Macedonia, but I have never been there, so …

CHIARA: I would go once to visit it then I would immediately come back here

So you are telling me that you would not go back to Macedonia, don't you feel Macedonia as your home?

CHIARA: If for instance I go and I speak in my language, I can also shout because it is my country, it is the same language. If for instance you go here to city centre and you speak our language and shout, some people notice it, because you have to speak Italian. And there I would feel also in my country, for the language, and for the food, the drinks.

DANIELA: No, I don't.

I found this part particularly interesting because it reflected an aspect that Sultan Dibran had raised during the interview concerning the negative consequences of living in a segregated village, namely, the alienation that it produces. The words of the two girls seemed to present the village or camp as their only real "home": a home that kept them separated from the external stigmatisation and, at the same time, connected them with their origin, namely a country they have never visited and that, consequently, could not be really considered as "home". The impression was that for them segregation represented a psychological, rather than physical, obstacle to integration – they went to school and spoke perfectly Italian but still felt like the village and the outside were two separate worlds. From this perspective, to say they were living in the village of Coltano did not simply provide a geographical information, but it became a confession charged with the meaning: "We are Roma, we are different".

Their account raised the question whether this alienation could ever be tackled or whether they would always lead segregated lives. When asked how they imagined/dreamt their future and future house, the answers revealed how, either way, they aspired to better accommodation compared to the current. Furthermore, they still did not have clear idea of their future, because of their young age.

If you could improve your house, what would you do? do you like it in your house?

CHIARA: We like it here because we have our childhood. Although there are difficulties, it is not that … some time we pay attention to them, but when we think to the positive side, there is our childhood, we have our memories.

DANIELA: What I would change of my house … the couch [she laughs]. No, jokes aside, I would add a room, because we have two, a living room, kitchen and one bathroom.

And, for instance, how do you imagine your house when you will be adult and will live alone?

CHIARA: A lot of imagination here!

DANIELA: A real house, maybe not in plasterboard, a brick house, I mean, normal with a kitchen aside, a living room aside, two or three rooms, two bathrooms, a garage because I put my car inside and, ok, a garden.

Ok, and what would you like to do when you will be adult, how do you imagine yourself?

DANIELA: My imagination is gone because meanwhile I go on with the studies then when it comes, it comes.

And, for instance, do you have plans on when to get married?

DANIELA: No.

CHIARA: At the moment we think only to – I mean, she studies – I [think] to hang out, like so … to have fun.

It was evident to me that Chiara and Daniela were two teenagers like many others: they went to school, listened to popular music, wanted to have fun and did not think too much about the problems and the future. They certainly did not reflect the stereotype of the "Romani female teenager" – not going to school to help the family at home and to get married early. For this reason, I thought that one day it might be possible for them to "exit" the "camp" both physically and psychologically and to feel also Italian, rather than Roma. Nevertheless, it was still surprising that until this point they still felt foreigners in the country where they were born and raised. The second interesting aspect of this interview was their "defence" of the camp. In contrast to their elders who considered it as something imposed, not belonging to them, they rejected this stigmatisation: the camp was the nest of their childhood – which, in their words, did not differ much from that of others – it was part of their identities, and, as such, it required respect.

Outside the camp: life in a flat and in a micro-area

Emma

Emma, a Romani woman originally from Macedonia of about 35 years, lived in an apartment found in the private housing market few months earlier by a local not-for-profit organisation. She lived there with her five children and made a living with small occasional jobs. The rent of the house was paid by the local social services, but not within the project "Città Sottili", and, as she explained, the possibility for her to remain was strictly connected to the renewal of her housing contract (lasting one year) and to the continuation of the financial support. The flat was located in an urban area of Pisa, just beside the city centre. The interview was organised thanks to the support of the organisation who helped Emma in finding the apartment. The president, indeed, was the one who contacted her to organise the interview, which was done in her apartment. She appeared immediately available and willing to take part in the interview, although she was not very talkative, giving the impression of thinking that there was not much to say. The flat appeared well kept but very modest and not particularly personalised, apart from some carpets on the floor.

The interview with Emma was the only one conducted with a Romani person living in a flat in Pisa, although others who took part in the study had previously lived in similar accommodation. Her account is therefore interesting because it shows the differences between living in a camp and living in an apartment and the advantages of the latter. Furthermore, the interview with Emma raised an issue which emerged in other interviews also: the exasperation of continuously fearing the possibility of eviction and of ending up again on the street. Emma, indeed, had changed accommodation often and had frequently lived in provisional and unauthorised shelters. She expressed this exasperation not only through the account of her story, but also through an evident anger towards Italian institutions that kept Roma marginalised.

As she told during the interview, she moved to Italy from Macedonia when she was 11 years old and did not remember much of her life in Macedonia. She instead immediately started talking of her life moving from one camp to the other:

> *Where did you live in Macedonia?*
>
> Ah, that I don't even know
>
> *Ah, don't you remember?*
>
> No, I don't remember, but you know how it is … . My goodness. I was before in Brigattiera [former nomad camp in Pisa area]. No, first I was in Coltano. From Coltano they sent me to Brigattiera. From Brigattiera I was going to Coltano. They are playing with people. And then when they came for the evictions, they threw me out. There weren't the permissions.
>
> *But how do you remember Coltano?* [when there was the camp]
>
> Ugly.
>
> *Why?*
>
> Because in a caravan there were ten people inside. Is it normal? I have to thank [names of two persons] because I wanted to go away. I did not want to stay here anymore.
>
> *Don't you have some positive memories of Brigattiera?*
>
> But what memories! They left us like dogs, without electricity, without water. The children could not go to school, not even the bus for the kids was coming. Also for me it was a mess, we were living with the power generator. What a bad life was there! Every day you have to put money on fuel, when you have them, ok, when you don't have them, you don't have. We were all burning. You could not see, sleeping. Do you know how many people died like this?! With candles.

When asked how she liked in the apartment, she highlighted the advantages of living in this kind of accommodation, especially in relation to the kids, but also the persistent fear of losing it:

And now how do you feel in this house?

Well. The children calmed down compared to the camp, where they were as crazy. They did not behave well the children, when I came here, they did not behave well, they were noisy, and all the people were putting papers on my door. Now they calmed down. And after, because I have contract for one year, I don't want that they put me once again there in the camp. Because now I have calmed down the children, and again they become messy.

And do you feel this a bit as your home?

Eh, I got used, yes.

How did you feel at the beginning? Meaning, why "you got used"?

Because it is not like the camp where the children are messy, go around. Now they are calm, they regularly go to school. And then they say that we don't want to send the children to school. It is normal that if you leave us like dogs, how can these children go to school? They take a shower to go to school. How do they go? Dirty? There we did not even have electricity … how do you live? Without anything … a mess … if you knew how I got this house, my goodness, with hundreds of problems.

This constant fear of losing again the house, to go back to the camp, seemed to deprive Emma of the possibility of dreaming for something better, beyond having a "roof over the head". This was my impression from these last passages, which, on the other side, also showed how she started creating relations outside of her apartment. Furthermore, she did not want to visit the Romani village of Coltano, neither to see her relatives:

And how would it be, your ideal house? If you could choose, what kind of house would you like?

For me a roof is enough. A roof is enough to start living decently.

But for instance, this house, if you could improve it, what would you like?

But for me the house is beautiful, it is big. This apartment suits us. I got used, people know me.

Eh, how do you feel with the neighbours?

Well. Only sometimes the kids are doing a mess. They cry, shout.

But it is normal, they are many …

Now they know it, now they say nothing to me. Before, yes. It is normal when people don't know you, it is normal that they do not have trust on you

[…]

And do you often go to Coltano, for instance, to your parents?

No, I don't go often.

Don't you like it?

No, I cannot stay, I am used to be relaxed.

And do they come here?

Yes, they come.

As highlighted, although Emma had a housing contract that could be renewed, the fear of being evicted remained vivid. The impression was that the possibility for her to feel really at home in the new accommodation was hindered by this fear. Indeed, despite saying she liked the new house and starting to have good relations with the neighbours, the fact that she did not personalise the space and she did not express desire in regard to her life in that house (like improving it) left me with the impression that she did not consider that space as hers. Nevertheless, it was undeniable the improvement of her quality of life on entering this apartment and the impact on the general integration of the whole family: the children could go regularly to school and take part in other recreational activities in town, she could more easily find a job thanks to the good connection with public transport and the regular contact with people outside of her community. Consequently, it was plausible to believe that support from the local social services would have resulted in a further improvement of the quality of life for her entire family, although the economic aspect would have continued to represent an important obstacle to her autonomy.

Agnese and Luigi

Agnese and Luigi, a married couple with three children attending primary school, both from Macedonia and around 30 years old, lived in a wooden house built on private agricultural land, in what is commonly called a "micro-area". This term is normally used to identify private land meant for agricultural purposes bought by Roma and Sinti families to place their mobile homes on or to build provisional shelters. This kind of accommodation was initially more common among Sinti living in caravans, because the acquisition of a private agricultural land allowed them to place their mobile homes somewhere safe at limited prices (lands intended for residential purposes are much more expensive). Nevertheless, this solution started being chosen also by Romani families who had previously lived in nomad camps. However, the most recent regulations on the use of agricultural lands had limited the possibility of placing mobile homes on these areas, exposing the risk of eviction for all families that opted for this solution. Agnese and Luigi found themselves in this situation, although, apparently, the local authorities had never threated to evict them.

Agnese and Luigi's micro-area was located near a suburban village on the outskirts of Pisa. Despite the rural surroundings, it was very close to the local services and well connected to the rest of town. The interview was conducted in their house, thanks to the mediation of a local organisation who knew them. Nevertheless, I had to go several times to their house before being able to interview them, because they were often busy with work. Despite this, once the interview started, they both appeared available and open to talk.

In Pisa, this is the only family that I interviewed that was living on private land bought on the market. Before moving to the micro-area, they had lived in an apartment rented independently and it seemed that they had never benefited from the support of local projects and social services. Probably because of this, the interview with them differed from the others in the kind of relationship they established with me. In all other cases, the hierarchical relationship between me, an external non-Romani researcher, and the Romani interviewees evidently affected the interview process. Namely, I had the impression that they were treating me as someone whose requests had to be accommodated (or not) because of her position, and that their participation in the study depended also on the kind of relationship established with other non-Roma (mostly social workers). Furthermore, despite the fact that some refused to take part while others evidently appreciated the possibility to express their opinion, the conversation always remained mostly limited to answering the questions. On the contrary, with Agnese and Luigi I had to adapt to their schedule in organising the interview but, at the same time, I had the impression that they were more "relaxed" in talking with me and they also asked several questions about my work and my life. In other words, I felt that they were treating me more as an equal – as a stranger and Gadjé who entered their house to ask some questions – rather than as a superior to obey or defy. This, obviously, did not mean that the interaction was not influenced by the respective positions, but the impression was that it was less touched by the relation of power. And this could maybe be explained by the fact that they had carried on an independent life, autonomous from the local authorities and social workers.

Agnese was the one more active in answering questions, although Luigi was present and sometimes added his point of view. They were very welcoming, and they often made jokes between them and with me. Overall they appeared to be a happy and close couple. As they told me during the interview, they both moved from Macedonia when they were children, and both spent their childhood in the nomad camp of Coltano. After they got married and had the first child, they moved into an apartment found on the private market, where they lived for about five years, before moving to the current micro-area in 2009. The land where they lived had been bought by an uncle of Agnese and Luigi, who then divided it between his relatives. Indeed, there were other two or three kin families living beside them, although each plot was divided and had its own private space. All the houses appeared very simple, built independently, mainly with wooden material; the quality of the structure did not differ much from the one of many shelters built in nomad camps. Unlike the nomad camps, here Agnese and Luigi had their own private space, divided from the outside and from the other houses by a fence. The couple's three children regularly attended the local primary school and Luigi could financially maintain the family with a series of jobs, such as gardener, repairs and driving.

Since they moved to Italy when they were children, they did not remember much about their life in Macedonia. Nevertheless, Agnese explained a bit how her family lived in their country of origin:

> *What kind of house did you have?*
>
> A brick-house. At the ground floor.
>
> *A house or a flat?*
>
> No, we were all relatives, we had small houses.
>
> *So were you living with all your family?*
>
> Yes, only my family, as here. Not strangers as there in the camp – different people, many Roma. While there we were all in family.
>
> *Everyone had their own house?*
>
> Yes, everyone was staying in their house with their families.

In her account of the house in Macedonia, she immediately highlighted one negative aspect of the camp: living together with many Roma who are not part of your family. Nevertheless, when asked about the life in the camp she did not present a negative picture of her memories there:

> *And what memories do you have of the camp?*
>
> Of the camp? I was going to school, as all other children. Then I grew up and I was always there in the camp, I never moved from Pisa: we always stayed here in Pisa, 24 years. Then I did my school and I stopped studying.

> *And how did you like it in the camp?*
>
> Fine. … With my parents … we were going to school, we were normal small children until we grew up, then we got married.
>
> *And do you have good memories also of the camp or you didn't like living there?*
>
> No, I don't have bad memories, we were fine, it was not messy. Normal people, in any case. I was fine there, I did not have problems there, then I was a child.

Regarding the flat where they moved when the first child was born she did not say much, apart from saying that it was fine but the expenses were too high:

> *Did you like to live in that house?*
>
> Yes, it was pleasant, but we were paying a lot. 800 euro the rent, electricity, water, heating, building's expenses. Basically, you were working one month, you were taking the money and you had to pay the rent. Then we found this land and we bought it.

On the other hand, while talking about the accommodation in the micro-area, she included more details and also the husband, Luigi, started intervening:

> *Did you decide to buy a land here because it was economically advantageous, or because you wanted to live more …*

LUIGI: We like it in here, we have our street, at least you don't pay the rent.

AGNESE: We like it because we feel good here. We are isolated. You pay only electricity and water, the rent you don't need to pay. Not even the gas, because we have the tanks. At least this helped us a bit. Nowadays with the rent it is a mess. Then we have a school here. And we feel good, we don't have any problem with anyone.

> *And did you have any problem here to build the house? Did you have any trouble? Like for instance of the issue of residential land, did the municipality ever raise an issue?*

AGNESE: I don't know that. Because my father-in-law went to talk with them. It is under his name, his property. We came here because they rented out the apartment, we did not have the possibility to pay it anymore. Then little by little, we paid this, by working.

The satisfaction with the current accommodation emerged also when asked how they would improve it. Nevertheless, the impression was that they were happy with it not because it was the ideal solution, but rather because it represented an improvement compared to the camp and something they could afford.

And the house here, if you could improve it, what would you do?

LUIGI: Give me the money and I will make you a four floors house [laughing]

AGNESE: No, no, at the moment I am fine, with one bedroom is already a lot.

[...]

AGNESE: No, because behind we have space. The bathroom is outside. We are good, because if we go back, we were in caravans with three four people inside. Now this is already a lot. My husband did this.

LUIGI: I did it myself, all alone.

As with the other interviews, Marta, Agnese and Luigi seemed to have got used to living in modest shelters, similar to the one present in the camps, and to consider it satisfactory to live in a space with basic space and services. Nevertheless, they also appeared quite proud of the house that they had built. Furthermore, they appeared happy and relaxed – namely, they did not seem exasperated with the continuous evictions, as Emma, or detached from the current accommodation, as Caterina.

The last part of the interview, touching their relationship with the rest of society, raised a surprising aspect. Indeed, although they both moved to Italy at an early age and said they liked living here, they had plans to go back to Macedonia, once the children were adults.

And here in Pisa, do you like it?

AGNESE: Yes, it is 24 years that I am here.

LUIGI: I never moved from here.

You never ... do you mean that this is your home?

AGNESE: Yes

LUIGI: This is our life.

AGNESE: Yes, the life is this. Then, when the children will grow ...

LUIGI: When the children will grow, we will go away.

And where will you go?

AGNESE: One day we have to go away. We must not die here. One day we go to our home. We have a house in Macedonia.

Ah, do you have a house in Macedonia?

AGNESE: Yes, we wait for the children to finish the school.

LUIGI: Why did I come here? I came on purpose to build a house there. With the war I did not have a house, it was destroyed.

AGNESE: If a day we are going away, where are we going? Under a bridge?

No, no, i thought you wanted to stay here.

LUIGI: If one day my son wants to go back home, to his origins, if he wants to see where it is, what is his country, he will go one day, then he will come back here, he will get married here, they will have a life here.

AGNESE: We are waiting for the children to grow little by little, to finish the school ...

To get married?

AGNESE: No, no. Before they find a job then they get married

The desire to go back to the country of origin surprised me, at first, because no other interviewee expressed the same desire and because they both migrated to Italy at a very young age. Nevertheless, the impression was that this desire was not so much related to a lack of integration in the hosting country, but rather to the project of a house in Macedonia in which they invested for years, working in Italy and saving money. In the end, it appeared in line with the immigration project of many other migrants, who work in other countries also to build or improve the house in the country of origin, where they plan to return one day. Furthermore, the words of Luigi highlighted the fact that they were aware that, for their children, Macedonia was not a real home, but just an origin, and that they most probably would have made their life in Italy.

In general, Agnese and Luigi appeared to be a happy couple who had not gone through any particular trauma and managed to carry on a "normal" life.

Furthermore, by living in the micro-area, they did not feel alienated from the rest of society and they did not suffer the stigmatisation of living in a nomad camp. From this perspective, the micro-area seemed a better solution than the camp. Nevertheless, the house itself was a provisional shelter that could not offer the same comforts and services as a brick house. Despite the fact that they did not complain about this, they also highlighted that the choice of moving there was almost exclusively due to economic reasons. Consequently, it can be argued that they considered the micro-area as a compromise between the discomforts of the camp and the high costs of an apartment; they had got used to living in provisional shelter, more affordable, while waiting to go back to Macedonia where they were building "the house". Doubts regarding their choice may arise in consideration of the children, who did not really have the perspective of going to Macedonia, a country they had never lived in. They may have still suffered from the stigmatisation of living in accommodation that is associated with the Roma, in a precarious structure that did not have the physical characteristics and services of other accommodation.

Vincenzo

Vincenzo, when I interviewed him in November 2016, was a Romani man about 50 years old living with his wife and four children, all over 15 years' old, in a caravan. I encountered him through a personal contact who gave me his telephone number. He immediately agreed to take part in the study and to talk about his story, marked by a series of events that brought him to live in a caravan, moving between the villages around Pisa and being *de facto* homeless. As in the case of Agnese and Luigi, Vincenzo had bought private agricultural land to park his caravan and build a provisional shelter, but, in his case, the local authorities had intervened by seizing it for inappropriate use. Since then, he had been living in the precarious conditions of a caravan without a stable place to park it. His situation was worsened by the fact that two of his children suffered from a serious disability that prevented them from being independent.

We met for the interview in a coffee shop in a village on the outskirts of Pisa, where he came alone. Despite his knowledge of Italian language not being perfect and, sometimes, it was difficult to fully understand him, he talked a lot and told his story with many details. Furthermore, he appeared to me humble while confident and dignified. His story and the way he told it moved and impressed me: on one hand, I was moved by all the misadventures he went through; on the other hand, I was impressed by the confidence and dignity he displayed while telling me the series of events. He had also brought me the newspaper article talking about his eviction from the land he owned and he appeared quite familiar with the Italian legislation and bureaucracy. He had the residence permit and had opened in the past a small business of recycling pallets. Therefore, my impression was that he was a tragic victim of the system that, because of complicated bureaucratic procedures and racism, hindered all his attempts to improve his situation. Nevertheless, few days after the interview, a volunteer of a local organisation that knew Vincenzo and was familiar with his story gave me a different perspective that partially questioned his position and words. The volunteer told me that Vincenzo was a problematic person, difficult to support. I sincerely did not have this impression of him but I realise the risk of emphasising too much his position of "victim", in such a complex context. I, nevertheless, decided to present his account because it certainly represents a significant example of the consequences of evictions and of the challenges that a person like Vincenzo, a foreign Roma, encounters in Italy.

Vincenzo was born in Bosnia-Herzegovina where he lived in a house on land owned by his family, which was destroyed during the war. The first time he came to Italy was 1991 and, back then, he kept moving between different cities.

> *When did you come here? can you tell me your story when you came here?*
>
> Yes, yes. From 1991 we escaped, we then went to Milan, in Milan we stayed a little, we then went to Turin, then to Voghera, to Vigevano, because there was not a nomad camp before 91, there was no camp.
>
> *Where?*
>
> In Italy. There was only in Turin, and in Rome. There were only two nomad camps. I was living two days here, two days there. I was travelling. Because there was no stable place. This for a while, until the war was over, then I brought my kids to my country. I made a shack there, then I built the walls. Like a small house, right? After, in 2000 2001 I found a job at a junkyard. From 2000 until 2002 I worked there [in northern Italy].

He subsequently moved back to Italy for work in the early 2000s. Initially, he was living in another town in Northern Italy, before moving to Tuscany and buying the agricultural land from where he would have been evicted 7–8 years later.

> *And there, were you living in nomad camps?*
>
> No, with the person [who hired him], in his house. Then, I came here in 2002. I found an apartment, I was living with another person, and also my aunt had a land. So, what happens … I stayed sometime there, I opened my own business of recycling pallets, in 2004. I opened the business, I was earning money, I took my kids from Yugoslavia, from Bosnia and I brought them here. But they are all born here in Italy, because they used to come, then after my wife delivered the baby when pregnant, after 2 3 months they were going back home. The kids were not going to school. Then, in 2005 2006 or 2007, I think, I bought the land. I started bringing the kids to school.
>
> […]

There I had my own land, I was making good money and so on. I stayed 7, 8 years on that land, my own property. I covered the land with some gravel, because the kids were getting dirty, they went to school always dirty, how can you tidy them up? They were dirty. I put the gravel, so it was clean, without using concrete, because it was an agricultural land. After eight years, police came and told me: "Look, you have to file an appeal to the Court". I filed an appeal through a lawyer, and he told me "Look that here the municipality took away the land from you"; and I: "How? It is my property, I don't know how the law works here". So he told me that the land was seized, they notified me before one year; with the disable kids that go to school I cannot [not understandable] so two years ago they evicted me. Then they told me: "Now we can help you with the social services and through a person we can find a house for rent". So I went to them and they told me: "No look, you have to find an accommodation on your own, we cannot".

[...]

But now are you living in the mobile caravan?

Yes, but in case they see my caravan here in the village, in front of the school, I don't live here – I leave the kids in front of the school and I go around, to city centre – they tell me: "You cannot stay here, you have to find a camping", and I say: "The camping costs 12, 16 euro. For me it is too much, today I cannot even earn 30–40 euros per day". And I cannot even leave the kids in the caravan along the street. If I leave it, they come with the tow truck and they take it from me, it is two years that I cannot work. What I had in the bank, money, I spent it all. The only thing left is this caravan, that I have it, if they take it from me, where do I go? Under a bridge? I cannot afford it. When I had the land, everything was fine, I was working, my kids were helping me, I had everything in order, the VAT number, the chamber of commerce, I paid taxes like all Italians do. My kids are all born in Italy, residence permits, I have everything, every year I pay taxes, I do the tax return, I am regular, and the municipality does not help me, they give me nothing.

But the land, when they seized it, didn't they propose to turn it into a building land?

No. They told me: we can take the kids and place them in a community. And I said: we still have what to eat, I do not send my kids to a community; if there is some way ... an emergency house, it is ok for me, otherwise I do not throw what is mine.

The newspaper article that Vincenzo brought me substantially confirmed his story: the land was seized because of unproper use and the alternative offered to him and his family was exclusively to place the minors in an institution. In the article it was also written that Vincenzo had been notified several times before the eviction, but he never filed an appeal to the local administrative Court. The eviction was presented by the newspaper as part of a process of redevelopment of the area and it was alongside an interview with the, at the time, Mayor of Pisa. It seems that the main issues that led to the eviction for unproper use was the gravel placed by Vincenzo and the draining system built for the bathroom. Indeed, according to the most recent legislation on the matter, it is forbidden to build or place any structure meant for living on agricultural land. Beyond the legitimacy of the eviction carried out against Vincenzo, which appears to be supported by national law, it is questionable that no adequate alternative was offered to him and his family. As highlighted in the previous chapter, international legislation in protection of housing rights engages national authorities to support evicted families in vulnerable positions to find an adequate alternative. In the case of Vincenzo, the only option was to leave his kids in a public structure. As a consequence, Vincenzo, along with losing his land, would have also lost his children. It is unfortunately not so uncommon that the alternatives offered to Roma after an eviction involve the separation of families or solutions that are overall no better than nomad camps, as also noted by Sigona (2002). For this reason, it is also common that those who suffer eviction prefer to refuse the offer and to live together, although in precarious conditions.

The conversation with Vincenzo moved to the housing solution that he would have liked for him and his family. In talking about it, he also described the difficulties that a foreigner who is not completely familiar with the bureaucratic procedures encounters in looking for a house in Italy.

> *And what would be the housing solution you would like now?*
>
> Now I have to do … how is it called … the request for public housing, the request for public housing. … I would like … the house! Because I have to do, how do you call it … integration! and also thanks to integration, stay here in Italy, because it is almost 12, 13 years that I have the documents, everything according to norms, children go to school regularly, they go every day. On Saturday they don't go, on Sunday it is closed. The municipality here, they don't give anything: "Make the request for public housing". I do that, but when do they give it to me? After one, two years. In those two years, where do I live? I cannot live like this. I don't have any criminal record, it is not that Roma steal. We are not all the same, like the Italians, there are those bad who steal. I don't have any criminal record.
>
> […]
>
> Every week I speak with the social services, for the rent. They tell me: "Yes, Vincenzo, you can do a request for public housing". I did it three, four years ago. Then, two years ago, when they took my land, I went there and they told me: "But did you make the request?" and I "Yes, I did

it, here is the request" and I showed them the request … . "But why did not you appeal?" they told me. "But you cannot say … . To a foreigner, he does not know it! He makes the request and that's it, he waits for the house. You can at least send me a notification, something, so I file an appeal." And they say to me: "We are sorry, you could file an appeal." I did not know it, and four years ago I had a house, I had the land, but it is better the house [referring to a brick house], the public housing, I would have paid 50 euro, plus bills, 200 euros. There wouldn't be problems: I have a job, I have everything.

In that moment, I had the impression that public housing for him was a sort of final solution, when no other alternatives were available. After all, public housing is often associated with neighbourhoods marked by neglect, poverty and deviancy and poorly accessed by public services. I thought that if he could have his land back, he would have preferred that to an apartment in public housing. But I was evidently wrong as he later started talking of the fact that he desired a brick house, because it is cleaner.

But now, if you could choose between an apartment in public housing and a land as you had before?

The land I don't want it anymore in my life. In my country, yes, the land, because you have a house on it. Because there it is my house, and everything else, it is fine. The land is cold, it is always dirty, because the kids play, right? And with the earth … they are always dirty. And you have to wash them, you have to yell at them. With the house, you are always clean, there is no dirt. With the house, I like it: you have the bathroom, you have everything, you are clean, the kids go to school regularly, they take the bus, they go to school, they go everywhere; my wife starts working, the son who is 22 now can also start working on something, while the one who is 18 studies. If they give me the house, thank god if they give it to me, because the land I don't want it if I have an apartment in public housing, 50 euros for the expenses, 50 euro is fine, then water and electricity, also 200 euro, there's no problem, I know that I can make money, that I earn it, that I sell, I leave my wife at 6 in the morning, I go to work and come back in the afternoon, at 7, 8, at night.

But why had you decided to take a land if you preferred a house? Because you had no other solution or. … When you took the land, why did you decide to take it?

Well … because I looked for a house for rent. Before I lived at someone's place in Livorno, two years, then I lived with my aunt, also my aunt has a land, like, a land on her own. What happens … I was looking for a house for my kids, I was going to the rental agencies, the agencies were bringing me to see the house, the owner was seeing that I am a foreigner and they were not giving it to me. Also there, when they took the land from me, since two years, all agencies of Pisa: "I am sorry, I can show you the house, but the owner does not give it to you". I have all declarations, I declare almost 9,500 euro per year, it is a little, right? It is a little, 9,500 10,000, these are my declarations. When I go, I don't say that I have four kids, I say that I have two. Me with the wife, if I say that I have four kids, they are afraid. With the kids, two rooms are enough, the kitchen and the living room. Because I can place four kids in a room, right? The house … . Thank god if they give it to me. Now I do the request for public housing, but still I have to wait a lot.

Initially, I had interpreted the "incapacity" of Vincenzo for desiring something better than a mere apartment in public housing as the consequence of the instability produced by the evictions. I thought that this insecurity prevented him from imagining a "home" and led him to wish for nothing more than "a roof over the head". Nevertheless, while rereading the transcription, I rather interpreted his account as a call for "normality": as with many other interviewees, his main desire was to have a "house, like everyone else". Although simple and poor, this would have allowed him and his family to find a job, send the kids to school, escape the stigmatisation of living either on the street or in a nomad camp. This call, also in this case, was supported by the claim that Roma want houses, like the other peoples. The stereotype associating Roma with nomadism and nomad camps was rightly perceived as one of the main obstacles to their inclusion, as also the initial prejudices that initially emerge among non-Romani neighbours which can be tackled with mutual knowledge.

And what people say: "Roma do not want the houses, they want the shacks" … who said that? They say this to us. What would I like? To live in a shack or in a house? In a house! More simple, cleaner and people don't look down on me as they do in a shack. Many Macedonian Roma, Bosnian Roma, many have the houses in Livorno, they also have four apartments. My cousins, they all have the houses … before five or six years ago they had the lands. Then they saw that they were seizing them, in Rome, everywhere … what they did? They sold the lands, they made a request for public housing, and they are in the houses. Roma who were living in the nomad camp of Coltano, where are they gone? The municipality helped them … . I don't know why they helped them, the Macedonians. I have two kids with disability and they don't help me … because Roma want the houses!

[…]

And how was the relationship with the neighbours when you were living in your land?

At the beginning they were a bit afraid, "But that one come to my house to steal, but that one … " You see in the newspaper what is written. After one two months, little by little, they were passing by, they were greeting, the people, they were relaxed, right? Everything started where I used to live, they were greeting me, people were coming close to my land, they were speaking to me. And then little by little they saw that we are diligent people, that we are good and they say. "Look at that people, they are intelligent people". There was no issue, nothing.

Conclusions

The interviews conducted in Pisa highlight some aspects which will recur also in other cases and that are common when policies for the housing inclusion of Roma and for the closure of nomad camps are concerned. The main insights that can be deduced in this case are the consequences of physical isolation and housing insecurity. The first issue, evident in the Romani village of Coltano, represents a serious obstacle to inclusion, as it does not only hinder the possibility of finding a job in the city, but it also creates a psychological barrier that prevents exchange and mutual understanding. The interview with Chiara and Daniela proved significant in this sense: although they were born in Italy, regularly attended school and could be considered completely integrated into Italian society, they still did not feel at all Italian. In the case of Caterina, the alienation produced by a life spent in nomad camps and in the isolation of the Romani village left the impression that she was living in a sort of *limbo*, in between the memories of the childhood's house and the dreams for a future, perceived as unachievable. While it is true that the Romani village of Coltano was the only housing solution that lasted after the closure of the project and that the lives of the families living there were surely better than in a nomad camp, the consequences of isolation from the rest of the urban structure remained too negative for considering this solution an example to follow. The analysis of this case, after all, is in line with other studies conducted on the impact of imposed physical segregation and isolation on inclusion of Roma and other marginalised groups (Claps & Vitale, 2010; Musterd & Murie, 2002; Picker, 2017; Sigona, 2005).

Housing insecurity and multiple evictions proved to be traumatic experiences that seriously prevent the possibility of building a feeling of home and of engaging in a process of inclusion. Indeed, they not only hinder the possibility to acquire the documents, to find a stable job and to regularly attend school, but they also provoke a psychological trauma that leaves the individual with the fear of "being evicted again". As other fieldworks on home-making processes in contexts of displacement have shown (Brun, 2015; Cancellieri, 2017), processes of inclusion are decisively boosted by the acquisition of housing security, especially through home-ownership. Indeed, the feeling of security and of attachment ensured by the ownership of the property brings the individual to invest in it and, therefore, to engage socially and economically with the surrounding context. This chapter presented the consequences of a continuous lack of security: Emma, despite living in an apartment with a regular housing contract, still feared eviction, and this evidently prevented her from being relaxed enough to invest in the house space and to feel at home; Vincenzo remained homeless after eviction and this brought him to lose the job, reducing even more the possibilities for him to find an apartment to rent. These examples show part of the serious impact that evictions have on the life of individuals and the importance of ensuring housing security. As a consequence, it highlights the absolute importance of implementing initiatives of housing relocation that can grant the sustainability of the alternative offered. Otherwise, the insecurity that follows, coupled with the trauma of the previous eviction, risks worsening the situation of the person, instead of improving it. This is what happened in Pisa, where the closure of the project determined the eviction of those families that could not pay the rent of the apartments and their return to conditions of total precarity.

The lack of sustainability of the project implemented in Pisa is associated with another issue that is also recurrent where Roma are concerned: the "special" character of the initiatives implemented. Here, the local administration, immediately after the first protests against the measure, specified that the initiative was "special", namely limited in time and space. As Bontempelli highlighted during the interview, to declare such policy as "special" immediately failed the main objective of totally dismantling the system of nomad camps. It is, indeed, not possible to replace a structural policy that affected Romani families for decades, such as the one of the nomad camps, with short-term and limited initiatives of housing inclusion. The lack of a long-term perspective that foresaw the support of those who lived in nomad camps as long as necessary, in order to ensure the sustainability of the initiative, unavoidably led to its failure. In Pisa, indeed, nomad camps basically never ceased to exist and most of the beneficiaries of the project lived again in conditions of precarity.

Finally, another common aspect recorded in almost all interviews is what I would define as a "call for normality". As highlighted, all interviews differed in many aspects, especially regarding the perspective on the accommodation provided and the expectations/desires for the future. Nevertheless, the majority of the interviewees claimed that they longed for a brick-house – "as everyone else, also us" – rejecting the evidently deeply felt stigma associating Roma with nomadism and precarious housing conditions. The desire of a "normal" house was therefore not only motivated by the comforts that this could offer, but also by the need to reject a stereotype that, evidently, was equally affecting their well-being. "Normality", as frugal and basic as that offered in public housing, became, in the words of those suffering from the precarity and the stigma of the camp, an unreachable dream.

Notes

1 A detailed history of the presence of Roma and Sinti in Italy can be found in (Piasere, 2004; Sigona & Monasta, 2006; Tavani, 2012)

2 The term "public housing" refers to residential units belonging to the State and allocated to families whose economic situation prevents the access to the regular housing market. In Italy, public housing represents one of the main measures adopted in protection of the right to housing (Conferimento di funzioni e compiti amministrativi dello Stato alle regioni ed agli enti locali, in attuazione del capo I della legge

15 marzo 1997, n. 59, 1998). "Public housing" should not be mistaken for "social housing", which, in the Italian context, refers to public/private initiatives aimed at the broader social inclusion within the housing context.

3 The list of interviewees involved in the realisation of the project "Città Sottili" (name, organisation, date of interview):

Antonio Minghi - Società della Salute, 12 December 2016
Elisa Mennucci - Coop. "Il Simbolo", 12 December 2016
Sergio Bontempelli - Africa Insieme, 15 December 2016
Public officer (anonymous) – municipality of Pisa, 15 December 2016
Sultan Dibran – Romani mediator, 18 December 2016

4 The list of Romani interviewees in Pisa - anonymous (fake name – kind of accommodation, date of interview)

Caterina – house in village of Coltano, 18 December 2016
Giovanni – house in the village of Coltano, 13 November 2016
Chiara and Daniela (friends – shared interview) – houses in the village of Coltano, 18 December 2016
Carlotta and Pietro (couple – shared interview) – hosted in the village of Coltano, 19 December 2016
Monica – house in the village of Coltano, 19 December 2016
Marta – informal shelter within the village of Coltano, 18 December 2016
Debora and Paola (daughter and mother – shared interview) – house in Coltano, 18 December 2016
Emma – private apartment in Pisa, 23 November 2016
Agnese and Luigi – private micro-area, 7 December 2016
Dora and Rosa (mother and daughter – shared interview) – nomad camp, 7 December 2016
Vincenzo – homeless, 18 November 2016

5 Nomad camps are divided by Italian institutions in "authorised" and "unauthorised". The firsts refer to structures created by local authorities, while the second to camps informally built, usually as consequence of the eviction of an authorised camp or to the arrival of new Romani migrants. See Manzoni, 2013; Tosi Cambini, 2013.

6 The absence of Sinti is probably due to the fact that, at the moment of the census, they already had independently found housing alternatives (flats or private lands), while the absence of Romanian Roma is justified by the fact that their arrival is subsequent to the census.

References

Azienda USL 5 (2004). *Programma Operativo – Le città sottili/Rom.* https://africainsieme.files.wordpress.com/2009/09/sottili3.pdf.

Bontempelli, S. (2006a). La tribù dei gagè. Comunità Roma e politiche di accoglienza a Pisa (1988–2005). *Studi Emigrazione, 164*, 947–967.

Bontempelli, S. (2006b). Vite di Scarto. Marginalita' abitativa degli stranieri a Pisa. *La Nuova Città, 11*.

Brun, C. (2015). *Home as a critical value: From shelter to home in Georgia. Refuge, 31*(*1*), 43–54.

Cancellieri, A. (2017). Towards a progressive home-making: The ambivalence of migrants' experience in a multicultural condominium. *Journal of Housing and the Built Environment, 32*(*1*), 49–61. https://doi.org/10.1007/s10901-015–9489-7.

Claps, E., & Vitale, T. (2010). Not always the same old story: Spatial segregation and feelings of dislike against Roma and Sinti in large cities and medium-size towns in Italy. *Multi-Disciplinary Approaches to Romani Studies*, 228–253. Central European University Press.

Conferimento di funzioni e compiti amministrativi dello Stato alle regioni ed agli enti locali, in attuazione del capo I della legge 15 marzo 1997, n. 59, n. Decreto Legislativo n. 112 (1998).

European Commission (2010). *Improving the Tools for the Social Inclusion and Non-Discrimination of Roma in the EU.*

European Union Agency for Fundamental Rights (2009). *Housing Conditions of Roma and Travellers in the European Union. Comparative Report.*

Furlan, F. (2011). Rom e sinti nelle legislazioni regionali. In P. Bonetti, A. Simoni, & T. Vitale, eds, *La Condizione Giuridica dei Rom e dei Sinti in Italia.* Milano: Giuffrè Editore.

Interventi per i popoli rom e sinti, n. Legge Regionale n. 2 (2000). http://db.michelucci.it/toscanarom/wp-content/uploads/2013/11/leggeregionale_2_2000.pdf.

Manca, M. C. (2013). *Il Paese dei campi. La presenza rom a Pisa e il progetto "Città Sottili".* Università di Pisa.

Manzoni, C. (2013). *L'uscita dal campo e dalla baraccopoli: Le carriere abitative dei rom, tra vincoli strutturali e strategie individuali.* Università Milano-Bicocca.

Musterd, S., & Murie, A. (2002). *The Spatial Dimensions of Urban Social Exclusion and Integration*, N. 22. URBEX Series.

Piasere, L. (2004). *I rom d'Europa. Una storia moderna.* Roma and Bari: Laterza.

Picker, G. (2017). *Racial Cities: Governance and the Segregation of Romani People in Urban Europe.* London: Routledge.

Sigona, N. (2002). *Figli del ghetto. Gli italiani, i campi nomadi e l'invenzione degli zingari.* Civezzano: Nonluoghi Libere Edizioni.

Sigona, N. (2005). Locating "the gypsy problem". The Roma in Italy: Stereotyping, labelling and "nomad camps". *Journal of Ethnic and Migration Studies, 31*(4), 741–756. https://doi.org/10.1080/13691830500109969.

Sigona, N., & Monasta, L. (2006). *Imperfect Citizenship. Research into Patterns of Racial Discrimination against Roma and Sinti in Italy.* osservAzione – Centre for Action Research Against Roma and Sinti Discrimination.

Società della Salute Zona Pisana (2007). *"Le Città Sottili" Programma della Città di Pisa con la comunità rom del territorio. 2002–2007.*

Tavani, C. (2012). *Collective Rights and the Cultural Identity of the Roma, A Case Study of Italy.* Leiden, Boston: Martinus Nijhoff Publishers.

Tosi, A. (2009). Abitare, insediarsi: Una integrazione possibile. In M. Ambrosini & A. Tosi, eds, *Favelas di Lombardia. La seconda indagine sugli insediamenti rom e sinti* (pp. 201–234). Osservatorio regionale per l'integrazione e la multi etnicità, ISMU.

Tosi Cambini, S. (2013). Accesso all'abitazione e problemi di salute delle popolazioni rom e sinti. In C. Saraceno, N. Sartor, & G. Sciortino, eds, *Stranieri e disuguali Le disuguaglianze nei diritti e nelle condizioni di vita degli immigrati* (pp. 225–250). Bologna: Il Mulino.

Tosi Cambini, S., & Solimano, N. (2014). Rom e Sinti in Toscana. "Un abitare amaro che non diventa casa". In Fondazione Michelucci, eds, *Case e Non-Case. Povertà abitativa in Toscana* (pp. 177–203). Firenze: Seid Editore.

3 Messina, the project "Casa e/é Lavoro" (House and/is Work)

The self-build solution: comprehensive, inclusive and cost-saving?

The city of Messina is located in Sicily, in front of the Straits that faces the region of Calabria, and hosts a population of over 200,000 inhabitants. This area is one of the poorest of Italy and, also because of this reason, the quality of life here is valued to be among the lowest in the country with an unemployment rate of about 20% (Gazzetta del Sud 2017; La Sicilia 2018). Furthermore, Messina is sadly known for the devastating earthquake of 1908 that caused thousands of victims and destroyed most of the city, including its cultural heritage. Since then, the city has never fully recovered: even today the most vulnerable sections of its population live in the precarious shelters constructed after the earthquake as temporary accommodation and, for this reason, it is known as the city of the shantytowns (Farinella and Saitta 2019). The Romani population in Messina is certainly limited compared to the numbers of Pisa and mainly consists of a group of Roma migrated from Kosovo and Montenegro between the end of the 80s and 90s. Their number decreased consistently over the years and, at the time of my fieldwork, it counted about 70 members. Apart from them, Messina, in the last few years, also witnessed the arrival of Roma from Romania, whose presence, nevertheless, was ignored by the local authorities. Even the volunteers traditionally working with Roma admitted that they never had contacts with them.

I selected this case because, similarly to Pisa, Messina has often been presented as an example of the use of public funds in the realisation of projects aimed at the relocation of Romani families living in nomad camps. Indeed, the project "Casa e/é Lavoro" (House and/is Work) was presented as a "good practice" within the Italian Strategy for Roma Integration (2012, p. 89) and during the conference "EU Inclusive" held in 2012. The solution proposed by the project foresaw the relocation of all the families living in the local nomad camp in housing units located in integrated settings with the reconversion of public buildings into apartments through the self-build method and the active participation of the families. This was done also with the aim of providing Roma with working skills that could then be used for the creation of a

DOI: 10.4324/9781003184539-4

cooperative in the construction sector. Apart from its supposedly innovative nature, the case of Messina has also been chosen to investigate inclusion processes within a socio-economic context different from the one of Pisa and Trento-Rovereto.

I visited Messina and conducted the interviews between September and October 2017. Before going there, I had collected information on the project "Casa e/é Lavoro", mostly through newspaper articles and institutional websites. I then contacted the organisations that were in some capacity involved in the project and the local social services. It was possible for me to quickly gather a satisfactory number of contacts, as the organisations and institutions involved in the project were many and they all expressed immediate availability to take part in the study. Indeed, the first aspect that impressed me about Messina and that, looking at it now, was telling of the situation of the Romani community there, was the high number of organisations and persons active in the promotion of their inclusion. Despite the limited number of Roma present in the area, the network of stakeholders active in this field was much more extended compared to Pisa or Trento.

The reason of such participation of civil society in matters concerning Roma can be found, in my opinion, in the central position of the nomad camp where Roma used to live before the project. The camp, commonly called San Ranieri, was located within a green area of the central harbour of Messina, quite close to the city centre. As a consequence, it was known by the rest of the population, the Romani children regularly attended the schools in the centre and, compared to other contexts, there was more exchange between the camp and the rest of the city. Nevertheless, apart from its position, the camp of San Ranieri suffered from a series of other issues usually associated with nomad camps: the housing units mostly consisted of self-made shelters; the provision of electricity was not always ensured; and the sanitary facilities were almost totally inexistent. Furthermore, according to many of the social workers and officers interviewed, the camp was considered a sort of "police free zone". This meant that local mafia groups used it to cover illegal activities and to hide money and weapons. Even during the relocation, a non-Romani person convicted for murder was found hiding there.

The nomad camp of San Ranieri was established by the local administration in 1992, by renting the area, as a temporary solution for the Romani community from ex-Yugoslavia who did not have permanent accommodation (Amante 2013). Nevertheless, this temporary solution became permanent, and the caravans were replaced with illegally constructed wooden and brick houses. As mentioned, a large number of organisations and volunteers consistently operated within the camp (ARCI, Caritas, CESV, Comunità Sant'Egidio), ensuring support for inclusion within the school system and promoting activities to improve the relationship between the camp and the rest of the city. This support and engagement also allowed the creation of a Romani organisation within the camp – Bahtalo Drom – which served as an intermediary in the relationships with the local administration. It is in this context that, in 2010, the municipality of Messina engaged in a dialogue with the civil society to design a project aimed at the closure of the camp and the improvement of the social inclusion of its inhabitants. The initiative was then implemented between 2011 and 2012, until the fall of the local administration brought its *de facto* immediate suspension and then closure. Despite most of the families being effectively placed in new housing units, also in this case the outcomes of the project did not completely meet the expected results. Indeed, some of the Romani families did not benefit from the project and others were placed in structures that never went through the planned works of renovation. Furthermore, as is going to be shown, some of the interviewees (both Roma and social workers) claimed that the project did not result in the effective improvement of the social inclusion of the beneficiaries.

During my visit to Messina, I had the opportunity to interview several representatives of the organisations involved in the implementation and monitoring of the project (Caritas, ARCI, Bahtalo Drom, CESV), two volunteers in contact with the community, a social worker of the local social services, the former Council Member of the Municipality of Messina who promoted the realisation of the project and the project developer who designed "Casa e/é Lavoro".[1] During the same weeks, I interviewed 13 Roma who used to live in the camp of San Ranieri, although not all of them benefited from the project.[2] As mentioned above, the Romani community here was quite limited, amounting to about 70 members and, therefore, they all knew each other. In this case, my only gate-keeper was the Romani representative of Bahtalo Drom, who I here call Giuseppe, because all other social workers and volunteers referred to him as the main contact within the community. Nevertheless, thanks to the availability of Giuseppe, it was possible for me to collect a satisfactory number of interviews, especially as they all concerned individuals living in different housing solutions. For this reason, the answers to my questions in some cases differed consistently between each other. The reconstruction of the project and of the events that preceded and followed it was also possible thanks to two previous studies conducted by Fortunato Amante (2013) and Silvana Salandra (2013).

The project Casa e/è Lavoro: objectives and results

As agreed by most of the social workers and officers interviewed, and confirmed by the Romani inhabitants, the nomad camp of San Ranieri lacked the infrastructures and services necessary for living, despite its central position. The housing structures present in the area were illegally built and the proximity with the coast exposed them to the risk of floods. For this reason, it was considered necessary to intervene in order to ensure safer living conditions. Nevertheless, the launch of the project "Casa e/è Lavoro" was not been instigated by the acknowledgement of this necessity, but rather by the request of the port authority to clear the area. This institution, indeed, owned the area where the camp was located and, in 2010, started planning new redevelopment projects for the harbour. Then, it requested the local administration to evict the Romani inhabitants in order to proceed with the works. Nevertheless, the Romani population, supported by local organisations, managed to oppose the eviction order by appealing to the legal authorities and organising a solidarity movement for the promotion of inclusive policies. The Administrative Court received the appeal of the community and ordered the administration to suspend the eviction: although the action itself was deemed legitimate, the Court required the provision of alternative accommodation for its inhabitants, especially in consideration of the high number of minors present in the camp (Tempo Stretto 2010).

At this point, the Council Member in charge of family and multicultural policies, Dario Caroniti, started engaging in a dialogue with the community to develop a project aimed at providing housing solutions and at improving the general socio-economic inclusion of the individuals concerned in the eviction. The project, developed in cooperation with ARCI and with a group of project developers, envisaged the restoration of a number of public facilities and their reconversion into houses through the self-build method. Consequently, the Romani families were supposed to be involved in training to acquire construction skills and to take part in the reconstruction works. In this way, the costs would have been reduced and the persons involved would have acquired useful skills, enabling them to enter the job market. It was also planned to establish a cooperative of Roma operating in the sector of construction and environment. Finally, it planned the implementation of a series of activities directed at Romani women: literacy courses and the creation of a working cooperative for women to operate within the hospitality market.

Following the approval of the Italian Ministry of Labour and Social Policies, which financed the project, the parties involved in its realisation started to identify a series of public structures that could be reconverted into flats. As Caroniti explained during the interview, the task was not easy, partly because of the difficulties in accessing the documents regarding public properties, partly because of the precarious conditions of the identified structures, abandoned and often subject to vandalism. After a long process of selection, three structures were identified: a series of non-residential spaces located on the ground floors of a series of public residential buildings (*Villaggio Matteotti*) and two schools. The second issue that had to be solved before the launch of the project was the legal status of the inhabitants of the camp. In order to receive accommodation, it was indeed necessary to possess a regular residence permit and to reside in the camp. Thanks to the support of the local lawyer, Carmen Cordaro, most of the persons managed to acquire the permit, although some of them remained out of the project because they were registered somewhere else. For two of these families, Caritas offered to pay the rent of two apartments while waiting for another solution.

After the identification of the buildings, on the night of 1 April 2011, the families living in the camp moved to the new accommodation. At the moment of the transfer, the works of reconstruction and reconversion of the buildings had not yet started. According to ARCI and Caroniti, the decision to move the families before starting the works was justified by the concern that the neighbours, once informed of the initiative, would have either occupied or destroyed the structures. This fear was justified by the fact that they had already received threats in order to block to operation and one of the structures initially identified was destroyed a few days after. For the same reason, the transfer was done during the night to maintain the secrecy of the operation and to avoid the organisation of protests against the arrival of Roma. Eight families were temporarily relocated within four apartments in Villaggio Matteotti, waiting to start the works on other four apartments, while two families were moved to a school (Cataratti), in another area of the city with the idea to transform it into two or three apartments. The families who remained outside the project were relocated into another school, which was meant to be a temporary solution before finding other accommodation.

This operation divided both public opinion and social organisations through its aims and modalities. First of all, while Caroniti and ARCI called the relocation of the families during the night of 1 April a "transfer", Tania Poguish from CESV and Chiara Pistorino from Caritas explicitly defined it as an "eviction". Indeed, as well as the fact that it was carried out because of the desire to clear the area and during the night, the operation was followed by a high number of police and the houses within the camp were immediately destroyed, with modalities that some defined violent. Furthermore, the project was criticised because the Romani families were transferred into facilities unfit for habitation. Those who were moved to Villaggio Matteotti lived for about one year divided into only four apartments, with two families in each, until the reconversion of the other four apartments was complete. Those who were relocated into the school in Cataratti with the idea of transforming it into two or three functional apartments continued living in a structure entirely unfit for habitation as the works of reconversion have never been carried out. At the time of the interviews, two families, for a total of ten persons, were still living in a decrepit structure that consisted of three rooms, one bathroom and one kitchen. Finally, the families that were excluded from the project lived one month within another school in worse conditions than the latter, before being transferred into apartments, whose rent has been paid by Caritas for one year and from where they have been evicted again one year later.

The beneficiaries of the project interviewed did not have the same opinion on the results of the project. While some regarded the new accommodation as a considerable improvement compared to the unsafe and precarious conditions of the camp, others claimed that their living conditions were better in San Ranieri. This was especially the case of the families living in the school of Cataratti, as the lack of the renovation works left them in seriously precarious conditions. Nevertheless, also some in Matteotti complained about the quality of the structures: since the apartments were placed on the ground floor, they all suffered from problems of humidity and mould. Furthermore, some complained that the new accommodation was located in decentralised areas and, in some cases, in neighbourhoods marked by poverty and deviancy. Consequently, while the relocation surely improved their urban integration and exchange with non-Roma, it was questioned whether it actually also improved their general social inclusion, in terms of school attendance and job opportunities. Indeed, another central issue raised by the Romani beneficiaries was the economic situation, which, according to some, worsened after the relocation. While in the nomad camp they could earn an income with the collection of iron or the management of small internal businesses (shops), these activities could not be maintained after the relocation. As other scholars have already highlighted, the marginality of the camp favours the creation of informal economies, which, on the one hand, reinforce the prejudices against Roma (Santilli 2017) but, on the other hand, ensure them a source of income and foster economic exchange with the exterior (Saitta 2010, Manzoni 2012). In Messina, the loss of the informal activities has not been replaced by new job opportunities; although the project foresaw the creation of two cooperatives (one for women and one for men), the sudden closure of the project left these initiatives incomplete.

For these reasons, according to both Pistorino and Poguish, from Caritas and CESV, the transfer, although necessary, had to be more progressive in order to provide Romani families with structures that responded to their needs and to ensure their sustainability. They agreed on the fact that the housing conditions of those living in Cataratti were not better than the ones in the camp and that the relocation did not always improve social inclusion. Furthermore, they stressed that the urgency of clearing the area prevented the search for housing solutions that could better respond to the needs of the families. Like in the case of Pisa, here also the attempt to involve the community in the project in order to find a solution that could satisfy everyone failed: the appointment of a representative and the organisation of collective meetings raised conflicts that could not be reconciled. As confirmed by Roma themselves, in order to avoid further arguments within the community they left the decision regarding the allocation of the families to the municipality.

Finally, the sudden closure of the project left the Romani beneficiaries without a lease for the occupation of the apartments. It was indeed agreed that the families would have paid a moderate rent after the signature of a contract, but this had never happened. When I conducted the interviews, the families had just received a request for payment for a not clearly defined overdue amount of almost 4,000 euro for each family, a sum totally unaffordable for them. Probably also because of this, the interviews with Roma reported a rather substantial dissatisfaction with the outcomes of the project.

Messina: life after the camp of San Ranieri

The interviews conducted in Messina concerned 13 persons, across seven families, that had previously lived in the nomad camp of San Ranieri. At the moment of the interviews, three of these families lived in the apartments built within the project "Casa e/é Lavoro" in the neighbourhood of Villaggio Matteotti, the other two in the abandoned school of Cataratti, while the last two families were among the ones who remained out of the project. One of them was living in an apartment found in the private market, another in a flat within a publicly owned building. All of them were interviewed between the end of September and the beginning of October 2017 and they were all contacted with the support of the local Romani representative, Giuseppe, who also took part in the study. All the interviews were conducted in the houses of the interviewees, except Margherita, who was interviewed in Cataratti, while she was visiting. Giuseppe accompanied me to all the families and took an active part in the discussion on many occasions. In some cases, the interviews were conducted together, in a sort of group discussion, especially within the same family.

The background of all the persons interviewed was similar: they had all migrated from ex-Yugoslav countries (mainly Kosovo and Montenegro) in the 90s and had lived in the Romani camp of San Ranieri before the launch of the project. Due to the shortcomings in the realisation of the project, such as the failure to renovate the abandoned school where two families lived and to create a cooperative for employment, none of the interviewees was completely satisfied with it. Nevertheless, the opinions on this regard varied considerably: while some claimed that the new accommodation was better than the camp and they did not miss that life, others affirmed that they would rather go back to the camp instead of continuing living in the current accommodation.

The differences mainly depended on the quality of the accommodation: for instance, for those living in the abandoned school (Marco and Giulia) the living conditions could be considered equal or even inferior to that of the camp. Nevertheless, in some cases, the interviewees living in better accommodation claimed to miss the camp and the life associated with that context. Although the nostalgic attitude was more evident in older generations, while younger interviewees generally appeared more critical, some to the latter also maintained good memories of San Ranieri and did not completely reject the camp.

Domenico, Angela and Carlo

Domenico and Angela were a married couple, and Carlo their older son. At the time of the interview, they lived in an apartment obtained through the project "Casa e/é Lavoro" in the neighbourhood called Matteotti. They have been introduced to me by Giuseppe, who remained during the interview but did not intervene significantly in the conversation. The couple was between 35 and 40 years old, while the son was 18 and attended a professional high school. They appeared to be one of the most integrated families interviewed, since Domenico was the only one who had a regular job and the son, Carlo, was considered an example because of his school achievements. The interview has been conducted in their apartment, located at the ground floor of a residential building. The flat was in a precarious state – as if it was under construction, with peeling walls and furniture temporarily placed – especially in comparison to other apartments in the same neighbourhood. The couple was previously informed of my arrival and were immediately available to take part in the study. Domenico was the one who started talking and who told their story with more details, while Angela remained rather in the background, simply emphasising some aspects that her husband was highlighting. Carlo arrived later and did not intervene until the end when I asked him some questions. He seemed very well integrated and mature in answering.

As Domenico explained, he and Carla moved from Montenegro in the 90s, Carla as a child, while Domenico later, during the war in Kosovo. They met in the camp of San Ranieri where they were both living. After they got married, Domenico found a job and rented an apartment in town. Nevertheless, after losing the job, they went back to live in the camp, where they stayed for about two years before being moved to the new accommodation. From the first question, Domenico started telling their entire story: on the one hand, he was very critical of the project but, on the other hand, he highlighted his attachment to the city of Messina.

> We stayed there another couple of years [in San Ranieri] then I found another job, well, always searching, I did so many jobs since I came to Italy. My life, I tell you, changed much since they moved us from the nomad camp and we came here. But I tell you the truth, it is not that it changed much … in a better way, no! Since we are here we only got punched in the face, hands over our faces, because all the demands we made, all the requests, we always found close doors. … Now I feel as a citizen of Messina, I don't feel belonging to my country, I feel like a citizen of Messina, I live here, I am with the people of Messina, in the morning and in the evening I wake and get up with the people of Messina, I work with the people of Messina, a person feels like that. But talking about our life … I mean, the children never felt sick while living in the camp of San Ranieri, we were along the seaside, yes, there was wind and open sea there but we never had problems, we did not know what is the medicine and now I show you everything … medicines, look, medicines, look, also here, medicines, look, it is full. Incredible … since we entered in the houses we are ruined … there, we were living in a shack, I am talking about a wooden shack, it was made of wood and there were also some houses built with bricks, let's say. And I am telling you, with time we got out and we entered the brick houses, these houses that they gave to us and that are ours. Ours … this we don't know, it is always a question mark. We are in the houses, but we don't know what is going to happen tomorrow

In this first passage, Domenico highlighted three issues related to the new houses that also emerged in other interviews. The first one was that the interest of the local authorities and of the civil society towards them, and the consequent support they received, decreased consistently after the transfer to the new accommodation. As also Angela explained better in another passage:

> *What Were the Problems with the House in San Ranieri? or Was Everything Fine There?*
>
> Yes, everything was fine, we were never sick, Italians always came to help us with money, with grocery shopping, with clothes for our kids, with books, with school bags. Since we came here, none is helping. Do you know how they help us? With our shoulders. If we work we eat, if we

don't work we don't eat. And do you know what they are saying now your Italians: "you have the houses, there is no help". But the house does not give what to eat, it is necessary to give a bit of support, it is necessary to give the kids what to eat, I am sorry. For me, I felt better in the camp!

The other two issues that Domenico mentioned, and that were confirmed by other interviews, were the problems with humidity in the new accommodation that were provoking a series of health problems, and the absence of a housing contract ensuring them security of tenure. As evident in the last passage, all these problems moved Angela to claim that she would have preferred to live in the camp. Domenico, on the other side, despite the various issues, did not seem completely unhappy about the situation and would have just liked that the above-mentioned issues were addressed. While talking of the contract and of the arrears bill just received, he said:

> If you have a normal contract, then things arrive little by little. On one side, we are happy, on the other, we are not.
>
> *But what are the positive aspects?*
>
> The positive aspects … let's hope that my sons will be happy because we won't be here forever. I am waiting the future of my sons, since the older one is 18 and I am waiting for him to finish the school, he still has two years, to give me a hand, to give me a support.

In another passage, he also emphasised the fact that they always lived in a brick house and that a brick house is what they aimed for. The dissatisfaction with the project was due to the fact that they were not provided with a house that could be considered "adequate", especially at the beginning, when they had to share one apartment with another family, as Domenico explained:

> *When you moved out from San Ranieri, were you happy to leave the camp?*
>
> No
>
> *Didn't you want to have a house?*
>
> No, I wanted a house, I grew up in a house, I know what a house means. … But that day when we left the camp of San Ranieri and we came here in the houses, I found myself living with other 20 people … two families, me and another. For two years we were together, right? … And we were not relatives, and according to you, can someone live with another and share the bathroom? It was one, one bathroom!

In the last part of the interview with Domenico, when asked about the relationship with the neighbours and the integration of the children in the school system, it emerged how his family was going through a process of integration, which, according to him, already had started during the life in the camp and was not really a consequence of the transfer:

> *Do you get along with the neighbours?*
>
> Very well, we don't have any problem, we never had any problems. I mean, they respect me, let's say I never had problems, my children get along with everyone.
>
> *And, for instance, do you think that the life of your children improved by moving from the camp to here, for instance, with the school?*
>
> Sure, sure … because they were going to school also there, they were not abandoned … my children they started first with kindergarten, from kindergarten to school, even if we were in the shacks, nothing changed. But in our shacks … you saw the house like that, but if you entered in our shacks, how can I tell you, it was … you entered like a president, you had to take out your shoes, because you could not enter like this, it was all well cleaned, carpets, all tidy clean and perfumed, you could not smell a thing.

After this passage, Domenico started talking of an issue that already Giuseppe, the Romani representative, mentioned during his interview and that recalled also here, namely the loss of "Romani language and way of life" because of integration. Giuseppe appeared sincerely worried in this regard, while Domenico recognised the issue, but did not seem to consider it as worrisome.

DOMENICO: Since we entered in the houses we don't know each other anymore. There is a division very … I mean, everyone thinks for himself, we took another mentality, we don't …

But why in your opinion?

DOMENICO: In my opinion … the houses changed us …

GIUSEPPE: Integrated, integrated, now we are more integrated, we are close to you gadjé because we are taking from you, because … how can I say … as the neighbour, so I take.

DOMENICO: You take another mentality, before we were in another way, and now …

GIUSEPPE: but I am happy for our children that are integrating but, as I told you, I am afraid for our Romani language that our kids throw it away. I hope that those books [Romani language books] will come and our children will also have to study Romani language.

DOMENICO: I start talking and my son doesn't understand me, he tells me "What did you say?" I mean, the language of their mother [Albanian], they understand it, while my Romani language they don't.

[…]

DOMENICO: Eh, I am telling you, yes, they are well integrated here, they are fine, our kids are good, and they go to school, and when they come home it is also correct that they go out sometimes, they are boys let's say. But our mentality is lost.

At the end of this conversation, as Carlo, the older son, arrived home, I asked if it was possible to ask some questions also to him. He assisted only partially in the interview with his parents and since it had already lasted one hour, I took only a few minutes more to ask him a couple of questions. Nevertheless, it was interesting to see how, despite being well integrated into the new location, he also had good memories of the camp and believed that a solution to their housing problems could have been achieved through a renovation of the camp itself, rather than a transfer. Furthermore, he highlighted another aspect common to other interviews with young Roma, namely the fear of being stigmatised by non-Romani peers.

> *How do you like it in here in Matteotti?*
>
> Quite well because at the end we were able to integrate with the other children and also because from the beginning they knew how to take us, more than everything. We have been happy with everyone, now it is not that because we are Roma then … [not understandable]
>
> *But do you have good memories of the camp or do you prefer to live here?*
>
> But it is normal, I grew up there, I am born there. Mostly now that I go there to see how it is all well fixed I think: "Instead of giving us a house, they could do something back then, not to take what was ours". But at the end, I am happy because, most of all, if I have to invite a friend home now I can, without having that fear that if I had brought him inside a shack before, to think: wait a moment, maybe he will criticise me.

This interview highlighted the complexity of the situation and how a series of factors intervened in the assessment of housing conditions. The impression was that, despite missing a "communitarian Romani mentality", Domenico and his family aimed at integrating and living in a brick house, as they did before migrating to Italy. Nevertheless, the precarious situation made them miss the life of the camp where they probably had more control over the management of their shelter. Furthermore, the camp of San Ranieri, unlike other nomad camps, was located in a central area of Messina and, probably because of this, it was not so marginal: the local associations collaborated with the Romani community of San Ranieri; they were also organising events within the camp open to the city; and the children were regularly going to school. Notwithstanding this, life conditions were not less harsh than in other nomad camps, and, as the following interviews highlight, not everyone had a nostalgic perspective on it.

Grazia and Francesco

When interviewed, Grazia and Francesco were a young married couple living in one of the flats built within the neighbourhood of Matteotti. They were both under 30 years old and had at least three small children. The interview has been conducted in their house and thanks to the mediation of Giuseppe, who was present during the entire conversation. They immediately accepted to take part in the interview, especially Grazia, who, nevertheless, appeared quite reserved throughout the whole interview and did not give many details in her answers. Probably because of this, her husband, Francesco, intervened and started providing more details. Their house appeared to me very well kept and decorated with beautiful furniture. The walls, as well, were well painted and were not ruined as in the other houses.

Grazia was born in Serbia and lived there until she was 13 when she moved to Messina, while Francesco spent his whole childhood in the camp of San Ranieri. After they got married, they continued living in the camp where their three children were born, until the launch of the project "Casa e/è Lavoro". Grazia did not say much about her life in Serbia apart from that she was living in a house that their parents owned and that she had to leave because of the war. Nevertheless, her account was interesting because of her perspective on the San Ranieri camp, completely opposite to that of many others. Indeed, similarly to Domenico, many of the interviewees were not that critical regarding life in the camp and some, despite aiming for a brick house, considered the camp better accommodation than the current one. Grazia highlighted a completely different opinion on this regard:

> *What kind of memories you have of the life in the camp of San Ranieri? Did you like the house that you had there?*
>
> We were living in shacks, when it was raining the rain entered … everything, it was a mess, cold, the children were always sick. … [she laughs] There was no house there, there were shacks! Then rats were entering inside, there were many things there, what should I tell you … we did not have a house there, there were the shacks, caravans, wind, rain, everyone was ending up in the sea.

So, are you happy with this house?

Of course, I am happy, because the house is the house, it is that.

And what are the positive aspects of this house compared to the camp?

Ehh, a lot!!Because before when the children were there, how to tell you? it was not like in the house, because in the camp when it was raining it was always all dirty, and everything, while here it is clean, it is different, obviously.

When asked about relationships with the neighbours and whether the children felt better in the new accommodation, neither Grazia nor Francesco provided much information, but just replied that yes, they got along with the neighbours and that they saw an improvement in the children. One issue that emerged was the lack of job opportunities: they were both unemployed and this situation did not allow them to feel secure regarding the future.

In the future, do you see yourself living in this house or going to live somewhere else?

GRAZIA: Where to go? At this point, I am here. Now also the kids don't want to go away from here. Only we don't have a job, if we had a job … That is what I and my husband need. And this is important because it is necessary to sustain the family, because with three children it is really difficult, with the school, then they grow up, they seek many things, it is not possible to continue … we need a job. Also the house doesn't give you what to eat, even if the house is beautiful, it does not give you what to eat, if you don't have a job.

FRANCESCO: I would have preferred that they had given me a job rather than the house, because when you have a job, you have everything.

The issue of the lack of a job emerged also when talking of another topic, namely whether they would have preferred to receive a plot of land to build their house rather than an apartment. This issue has been tackled in some interviews in Messina because the social workers, while discussing on the possible solutions to the eviction from San Ranieri, told me that some Romani families proposed leaving the camp in exchange of another plot of land where they could build new houses in cooperation with the authorities. This fact was confirmed by Giuseppe who stated that he would have preferred to receive land where they could live all together, in order to maintain the community life and the small economic activities carried out within the camp. In this regard, Francesco did not seem to lean towards the plot of land, but highlighted the fact that with land they could at least earn some money with activities, like the iron collection, that could not be carried out in Matteotti:

When you left the camp, if you had the possibility to choose between a house and plot of land where to build the house, what would you had chosen?

FRANCESCO: It is the same thing … yes if they gave a land and they gave you the money to build a house, let's say than you could do any job, even if you did not have a job let's say … regular, then you could collect the iron. Also here we are fine, yes, but without a job, we cannot move on.

Because in the camp it was easier for the iron collection?

Yes, you had the space … then always someone was calling you for some small jobs, one or two hours. Here instead you cannot do anything, what can you put in front of your door? Nothing.

Finally, the last issue that emerged was the lack of a clear housing contract that, as in the case of Domenico and Angela, prevented them from feeling secure and, consequently feeling at home. This issue arose exactly when asked whether they felt the current house as their own.

Do you feel this as your home/house?

GRAZIA: We still don't know if this is my house [she laughs]

FRANCESCO: The house is ours if I buy it, then I can say that it is mine 100%, but like this … because we don't have any paper, any documents. If you have in hand the papers you can say yes, but if you don't have the papers, you cannot say yes. Yes, I fixed it up, because if you stay one month or one year, at least you live like God intended, but I still cannot say that it is mine.

The interview with Grazia and Francesco confirmed how a broad series of factors intervene in influencing housing choices and the level of satisfaction with a housing solution. The comparison with the case of Domenico and Angela is significant in this regard. Both couples lived with their children in apartments provided by the local authorities in the neighbourhood of Matteotti and they both had similar backgrounds. Nevertheless, their opinions on the project, as with their problems and wishes, differed consistently: despite the fact that his family was well integrated, Domenico was very critical of the project and the house he had been provided with, while Grazia and Francesco were happy with the accommodation and did not regret leaving the camp. Although the house of Domenico and Angela appeared in worse condition, it was not possible to know whether this difference was due to the construction works or to the tenants' different ways of maintaining the apartments. Furthermore, the possibility of living on land rather than in an apartment was considered by Francesco only in the context of carrying out economic activities like iron collection, in the absence of other job opportunities. It was not motivated by the desire to maintain a communitarian life-style, as in the case of Giuseppe. The only common issue was the insecurity due to the lack of a clear housing contract, which, if solved, would have evidently improved the condition of uncertainty and probably boosted a process of inclusion.

Dario, Elisa and Antonio

Dario and Elisa were a young couple (around 25 years' old) living with their children and parents in a flat found independently in the housing market. The both grew up in the San Ranieri camp, after migrating from Kosovo as toddlers, but they did not benefit from the project "Casa è/e Lavoro" because they did not have regular documents. Since being evicted from the camp, they have lived in different flats paying regular rents. At the time of the interview they lived in a flat located in a peripherical neighbourhood of Messina, and, as they explained, they were about to leave that apartment because the owner wanted to sell it. The interview was conducted in this flat, together with the father of Dario, Antonio, who lived with them, and Giuseppe, the Romani representative who accompanied me.

The interview with them was particularly interesting not only because they did not benefit from the project and had to find an accommodation independently, but also because the participation of Antonio and Giuseppe enriched the conversation. The initial interview with Dario alone turned into a discussion that highlighted the different perspectives and expectations in regard to the San Ranieri camp and the house. The apartment in which the family lived was very well kept, but very little personalised: the furniture present in the flat was essential and appeared almost new – part of it was even still covered with packing paper. This, added to the total absence of other decorations, gave me the impression that they lived the apartment as a "transition", probably because they already knew that they had to leave it soon. Dario, who was the first taking part in the interview, appeared open to answering questions but not particularly talkative. This changed once Antonio and Giuseppe started intervening and the interview took the shape of a conversation. Elisa did not intervene much initially, but I included her in a later stage by asking some questions.

From the beginning, Dario highlighted the he did not like living in the camp and wanted to find other accommodation. Nevertheless, when talking about this topic, the father, Antonio, intervened, showing a completely different point of view.

Did you like it? [in the camp]

DARIO: Mm, yes and no, that one is our life … but at some point, I said: enough with that life. If you were saying to your friends around that you were living there.

[…]

And do you like it in the house here?

ANTONIO: Yes, but we always paid what we had to pay … rent, electricity, the water bill, 800 euros go away each month. I am sorry, but where do we take 800 euros?

But, apart the costs, do you prefer to live here or in the house you had in the camp?

ANTONIO: Better in the camp!

Did you also prefer the house in the camp? [To Dario, who is smiling at the answer of the father]

DARIO: Better a house than the camp.

ANTONIO: But there you did not have to pay anything.

GIUSEPPE: No, be clear [to Dario] here they command you. There, who was commanding you? What was there, it was yours! I spent the best years of my life there … you grew up there!

[Dario laughs and makes fun of Giuseppe by singing the Italian song *I Migliori Anni della Nostra Vita* (the best years of our life)]

GIUSEPPE: That piece of land, that life, you will never have it again.

ANTONIO: True!

[…]

DARIO: It was worse than a prison there, worse than a prison! We had a life with rats, snakes.

Later, Elisa also expressed a negative opinion regarding the camp and stated her preference for a house outside. Furthermore, when asked about which kind of accommodation she would have liked to live in, Elisa did not appear to have particular preferences, as long as it was decent and allowed a certain level of privacy. In this case, the difference with the desires of Giuseppe was evident, since he would have preferred a piece of land where he could live with all the other Romani families.

Are you happy not to live in the camp anymore?

ELISA: Yes, having a decent house, a normal bathroom.

But on the fact that you were saying about living all together, would you still prefer to live all together or to have your own house?

ELISA: To have our own house, yes.

But in a place with other Roma, or on your own?

ELISA: No, no, it is not important.

GIUSEPPE: I would like that. In a future if they give me a piece of land, I sign for it, ten times!

Also you [to Dario and Elisa] *would prefer to live on a piece of land?*

[Dario and Elisa do not reply]

GIUSEPPE: They give me the material [Dario keeps laughing on what Giuseppe is saying] They give the material, what it is for you … with your family. The design of the house, they bring me the electricity, they bring me the water, and we make the works … and they give me a job … I sign for it! Because one thing, the way we were celebrating the holidays, we don't do it anymore.

Despite the fact that Dario and Elisa did not appear very interested in Giuseppe's project of living all together, they nevertheless seemed to sincerely miss some aspects of the communitarian life of the camp. Indeed, just after Giuseppe mentioned the way they celebrated holidays in the camp, I asked them whether they also missed that. In that moment, they stopped being ironic and displayed a sincere nostalgia for that aspect.

And do you miss that? [the way they were celebrating the holidays]

DARIO AND THE OTHERS: Of course!! This is our custom!

ANTONIO: We were eating all together, we were united.

Because maybe there are some who prefer to stay on their own …

ELISA: No

GIUSEPPE: No, you see, I think everyone misses that. Because, you see, when there was something, like: he has a guest in his house tonight or tomorrow, and everyone would be there to talk until midnight.

DARIO: It was beautiful!

Finally, another interesting aspect that emerged in the interview with Dario, Elisa and Antonio was their relationship with Messina. Like other interviewees, they felt completely part of the surrounding society, without denying their Romani identity. As in the other cases, they did not think that the transfer from the camp represented a turning point in this sense, since they already felt integrated. Furthermore, the sense of belonging was also confirmed by the fact that they did not perceive discrimination on a daily base.

Are you proud of being Roma?

ELISA: Yes!

DARIO: Yes, I am proud, really! And I say it.

But do you also feel to be citizens of Messina?

DARIO: Yeees, yeees … . They say to us: you are from Messina more than us.

ANTONIO: It is 40, 35 years that I am here.

Eh, yes, of course. But do you think that you have more contacts with Gadjé since you got out from the camp?

DARIO: It depends …

GIUSEPPE: We had them also before.

ANTONIO: we respect each other, they respect us, they have respect towards us.

[…]

Did you have difficulties finding a house?

ELISA: Yes, yes.

For the discriminations?

DARIO: No, no. Because they ask for the documents, things like that. Here in Messina there isn't discrimination, no.

Conclusions

This last interview showed once more the fact that perspectives on the house and on the closure of the San Ranieri camp varied according to the speaker. It was undeniable that the conditions of the nomad camp of San Ranieri required an intervention aimed at ensuring a certain level of safety, hygiene and access to services. Nevertheless, the solutions proposed were not considered by everyone as an improvement to their living conditions. This was true especially for those who had been living for long time in precarious accommodation, but also in the light of other aspects that worsened after the transfer, such as the lack of job opportunities. These issues, together with the desire to maintain communitarian traditions, led some interviewees to wish for accommodation that reflected some aspects of the camp (land where they could all live together). Nonetheless, this wish was not shared by all members of the community: others preferred to live in apartments, the same as other citizens of Messina, because of the comforts, because of the fear of stigmatisation, because of not being attached to a communitarian way of life. Their accounts show how one solution may not fit everyone's needs and that an accommodation outside the camp is not always better than the latter. The first aspect was confirmed by the social workers who highlighted that, during the development of the project, the community of San Ranieri was asked to propose a housing alternative to the camp for everyone and they did not manage to find an agreement, leaving the decision to the policy makers.

As in the case of Pisa, here also the collective mechanisms of participation failed to effectively involve the community in decision-making, and they actually created lasting conflicts between some families. These two cases, therefore, show how addressing the housing issue collectively may not result in satisfactory outcomes. This can be explained by the fact that, as highlighted in this work, the house has a broad impact on the individual, not only in terms of its physical state, but also as emotional nest, identity-maker, space of social interaction, economic asset, etc. Consequently, on the one hand, housing needs are affected by a large series of factors that vary from person to person; on the other hand, their importance prevents the possibility of the individual easily giving up their housing claims within a collective discussion. It is, therefore, legitimate to suppose that involvement of the families individually may have led to more satisfactory results. Surely, in this case the exit of the families from the camp would have been more progressive, but it may have ensured a major sustainability of its results.

In the case of Messina, the decision to move all the families together, in one night, was justified by the intention of keeping the operation secret so not to raise protests among the non-Romani population. Indeed, here, as in Pisa, the news of the relocation of the Romani inhabitants to non-Romani neighbourhoods has led to the vandalization of some structures and to the organisation of protests. Nevertheless, the protests vanished shortly after the relocation was completed and the Romani interviewees did not experience particular discrimination against them in the new neighbourhoods. Most of the persons involved in the realisation of the project highlighted, as well, that the protests organised in the neighbourhoods were immediately followed by a reconciliation when the two parts saw and recognised each other. This example shows how prejudices against Roma are, most of the time, the product of irrational fears that can easily be deconstructed by reciprocal knowledge. It looks, therefore, recommendable to foresee initiatives aimed at fostering mutual knowledge between future neighbours and to fight mis-representation of Roma by public and media discourses. Fighting prejudices is indeed essential in order to ensure the smooth implementation of the projects and their sustainability.

The interviews conducted in Messina highlighted also important differences with the situation of the Romani community in Pisa. Despite the similarities in terms of composition of the communities living on the territory – namely, Roma migrated from ex-Yugoslavia in the 90s – and size of the municipality, the Roma interviewed in Messina felt more integrated into the surrounding society than in Pisa. It is significant how those living in the village of Coltano in Pisa still experienced forms of alienation, due to the distance of the village from the rest of the urban fabric, while in Messina they felt as part of the town already in the San Ranieri camp. One of the reasons of this difference is surely represented by the central position of the former nomad camp that probably also triggered a higher involvement of the civil society in the issues concerning its inhabitants. Indeed, the number of persons and organisations involved in the promotion of initiatives aimed at improving the overall inclusion of the Roma living in San Ranieri was higher than that in Pisa. This had already had important repercussions before the project, because it allowed a larger mobilisation in favour of a solution that did not leave the Romani inhabitants homeless.

Finally, one of the main concerns of the Romani interviewees here was also the absence of a housing contract that ensured them security of tenure. As explained in the previous chapter, social inclusion can be boosted effectively when a feeling of security is ensured. In Messina, the lack of a housing contract was probably the main issue that emerged, not only because it evidently left Roma with a sense of insecurity and precarity, but also because it effectively exposed them to a new eviction, in the case of sudden changes in the conditions that allowed them to live in the apartments without any kind of lease.

Notes

1 The list of stakeholders interviewed regarding the implementation of the project Casa e/é Lavoro (name – position/organisation, date of the interview):

Dario Caroniti - former Council Member Municipality of Messina, 27 September 2017
Silvana Salandra and Stefania La Malfa – volunteers, 28 September 2017
Tania Poguish - CESV Messina, 29 September 2017
Carmelo Lembo – project developer of "Casa e/è Lavoro", 29 September 2017
Rosaria Tornesi – social services of the municipality of Messina, 29 September 2017
Giuseppe (fake name) – Romani association, 3 October 2017
Carmen Cordaro and Patrizia Maiorana – ARCI, 3 October 2017
Chiara Pistorino – Caritas, 6 October 2017

2 The list of Romani interviewees (fake name – kind of accommodation, date of the interview):

Giuseppe – flat built through the project, 3 October 2017

Lidia – flat built through the project, 3 October 2017
Domenico, Angela, and Carlo – flat built through the project, 4 October 2017
Grazia and Francesco – flat built through the project, 4 October 2017
Marco and Giulia– abandoned school, 6 October 2017
Dario, Elisa and Antonio – private flat – 6 October 2017
Margherita – flat in publicly owned building – 6 October 2017

3 In Italian: "La senti come casa tua, questa?" was intended to mean "Do you feel this as your home?" (emotional ownership), but can easily be interpreted as "Do you feel this house is yours?" (physical ownership)

References

Amante, F. (2013). Dinamiche e processi d'integrazione comunitaria a Messina: Lavori in corso nella città dello Stretto. *Humanities, 2* (*1*). https://doi.org/10.6092/2240–7715/2013.1.65–87.

Farinella, D., & Saitta, P. (2019). *The Endless Reconstruction and Modern Disasters. The Management of Urban Space Through an Earthquake – Messina, 1908–2018.* Cham: Palgrave MacMillan. https://doi.org/10.1007/978–3-030–19361-4.

Gazzetta del Sud (2017). Qualità della vita. Messina verso il basso. www.gazzettadelsud.it/news/messina/268442/qualita-della-vita-messina-verso-il-basso.html.

La Sicilia (2018). Istat fotografa disoccupazione in crescita in Sicilia: Catania e Messina le peggiori. www.lasicilia.it/news/economia/146505/istat-fotografa-disoccupazione-in-crescita-in-sicilia-catania-e-messina-le-peggiori.html.

Manzoni, C. (2012). *L'uscita dal campo: L'impatto delle politiche pubbliche sulle carriere abitative dei rom.* Paper for the Espanet Conference "Risposte alla crisi. Esperienze, proposte e politiche di welfare in Italia e in Europa" Roma, 20–22 September.

Saitta, P. (2010). Immigrant Roma in Sicily: The role of the informal economy in producing social advancement. *Romani Studies, 20*(*1*), 17–45. https://doi.org/10.3828/rs.2010.2.

Salandra, S. (2013). *Percorsi di cittadinanza. Case per i Rom nella città di Messina.* ESPAnet Conference "Italia, Europa: Integrazione sociale e integrazione politica", Rende, 19–21 September, 2013.

Santilli, C. (2017). I rom che raccolgono il ferro a Roma: Vuoti normativi, economia informale, antiziganismo. *ANUAC, 6*(*1*), 141–163. https://doi.org/10.7340/anuac2239-625X-2929.

Tempo Stretto (2010, May 5). Rom villaggio Fatima. Il Tar di Catania sospende il provvedimento di sgombero. www.tempostretto.it/news/cronaca-rom-villaggio-fatima-tar-catania-sospende-provvedimento-sgombero.html.

Ufficio Nazionale Antidiscriminazioni Razziali (UNAR). (2012). *Strategia Nazionale d'Inclusione dei Rom, dei Sinti e dei Camminanti 2012–2020.*

4 Trento-Rovereto

micro-areas and public housing

The provincial law on micro-areas and inclusion in the housing market

Trento and Rovereto are two towns belonging to the province of Trento, located in the Northern Italian region of Trentino Alto-Adige, in the Alps. Throughout history this area has been contested between Italy and Austria and there are both Italian and German-speaking groups. For this reason, the province of Trento, together with the province of Bolzano, benefits from significant autonomy, allowing the local approval of laws in a wide range of matters. Trento and Rovereto are the two main towns of the province, the first of about 120,000 inhabitants, while the second 40,000. This area is among the wealthiest territories of Italy and Europe, and the province appears at the top of every statistic on the quality of life (Il Sole 24 Ore, 2019; Italia Oggi, 2019). Its economy is based on mountain tourism and farming (especially wine, fruits and diaries) and it benefits from the autonomy accorded to the whole area by the Italian State.

Here, the Romani and Sinti population is mainly composed of Sinti, whose number exceeds 500 members spread between Trento and Rovereto. Among them, there are also Roma from Istria who have been living in the region for decades and, for this reason, identify with the local Sinti (Piasere, 2004; Setti, 2015). Also, in the few last years, Trento has seen a rise in the presence of Roma from Romania, who regularly migrate to the area for seasonal jobs and temporarily live within illegal settlements. When I conducted my study, their presence was not well known by the social services who were just starting to move to assess their conditions and needs, as in the case of Messina. Finally, there was a group of Roma from Kosovo, who moved to Trento during the war and represented a compelling case, as they all lived in apartments found in the housing market and did not need the support of the local social services.

These two towns have been considered with the aim to analyse the adoption and impact of the provincial law adopted in 2009 by the local authorities for the creation of micro-areas (Misure per favorire l'integrazione dei gruppi sinti e rom residenti in provincia di Trento, 2009). Indeed, this case represents the first attempt in Italy to regularise and support this kind of accommodation for Roma and Sinti (Furlan, 2011), and it has been followed by other local

DOI: 10.4324/9781003184539-5

authorities in more recent times, as, for instance, by the region of Emilia-Romagna in 2015 (Norme per l'Inclusione Sociale di Rom e Sinti, 2015). Furthermore, this case proved to be particularly interesting also for a series of minor initiatives that have been implemented for the inclusion of Roma and Sinti in the housing sector and these emerged during the fieldwork. I conducted the study in this area between July and September 2017. At that time, in Trento and Rovereto there were two institutional nomad camps established in the 90s that hosted a limited number of Sinti families. Here, unlike in other Italian contexts, Romani migrants who arrived from Yugoslavia in the 90s have not been placed in camps but allocated in public housing through the services assisting refugees. Furthermore, the great majority of Sinti who lived in nomad camps have already moved to private flats or accessed public housing. This was possible thanks to the great availability of public housing in the area, offered by the province's welfare state, which surely is among the best in Italy.

During my visits in Trento, I was able to interview one social worker in charge of the Sinti nomad camp in Trento for the municipality, a Sinti mediator, the president of a local Romani organisation and three cooperatives/organisations working in this sector in Trento and Rovereto.[1] Thanks to them, I was able to also interview ten Roma and Sinti, living in different accommodation – nomad camps, private flats, public housing and informal micro-areas.[2] The main issue that emerged concerned the law on micro-areas, which, as I am going to present, has never been applied, although it responded to an explicit request of the local Sinti community. Nevertheless, the different interviews highlighted how the creation of these structures did not represent a priority for everyone as some actually preferred accommodation in flats rather than in a micro-area. Despite the failure to apply the law, the analysis of this case is interesting because it allows a further investigation of the reasons behind the choice of the micro-areas, its feasibility and its connection with the general social inclusion of the person. Furthermore, the case of Trento and Rovereto raises some new insights into the processes of housing inclusion concerning Roma and Sinti and it highlights once more the impact of the system of the nomad camps on the life of its inhabitants.

The law on micro-areas as a way out of nomad camps

The law adopted in 2009 in order to regularise the creation of micro-areas and to favour social inclusion of Roma and Sinti was meant to offer a housing alternative to those who refused to live in apartments. This issue was immediately raised by both social workers and Sinti interviewed during my visits. Apparently, those who were still living in the camps were doing so not because they did not have the possibility of accessing public housing, but because they did not want to live in apartments or because, once in flats, they understood that they could not live there, as they were used to living in the "open air". According to Ottavio, a Sinti mediator living in the camp of Trento, those who moved into apartments did it because of the lack of alternatives, not because they wanted to change lifestyle. As a consequence, the law was adopted with the intention of closing the nomad camps, which also suffered from a series of issues typical of these structures, by providing micro-areas to those who preferred this solution. It was drafted and promoted by Council Member, Matteo Civico, in cooperation with the Sinti community and it did not concern only the creation of micro-areas, but also a series of other matters connected with the socio-economic inclusion of these groups.

Regarding the micro-areas, here called "community residential areas" (*area residenziale di comunità*), the law established that they had to be identified by the "community" – namely local authorities, in cooperation with an *ad hoc* Council and experts – and assigned to families that respected the requirements. According to the law, these areas had to be fenced, with a surface of 500 and 2,000 square metres, to be located in a way "to avoid any form of marginalisation" and to be equipped with a sewerage system, electric and water plant and a space for the waste collection. The families, to be eligible, had to demonstrate a sufficient income, give their availability to training and job offers in case of unemployment, engage in the payment of a lease housing expenses and to participate in training activities. Once assigned the micro-area, the families were responsible for their maintenance and signed a contract with the local administration comparable to the one for the assignment of publicly owned houses. The main difference with nomad camps consisted in the fact that, while camps hosted different families living in a sort of camping area where the maintenance was supposed to be the responsibility of the administration, micro-areas ensured privacy and control of the property where the families lived. Furthermore, each area could only host one or two families, in order to limit their extension.

For these reasons, the majority of the interviewees considered this law a positive outcome of the cooperation between Sinti and local administration, as it responded to their housing needs and desires. Nevertheless, the law has never been applied and micro-areas have never been created. According to those who took part in the first phase of its application, an *ad-hoc* Council was created with representatives from the authorities, third sector organisations and Romani and Sinti communities, to start identifying land where these areas could be established. Despite all of this, lack of political will and funds prevented its implementation, failing to meet the hopes of Sinti living in camps. The consequent disillusionment was well expressed by the words of Ottavio, who, referring to the law, said: "the law was studied, it was done quite well. But then for political reasons, it was never applied, never taken into consideration. It was done only to silence us, at the end".

According to most of the interviewees, both Sinti and social workers, the application of the law was necessary to dismantle the policy of the nomad camps as not all families wanted to move into apartments, which they saw as an imposition by the Gadjé. This perspective was also shared by some of the officers working on these issues. Alessandro Bezzi, from the cooperative Kaleidoscopio, declared on this matter:

> Then we talk about it [inclusion in housing] with Sinti and they say: "Eh, but we always lived outside and Gadjé want to oblige us to live in the

> house". Surely, this is a strategy: "Let's send them into a house so they do not bother anymore", surely at some levels this idea exists. [...] In my opinion, all in the houses is not possible, because some really do not want to enter, old people who lived all their life outside. They also tried, for instance, this man ... a very good person, smart, they entered in a house, but the wife was going crazy – he told me – they could not stay, they were not used so they went out. For instance, this man will never enter in a house.

A few days after this interview, I had the opportunity to talk and to interview the Sinti person mentioned by Bezzi (Davide), and he confirmed his version. He had tried to live in a flat but had to leave it after few years because his wife, especially, could not stand living enclosed in "four walls". He then acquired private agricultural land and built his shelter, there with a caravan and a wooden veranda, illegally, although tolerated by the local authorities. Despite his aversion to life in an apartment, Davide should not be considered as a person who "does not want to integrate": he was, indeed, considered an important figure within the Sinti community in Trento, because of his commitment and work for the social inclusion of Sinti, especially in education.

The perspective of Bezzi was also shared by Davide Lasta, from Trento social services. When asked whether there was any project aimed at providing a housing solution to all Sinti, he replied: "Like all in the house? No, but I think this is an approach too deterministic: it is me who decides for you what is your favourite housing solution". In addition, the interviews conducted with Sinti already living into apartments also confirmed the fact that some of them opted for this solution due to the lack of alternatives. The solution of the nomad camp, indeed, was perceived by everyone as degrading, because of its stigmatisation, the lack of privacy and the impossibility of having control of the management of the area. Furthermore, according to Sinti interviewees, the nomad camp represented a major obstacle to integration, while the solution of the micro-areas was considered a good compromise between the need for integration and the will to maintain a certain lifestyle.

The preference for this solution was justified by a series of reasons. The main one was the wish to maintain a community way of life: with a piece of land in the open air, it was indeed possible to organise bigger family gatherings and to live with the extended family. Also, the local officers highlighted that many of those who entered public housing kept a bit of private land with the aim to organise gatherings with the rest of the community. Another issue, nevertheless, raised by Sinti themselves, was the wide-spread anti-Roma sentiments that prevented them from feeling welcome in the non-Romani context of public housing. Often, the neighbours protested against the allocation of public flats to Sinti or loudly complained when major family gatherings were organised in the apartments. The impact of anti-gypsyism in this context was also recognised by Bezzi: he explained how small problems provoked by Sinti families – like noise during family gatherings – were then "used" and "manipulated" to complain about their presence after many years.

At the time of my fieldwork, along with the debate on the application of the law, the municipality of Trento, in cooperation with the cooperative Kaleidoscopio, was implementing small initiatives aimed at providing a house for those families who had the will to live in an apartment, but who did not have access to publicly owned houses. The project, therefore, was based on individual necessities and possibilities and provided selected families with a house, covering the initial housing expenses until the beneficiary could reach economic independence. When the interviews were conducted, the initiative had provided two families with a house and was about to include another one, while waiting for public funds in order to extend this experience to others. Thanks to the support of the cooperative, it was possible for me to interview two members of these families, who both expressed satisfaction with the solution provided, as they did not wish to receive a micro-area.

Finally, the story of the Roma from Kosovo who arrived in Trento as refugees during the war is very significant. Instead of being treated as "Roma/nomads", like in other parts of Italy, they have been assisted as "foreigners/refugees". Consequently, they have not been placed in camps but provided with apartments, and they have progressively become independent from social services. It was telling that the social services basically did not know them since they did not need and request their services. The only Roma I had the possibility to interview here, Baskim Berisa, president of a local Romani organisation, was studying Law at the University of Trento and living in an apartment with his girlfriend, a non-Roma. He claimed that the Roma are not interested at all in "micro-areas" because this is not their way of living. He strongly opposed their creation because he considered them a new form of segregation, hindering the process of integration.

Micro-area or apartment? The contested intersection between life choices and social inclusion

In the area of Trento and Rovereto, the majority of the persons interviewed belonged to the local Sinti community, present on the territory for centuries. Since Sinti have been Italian for generations, their stories and backgrounds differ significantly from the ones of the Roma interviewed in the other contexts. Furthermore, their ancestors were mostly nomadic and used to carry out traditional crafts associated with travelling. Like Roma, Sinti have often suffered discrimination and persecution and have been placed in nomad camps (Bonetti et al., 2011; Marinaro & Sigona, 2011; Trevisan, 2018). For this reason, they have been included in the National Roma Integration Strategies and considered in this work. Here, I interviewed ten Sinti persons and only one Roma, Baskim, the president of a local Romani organisation.

I intentionally tried to reach individuals living in different housing conditions and this was possible thanks to the availability of the local social workers who took part in the study to contact Sinti families and to accompany me in the field research. Out of ten, five were still living in a nomad camp – although two were about to move to public housing, two in flats founded within the housing markets thanks to the support of a local organisation, two in a flat within a public building and one in an occupied area. All the interviews were conducted in the houses of the interviewees, except one, with Maria, that was conducted in a coffee shop. Most of the interviews were conducted singularly, without the presence or intervention of the gatekeeper. Only in a couple of cases did the gatekeeper remain during the interview, without intervening (with Daniele and Lorenzo), while in another case I explicitly asked his participation because of the lack of trust of the interviewee (Davide) towards me.

The main objective of the interviews in this area was to investigate the opinion of the local Sinti and Romani population in regard to the law on micro-areas: did it really respond to a necessity of the community? What were the reasons behind it? Was this necessity shared by everyone? As described in the previous section, the welfare state in this area ensured a greater access to publicly owned buildings, compared to the other two cases analysed in this study, and Sinti generally did not have problems with documents in having access to social benefits, since they were all Italian citizens. For this reason, over the years, many Sinti families had the possibility of leaving the camps and receiving a publicly-owned apartment. Nevertheless, according to the social workers interviewed, some of these families went back to live in the camp because they could not stand living "between four walls" and others refused to leave the camp. Furthermore, the majority of the Sinti families who adapted to the life in the flats still maintained a space outside, to park the caravans and meet the relatives.

The interviews conducted with Sinti confirmed the fact that some of them perceived the apartment as an imposition by the Gadjé. For this reason, they had great hopes in the provincial law for the creation of micro-areas, which they considered the best solution. This emerged also during the interviews with Sinti who already lived in apartments or were about to enter one. Everyone complained about the unsustainable conditions of a nomad camp, but many declared that they would have preferred a micro-area and had requested an apartment because of the lack of alternatives. Fabio explained his point of view on this issue very well. At the time of the interview, he was living in the Trento camp and was about to enter an apartment in publicly owned building. He told me that he would have preferred the micro-area, but the law had never been applied and to acquire private land independently was too complicated and expensive. When asked what were the reasons moving him to prefer a micro-area, he replied:

> That in a micro-area you have all your family, the children grow, they get married and remain close to you. But if there is no alternative, it is not possible to always live in camps, it is not possible. There is no integration. Also the kids grow, but they always do the same life that their father did, that their grandfather did, no … they also have to change by now. We are almost in 2020, eh.

Nevertheless, not everyone desired a micro-area, as some expressed preference for an apartment. The reasons behind this choice varied greatly: some preferred the comforts offered by an apartment; others aimed to abandon what they associated with "Sinti way of life"; others did not consider the apartment as a problem and did not feel the need to have a micro-area.

Due to the impossibility of reporting thoroughly all the interviews conducted in Trento and Rovereto here, four of them have been chosen because they represent three opposing points of view. The first two have been conducted with two Sinti who, at the time of the interview, still lived in the camps and were waiting for the micro-area; the third with a Sinti woman who lived in an apartment and did not regret the life "outside"; the fourth is the interview with Baskim, who presented his story as a young Roma from Kosovo living in Trento. The houses of the Sinti in the camps or micro-areas usually consisted of a caravan enlarged by a veranda constructed with prefabricated material. As in other contexts, in Trento and Rovereto, the interviewees often used the term "house" (casa) to refer exclusively to the "brick-house". For instance, when they said: "I never lived in a house", it did not mean that they were homeless, but that they had never lived in a brick-built house, as an apartment.

Anna and Lorenzo

The interviews with Anna and Lorenzo were not conducted together. The first one was conducted in the nomad camp of Trento, where Anna lived, the second in the nomad camp of Rovereto. I present them here together because they reflect a similar point of view from two different backgrounds. Namely, they both declared that they did not want to live in an apartment and that they were waiting for the provincial law on micro-areas to be applied. Nevertheless, while Anna could be perceived as a woman of the "old generation of Sinti", Lorenzo belonged to a younger generation and was also very active in society as a musician and activist. I found this aspect particularly relevant because the social workers that I interviewed here, although supporting the application of the law on micro-areas, still considered this necessity as something pertaining exclusively to the older generation more attached to the "Sinti identity". As I am showing here, the interview with Lorenzo seems to confute this assumption.

Anna was a Sinti woman, about 60 years' old, who lived in the Trento camp. She was introduced to me by the Sinti mediator living in the same camp, who also took part in the study, and she accepted taking part in the interview although she appeared quite shy and embarrassed. She also appeared cheerful and decisive in replying to the questions. Her house in the camp was made of a caravan surrounded by a veranda built with prefabricated material. It appeared well constructed and maintained, like the majority of the other houses in the same area. The camp was located in a forest area at the outskirt of Trento. The closest bus departed ten minutes by walk from the camp. As she explained at the beginning of the interview, when she was a child she used to travel with her parents who always lived in a caravan. When she got married, she moved to Trento and always lived in camps.

> *What memories do you have of the life in caravan traveling? Is it a pleasant memory?*
>
> Yes, yes, pleasant, because I always lived in the caravan, I mean, I never moved from the caravan to the house, I always lived in caravan, so it is not that I had to do an effort … I am born, raised and have lived in caravan! So I don't see the difference, because that was my life. And now let's see, even if they give me a house for rent, I would not stay there. I cannot, I really cannot stay there.

Interestingly, Anna immediately highlighted her intention not to move into an apartment, despite the fact that I still had not mentioned the issue of the law on micro-areas. This was probably due to the fact that, in that period, many were moving into apartments as the creation of micro-areas was blocked. It was therefore evident that the issue of whether "to accept an apartment" or "to stay in the camp" was felt to be particularly urgent. Immediately after this answer, I asked what were the reasons preventing her from adapting to a "house". Her reply, somehow, emphasised a series of elements that could be associated to the romantic idea of "old Sinti life":

> *And what are the reasons that, according to you, prevent you to stay in a house? What don't you like of a house?*
>
> I don't take it well, I mean, I don't know, I don't take it well, the house! Because it is closed, I always have been in the open-air, I like being like those little birds, outside in the air. In the house you have to stay 24 hours a day. No, no, no, no, let's not talk at all of a house, that also at my age, it is not that I get used immediately, eh! If I had less years, maybe, but at this age … no, rather, it would make me anxious, because I always lived outside, that in a moment, to be closed in a house it would look to me like being in a prison. No … there are the comforts, but also here I have everything, but I live in the camp. Nevertheless, I have all my services as if I was living in a house, yes, yes … I don't see the difference.

The account of Anna reflected somehow the stereotyped image of the Sinti who aims for a free life in the open-air. This quite surprised me at first, because her answer seemed to confirm the prejudice at the base of the creation of the nomad camps. As a consequence, could the nomad camp be considered a suitable housing solution for her? The answer to this question was found in her reply to the question of how she liked to live in the camp and what would be her ideal house.

And how do you like it here in the camp?

A bit boring … not because I am not settled in. Sometimes it is a bit boring, sometimes I am panicking … therefore, look.

But because it is always the same people?

That's it! yes, very good, very good, very good, you got me immediately! Because it is always the same people, right!

[…]

What would be your ideal house?

[She takes sometimes to think] Yes, to stay with my sons, to have a piece of land, something, a micro-area, but to stay with my sons, that's it. If I had to choose a life, I would choose this one: to have a piece of land that is mine, with all my kids, only with my kids, and to live all together till death do me apart from my sons, that's it. But in a house no, absolutely not, a piece of land, yes, with my sons I would live my dream. My dream would be, with none else, but my sons … I would get along very well with my sons.

On one side, Anna rejected the nomad camp because of the obligation to live in close proximity with other families, but, on the other side, she seemed to confirm another stereotype associated with her group: the desire to live with all her family, separated from the rest of society. This still is the stereotype often used to claim that Roma and Sinti do not want to integrate and do segregate themselves in order to maintain a supposed "Sinti way of life". In this case, nevertheless, the stereotype was confuted by Anna herself when talking about her desires concerning the future life of her kids. Indeed, when asked about it, she evidently wished for her kids to be integrated into society, although this may lead them to live away from her.

What kind of life you wish for you sons?

That they find a job.

A permanent job?

Yes, a permanent job. That is what I wish for my sons, that they have a permanent job and that they go ahead like this. Then, if they want to live in the camp, that is their choice, or if they want to apply for a flat to social services. But for my sons I wish that they have a permanent job, that, with a job you can live, survive, without a job you cannot … that is. I would like this for my sons.

The interview with Anna was interesting because it reflected the old idea of a Sinti life, despite her being aware of the changes in society and its implications. As already mentioned, according to the social workers this idea mainly belonged to the older generation and was progressively disappearing. It is not possible here to assess whether this tendency is real or not, because of the limited number of interviews collected, but Anna was not the only one to reject the apartment so decisively. Lorenzo, 40 years' old, also appeared to have a similar point of view. At the time of the interview, he lived with his wife in the nomad camp of Rovereto. The interview with him was conducted thanks to a social worker from the organisation Gruppo 78, who accompanied me to meet and interview him. As the same social workers explained, the camp where Lorenzo lived was inhabited by a couple of families who had refused other housing solutions, while all the others had already entered flats in public housing. As in the Trento camp, the houses consisted of caravans added to prefabricated structures, all quite well built and maintained. Nevertheless, in this case the camp was more isolated, in a rural area that could be reached only by car.

Lorenzo, as he said during the interview, was a musician and he used to collaborate with a local organisation in activities aimed at promoting the knowledge of Sinti history in schools. He immediately accepted taking part in the study but at the beginning he appeared a bit reserved, while at the end he started opening himself more. Once the interview was finished, I continued the conversation with him and he displayed a strong political consciousness. He reaffirmed that the creation of micro-areas was a priority for him. He also harshly criticised the organisations and programs that deal with Roma and Sinti in a paternalistic manner ("we come and we help you") and those who oppose the creation of the micro-areas.

During his life, Lorenzo had lived in different places and in different accommodation: he travelled with his family when he was a child, then they settled in a camp. At some point, he lived in his caravan on a private land (when it was still possible, by law) that he later left because he did not like the area. He also moved to an apartment twice, but then always returned to the camp of Rovereto. One of the first questions regarded his life in an apartment, why he chose this solution and why he left:

> *Why did you decide to live in an apartment?*
>
> Because we did not have any more places where to go, let's say, places where to stop, at least during winter. Then, they gave us the possibility to come back here, and we came back.
>
> [...]
>
> *How did you like in the apartment?*
>
> I did not like it, because people did not want us there. Look, as we were just preparing the flat, we were placing the kitchen, we were assembling it, 20

people gathered in front of my house and they were shouting "you steal the houses from us!", as we were not Italian. How can you pay a rent, when nobody wanted us? I clarify that I am not a person that makes noise … I, I am not … I am a quiet person. I don't make receptions, parties. And then, I did not like it. I like more to live in the open-air, as I am now.

But, were there some positive aspects of living in an apartment?

The positive sides … for me, I see them more here: I am close to my family, I am out, in the open-air, there is none who does not want me … A positive there was that you had a roof over your head.

The experience of Lorenzo living in an apartment resulted particularly negative because of the bad relationship with the neighbours. Nevertheless, he also pointed to the preference for a life open-air. Both aspects were reiterated in a second passage at the end of the interview:

We are used, I mean us, Sinti, to live with extended families. Over there live my parents. Over there, there are my parents-in-law, for instance. Here my parents live, I live, my wife, my brother, so … we are used to live like this. In the apartment there, on the other side of Rovereto, I didn't. … It feels like a separation, you know. Then the problems with people I had … look, they were saying to me, how was he called, [name of the responsible for the building]. He was coming to me and telling me: "You should not let people come to visit you anymore", but, are we crazy? I have my parents, friends, relatives and what should I do? Sit there and stare at the air? Understood? We did not like it and we did not make noise, eh. But they told me: "We will proceed with the signatures, people want to send you away". I said: "Well, and I bring you all in front of the judge for racism" because I don't make noise, I am not a vandal. And let's say that I had all these problems. The Gypsy is seen as an annoyance.

When talking about the camp where Lorenzo moved in again few months before the interview, he looked quite satisfied. Nevertheless, he also expressed the preference for a micro-area. He had already experienced this kind of accommodation a few years before, when it was still possible to place a caravan on agricultural land. On this regard, he said:

How did you like it? [living in a micro-area] *Why didn't you stay there? Did you have some problems?*

I had some problem with work … than there, have you even been there? [surrounding area of Verona] No, it is better to live on a peak, you are isolated, you are out of the world there, something incredible. Because there you cannot find a job. And little by little we started having some difficulties, we were starving, I mean.

No, I meant if you had difficulties with … since you bought a private land that the local authorities sent you away.

No, no, actually, the municipality there … once laws were different. You were taking a private land, you could place a mobile home, with the wheels, with a caravan you could stay there. Now you cannot anymore … not with the agricultural lands. … Then after a while, if you stay there, they come to send you away, by practice you stay … then the municipality gave us the permission, we connected with the electricity, the water well was already there, the municipality gave us the street number, the residence, so we could … once it was like this, I am speaking about … now I am 40 years old, at least nine years ago. Now you could not anymore, not even a caravan you can place.

If you had the possibility to have your own land, would you prefer it?

Who wouldn't prefer it? Do you prefer a publicly-owned flat or a house for yourself? Who wouldn't like it, with his own family?

And in this house, do you like it? would you like to improve it?

I have to finish to place the kitchen. I am sleeping in the caravan. I built the room for the music, where I study, play and teach. I feel good here.

These two accounts represent a new facet of the universe of housing perspectives and desires, only partially collected during the research. In these cases, the arguments seem to be more in line with a certain stereotyped idea of the "Romani way of life". Nevertheless, the desire to live with the family in a micro-area did not appear to affect their desire and capacity for integration. It appears, therefore, legitimate to take into consideration the micro-area as an effective housing alternative for those who, for a series of reasons, after a life spent either "on the road" or within the nomad camps, do not want to move into an apartment. It is, nevertheless, important to stress that it lies within the capacity of the local administrations to ensure that such structures remain connected to the local services and do not become new sites of segregation and stigmatisation. Furthermore, as the following interview shows, not all Sinti prefer the micro-area, as some wish to live in a different kind of accommodation.

Teresa

Teresa was a Sinti woman interviewed in an apartment provided to her by a local organisation that supported Sinti who could not have access to public housing. Back then, she was about 40 years' old and had been living in that apartment for two years with her three kids. After being financially supported in the payment of the rent, she became economically independent. The house was located in a rural and residential neighbourhood of Trento. Its interior looked modest but well kept. Before entering this apartment, Teresa had always lived in a caravan, travelling with her family most of the time. Nevertheless, as she explained, she never liked that life and had always tried to move into apartments with non-Sinti friends. She immediately appeared very open to the interview and very talkative. Therefore, the interview proved to be particularly interesting because she provided a lot of details in telling her life story and her perspective on the house.

From the beginning of the interview, Teresa highlighted the difference in perceiving the house between her parents and her, who never liked to live "on the road". On the contrary, her parents were so used to living in caravans that they never accepted the apartment that was offered to them by the local authorities.

> When I was little, it was given to us a house in the municipality of Fiavré, but my father was not going to live there, he preferred to place the caravan there. [...] And my father was rather going to live in that municipality, in that area, but not inside the house.
>
> *And inside the house, it was you and your mother?*
>
> No, none, none.
>
> *And why were you looking for the house, anyway?*
>
> I don't know, the municipality at the time decided – I was little – to give this house to my father, where he had the residence and everything, then my father was not going into the house.
>
> [...]
>
> *But why they were not going, according to you?*
>
> Because they had this free spirit – how can I say? – going around one day here and one day there, then they were travelling in Trentino, they were not going very far, they were always moving, they did not stay long in a municipality.
>
> [...]
>
> *Do you have good memories of this period, when you were a kid and you were travelling with your parents?*
>
> No, no, I never liked to move.

Why?

> Because in the villages where we were moving, I was a girl who gladly talked with other guys and I was immediately making friends. Every time we were moving, I was losing the friends and then I had to make new ones in other places where I didn't know anyone. Basically, when it was getting good that I knew the person, they were leaving. And you were thinking: "Look, I had found a friend" or "Look, there I was fine, I could learn so many things", but it was going bad because we had to leave ... because maybe the police came and told us to move. Maybe we were not moving very far from where we were, but I knew that I was about to lose everything that I had found in that village.

The aversion of Teresa to a nomadic way of life was reaffirmed in a second passage where Teresa linked her feeling of unease to a sense of belonging to the territory of Trentino, which made her suffer every time she had to move out of the region.

> I never liked it [the nomadic life] exactly because every time that we had to move from the hometown or the village of residence – because at the end we are from Trento [emphasised] – I found myself living 150–200km away from Trentino, I was not feeling fine because there I did not know anyone and at the end this was my home. Even if I was living in a caravan, Trentino has always been my home, where I grew up. I was born in Iseo, in Brescia's province, but immediately after my birth, after seven days, I moved to Trentino. Because my parents grew old and now died in Trentino. I had my friends, I had ... everything I have now, and I had at the time, I had it here. And maybe they decided: "You know, tomorrow we go to Treviso". In Treviso, it took months before we were going through all the area. I had my friendships here. Everything that was important to me, I had it here. But we were there and, unfortunately, I was young and I could not go and move when I wanted and come here again alone. ... I could not do it back then ... everything was a problem to me. A real tragedy.

In this passage, Teresa highlighted a sense of home strictly associated to her sense of belonging to the territory, which was probably reinforced by the trauma of constantly losing friendships by moving to other territories. Once adult, she moved to live with non-Sinti friends for some periods but then always had to go back to a life in a caravan. Her parents at some point stopped travelling and moved into a camp, but she refused to go there and instead decided to live in a caravan with her grandparents, who owned some private land. In talking of this experience, she emphasised again her idea of "being fixed", of "having a point of reference", strictly connected with a brick-house.

> *But the grand-parents also lived in a caravan?*
>
> Yes, also them, but they were in the countryside, where there were no other Sinti, but only them.
>
> *And were they fixed there?*
>
> Fixed … actually, outside the Sinti person is never fixed. This I can ensure it to you, believe me, because I lost some years of my life for it. You are fixed when you are here inside, when you can say: "This is my house, I am fixed, I can do whatever I want, I can go and come back when I want, because this is my point of reference and everything".

Because she always refused to enter a nomad camp, which would have ensured her a permanent residence – a necessary requirement for receiving a flat in public housing – she could never benefit from this social service. The difficulty of acquiring a fixed residence because of living in a caravan on the road was considered by Teresa one of the main problems of the nomadic life. As she explained, this affected also the possibility to find a job, which would have allowed her to rent an apartment. This added to the other difficulties of living in a caravan that does not have direct access to electricity, water and sewage.

> But also going to work is difficult when you live in a caravan. Because people often ask who you are, they don't give you the job because they don't know you, cooperatives come to look for you, but where to go to look for you? Where do you live? They don't know if it is true what you are saying or not. Because you don't have the walls that confirm that a person is there and is like that and that. […] With three children I always had many difficulties in the caravan. I don't tell you what I had to face with the kids. Because anyway the kids go to school and you have to wash them, clothes need to be washed, to be ironed, you need to clean and if you are without electricity and without water, it becomes difficult … it becomes a work that I think is like the one of the bricklayer, the same … because you have to go to pick up water with the jerry can if you live as a Sinti person, you have to warm it up with the gas tank, you have to wash the kids with the tank, to wash and iron … to iron with a normal iron, but to warm it up on the gas, and so everything becomes difficult … to do homework during day light hours, never at 7.30–7 or 6 p.m. in winter … everything becomes difficult.

Fortunately, after years trying to settle without succeeding, Teresa benefited from a project that provided her with an apartment and helped her in paying the rent at the beginning. When asked about the current accommodation, she appeared satisfied, as was already evident in the comparisons she made between the current house and the life in a caravan. I also asked her whether she would have preferred a micro-area but she was firm in replying no, as for her a house is "four walls".

> *Do you like it in here, in this house?*
>
> Yes, very much.
>
> *If you wanted to improve something of this house?*
>
> Nooo, to me it is very good like this. I always accepted it like this. For me it was really a Godsend, for me this house, for me and the kids, we are all happy of this house.
>
> [...]
>
> *And if you could choose between going to live in an apartment or in a micro-area, what would you have preferred?*
>
> Into an apartment, for sure.
>
> *Why?*
>
> But because in a micro-area you are always out, so it is meaningless for me. While here I am indoor, I have all things I need, I have more hygiene, more cleanliness, I am not beside other people, I am in my house, I am in my private. I am in my private here. While in a micro-area they put you beside other people and you never live your life.

Teresa's account is probably one of the most interesting of the ones collected in Trento, because it reveals how the way of conceiving the home and the house is highly personal and depends on a broad range of factors. She showed how the creation of housing policies based on the group, rather than on the individual, can cause unease and serious distress to individuals who have different needs and desires. Furthermore, her account is also interesting from another aspect: the difficulties for a Sinti who lives in a caravan but outside the camp. Indeed, Teresa always refused to move to a nomad camp and live with other Sinti, but this choice resulted in a further obstacle to her social and economic inclusion – the impossibility of having a fixed residence. Consequently, as already highlighted by other scholars (Sigona, 2002; Tosi Cambini, 2013), the necessity of a fixed residence to access general services and job market makes nomad camps an obligatory step towards it, despite the fact that the camps themselves, most of the time, hinder social and economic inclusion.

Baskim

The last interview presented here is the one conducted with Baskim Berisa, the president of the local Romani association "Rom Stanziali del Kosovo in Trentino". Since Baskim was the only Roma interviewed in Trento, I asked him to take part in the study not only as an activist but also by telling his story. His account is particularly interesting because it differs substantially from those of all the other interviewees. After migrating from Kosovo as a child, his family was provided with a house by social services from the beginning and he never lived in a camp. At the time of the interview, he was 32 years' old and was living in an apartment in the city centre of Trento with his girlfriend, a non-Romani foreigner girl. He had the possibility of reaching a higher level of education, enrolling in the University and achieving economic independence. Although Baskim was considered an example within the Romani community in Trento, his story was not seen as an extraordinary case, because all the community in this context was well integrated. This was especially evident from the fact that the social services and local organisations had no contacts with them, as they were independent and did not require their support .

The interview with Baskim was conducted in his apartment, a flat furnished and decorated as many other apartments belonging to young couples in the same area. He was available to take part in the study and very talkative. It was evident that he wanted his story to be known since he was very well aware of the difficulties encountered by Roma in other regions. Furthermore, the fact that we shared similar backgrounds in terms of age and level of education surely reduced the distance between the two of us. For this reason, the conversation was very relaxed and informal.

Baskim migrated from Kosovo when he was a child. In his country of origin, he lived in a house within a Romani neighbourhood and his family was quite wealthy, because his father and grand-father were business men who traded goods through the whole Yugoslavia. With the dissolution of the country and the closure of the borders, trade could not be carried out any longer and, for this reason, his father decided to migrate to Trento, initially alone with other families. Arriving in Trento, they settled in a camp called the "camp of Kosovo" and, after a while, the municipality decided to intervene and to move all the persons living in this camp into a building, where only Roma lived. In that moment, in 1996, because of the war starting in Kosovo, Baskim's father brought all his family there.

Baskim and his family lived in this building for about one year and he did not have good memories of this period, because of the precarious conditions of the building and the discrimination suffered in school.

> Therefore in 96, I also moved here with three of my brothers and we went to live in this house, with three floors, but to us they gave one floor where I lived with seven brothers, parents, grand-parents and uncles, so we were 15, 16 people, for you to understand, there were two bathrooms but one was not working, so one bathroom, three rooms and a sort of living room-kitchen … ok. We were in pitiful conditions and there we lived until 97,

one year. Then, well, there has been an important process of inclusion into schools concerning us, we were gladly going to school and the teachers noticed the situation of discomfort caused by that house and, for this reason, they allocated to my family a sort of public housing [here, he explained that the house was allocated through the services for foreigners]. They gave us the possibility to have this house which was much bigger in order to live decently. […] Then later the municipality decided to close that house and it was a good decision because that building really was a ghetto.

Because they were only Roma living in that house?

Yes, yes, but only that house was there. Basically, on the right there was the road and on the left there was this white house with a waterfall on the back, very beautiful with a view on the back but completely isolated from the world, where you did not have the possibility to socialise. Let's say that it was a vertical camp, that is, isolated from the world. We were socialising, me especially, with my brothers we were going to school and we were socialising with our school-mates but also there you were always an immigrant, the first foreigner you were seeing in that school, which was a school for wealthy people, for you to understand, I mean, there wasn't really this possibility. … I personally suffered the initial racism very much, a bit the language, a bit the skin colour, a bit this and that … I was the strange one, the different and so I was treated very badly, that is.

[…]

Then, by changing the house, changing the school, I went into a school where the kids were from families closer to our characteristics, workers … like us. Therefore, it was easier, it has been easier to start socialising. I remember that me and my class-mates were gathering to go playing football, or to go to the cinema, and things like these

As is evident from Baskim's account, he was used to living in an extended family, with many brothers and sisters, uncles and aunts around. For this reason, I asked him whether this had an impact on their inclusion within a housing system designed around the needs of nuclear families with a maximum of two or three children. As he explained, this represented a problem and a reason for distress caused by the separation from other members of the family. Nevertheless, he also considered positively the impossibility of living all together as it would have prevented them from socialising with others.

Talking about the habit of living within extended families … did you ever have difficulties in going to live in a reality as the apartment that is anyway built around an idea of nuclear family with two-three children, rather than in a house where grand-parents, uncles live?

> But look. … Initially I felt this thing a lot, because I was … still today I am very attached to my uncles and to my grand-parents, because I grew up with my grand-parents and my uncles. We were living in this house in Kosovo, as I was telling you, and already when I was a child, I was going to sleep with … because then we had a big room where we were all sleeping, parents and sons together, and this house was three-four rooms on two-three floors. So I was going to sleep with my grand-parents, with the uncle, close to the aunt [he laughs] I was four five years old, imagine … so this thing of the sense of belonging no … when they gave to us this house, we had to leave the grand-parents and there I suffered a lot, but every week-end that I was not going to school, once it was Friday I was going to the grand-parents. This thing struck me a lot and I noticed that generally it is preferred to have a small Romani neighbourhood, which is not possible, and luckily, because otherwise you isolate and you don't socialise with others, so does it make sense? Nowadays with some difficulties … because what happens: you find yourself alone with four or five children in a flat maybe close to other foreigner families, but especially to families from Trento, to understand … the person from Trento sees us so numerous, he gets scared, because if someone comes to visit you, he does not come alone, he comes with the entire family, so he sees full of people [he laughs] … that they never did anything wrong, but to go visit someone, that here there is the culture to gather together. […] So this thing bothered and they were complaining.

Thanks to the progressive process of inclusion in the sector of education and housing, all Romani families became financially independent. As Baskim explained, everyone had the possibility of finding a job or opening a small business, despite the difficulties that every foreigner encounters and the persistent discrimination against Roma. It was therefore interesting for me to understand whether this process of integration affected their sense of belonging to the Romani minority.

> *Do you manage to maintain romani traditions, how to say, as integrated Roma do you still keep … ?*
>
> No, absolutely, we … it is still strong our sense of belonging, the language especially. For instance, the language still remains robust, we still speak Romani language, also the children, that my fear was that one, that at the end one day … but no, I noticed that there is still, fortunately, this conservation of the language and also of traditions, weddings. Although in the last years … and let's say that I am the one who started this thing because I did a process of integration in all aspects: I am now 32 years old and still not married, I still don't have children, and I live with a Ukrainian girl. My parents at the beginning were considering her a bit as the usual Gadjé passing by, not really well, but now it is six years that we are together, and it was me starting a bit this revolution of the wedding and I

> saw also others. For instance, my uncle lives together – they are like married – with a Moldavian girl, another cousin with a Romanian.
>
> [...]
>
> But the base of the wedding between Roma still exist within the sphere of Roma. But I think that this process of change already started.
>
> [...]
>
> It is normal because anyway a dynamic culture, there is this process and fortunately I would say, although keeping the roots, because it is true that I did this path of change and integration, but, in any case, I still keep the fact of being Roma, the language, I gladly go to weddings, to talk with another cousin that I haven't seen for years, to meet.

The final issue addressed during the interview was his relationship with Italy and Trento and with his country of origin, Kosovo. He evidently felt part of the context in which he lived, although still maintaining a connection with his origins. Nevertheless, as he told me, this was not the same for all the members of his family, since the older ones did not consider Trento and Italy as their home.

> He [the grand-father], unfortunately, always tells me: "Ehh, damn the day that I came here because in any case your own land … you can have everything but … I've never been happy in Italy and I will never be, I am fine for the family, yes, I don't miss anything". But I think that at a certain age there is this lure of your own land, I don't know how to explain. Also my grand-mother, the same, while my father doesn't care at all, but my father is born in 1970, he is still young.
>
> *While do you feel belonging to Trentino, in some way?*
>
> Well, I [he laughs] … it happened to go back to Kosovo two times and I was feeling as a foreigner in my own country, meaning that could I see myself there? Absolutely not. For instance, I went there with my uncle and he went crazy: "Kosovo is so beautiful, fantastic! Look here when I was a kid, look there … my goodness, I would … I don't know really, but if one day I make up my mind, I really come back to live in Kosovo". While me, no please. … Then the first time I went there I was 22, 23 years' old, I mean, I was young, I had small braids, I was dressed quite well, so I was entering in the shops, in the bars, and they were speaking to me in Spanish: but look that I am from here, I just live in Italy. For you to understand, right? I was feeling really uncomfortable … come to live here? Forget about it!

Despite his feeling of discomfort in going back to Kosovo, Baskim still kept contacts with his country of origin and his association decided to carry out activities also aimed at helping Roma there. It was nevertheless clear that he had made his life in Italy and he would probably continue living there. However, the conclusion of his inclusion process was hindered by the fact that he had still not managed to acquire Italian citizenship because of the complexity of the procedure and because of the impossibility of retrieving some requested documents from Kosovo. For Baskim, this issue was a source a great distress because of the frustration of being unable to benefit from citizenship after growing and fully integrating in the local context.

The story of Baskim differs substantially from all the others and it provides an example of the results of inclusion policies that are not influenced by anti-gypsyism and stereotypes. Namely, his family was not labelled as "nomad" and placed in a camp but given the possibility of receiving a house, which contributed to their integration. The analysis of his story may raise the legitimate question whether his inclusion process could be applied to all Roma living in Italy. His family, indeed, initially encountered some difficulties in adapting to the new accommodation, but finally it managed to fully integrate. Would that be possible for everyone? Other interviews showed that this is not always possible or, in some cases, desirable. In analysing Baskim's case, it is indeed necessary to consider the fact that his family never lived for a long period within a camp. His initial situation, therefore, differed from those who spent decades within the camps, which may have inevitably impacted their way of life.

Conclusions

The interviews conducted in Trento display even more the impact of diversity in the development of housing needs and the individual perception of public policies that do not take into account this diversity. Here, indeed, the solution of the apartment in "public housing" is seen as an imposition by the "gadjè" by many, and this aspect is also recognised by the social workers who operate daily in this field. In this context, the flat can be seen as a physical and symbolic imposition for those who would like to keep living in the "open-air": physical because it obliges the person to adapt to the spaces of an accommodation built around the housing needs of others; symbolic because it is perceived as an abandonment of part of the "Sinti identity", as a further step towards assimilation. Despite all of this, here the nomad camp appears as a degrading and failing solution. This not only because of its stigmatisation, but also because of the substantial lack of privacy and control that this kind of structure presents, even where the general infrastructures are not as poor as in other nomad camps. Furthermore, despite the recognition of the negative consequences of these structures for the social inclusion of its inhabitants, they remain the only solution for those Roma and Sinti that cannot have access to the regular public and private housing market. The story of Teresa is exemplary in this sense: the difficulties of finding a regular job and of having access to public housing were worsened by her refusal to live in the nomad camp, where she could have acquired the residence status necessary to apply for public housing. This shows the necessity of implementing policies that replace the system of the nomad camps with solutions that ensure inclusion within the housing market, while respecting different needs.

With this objective in mind, Trento province can be considered a positive example for its broad access to public housing, the way social services have dealt with Roma migrated from Kosovo and for the initiatives that have been implemented to provide Sinti families that did not have access to public housing with a different solution.This last example shows the importance of considering individual cases in the implementation of inclusion processes into housing, instead of designing policies intended for an entire group of people. In the same way, the broad offer of apartments in public housing proved to be a good alternative to nomad camps: the opportunity to enter public housing had moved many families out of the camps, where a very restricted number of families was still living, although some would have rather opted for a micro-area.

In this regard, the analysis of this case has shown the necessity of engaging in a serious debate and dialogue with the local community on the feasibility of these structures. Indeed, although concerns regarding the risk of preserving forms of segregation may rise, the desire expressed by many to live in structures that allow the maintenance of a community life with open spaces should be considered. Indeed, this example shows, once more, the importance of listening to the individuals when housing is concerned, because of its importance in the processes of inclusion and because of the plurality of factors affecting housing needs. For this reason, offering a range of different housing solutions that individuals can access by choice may prove to be a better solution than the resettlement of entire communities in accommodation chosen by others.

Finally, the case of the Roma who migrated to Trentino from Kosovo efficaciously highlights the consequences of anti-gypsyism in the development of the nomad camps system. Unlike the rest of Italy, here Roma were treated as refugees and, as such, were provided with the social support reserved to this group. This allowed them to integrate into the local society and to become completely independent from the support of the social services. As Baskim emphasised during the interview, if his family had decided to move to another location in Italy, where Roma were placed in nomad camps, his life would have been completely different. This example should be seen as a lesson for future policies: measures designed around ideas that Roma are "different" and "special" and require a different treatment may lead to negative outcomes.

Notes

1 List of public officers, representatives and activists interviewed in Trento and Rovereto (name – role/organisation, date of the interview):

Davide Lasta – social services municipality of Trento, 24 July 2017

Ottavio – ROMACT mediator, 25 July 2017
Costanza Righetto and Santo Boglioni – Gruppo 78, 25 July 2017
Alessandro Bezzi – Coop. Kaleidoskopio, 26 July 2017
Gianluca Magagni – AIZO rom&sinti Rovereto, 21 September 2017
Baskim Berisa – Rom Stanziali del Kosovo in Trentino, 21 September 2017

2 List of Sinti and Romani interviewees (name, kind of accommodation, date of the interview):

Anna – nomad camp (Trento), 25 July 2017
Fabio – nomad the camp (Trento), 25 July 2017
Daniele – nomad camp (Rovereto), 18 September 2017
Lorenzo – nomad camp (Rovereto), 18 September 2017
Teresa – private flat (Trento), 20 September 2017
Davide – occupied area (Trento), 20 September 2017
Maria – private flat (Trento), 20 September 2017
Giacomo and Anita – flat in publicly-owned building (Rovereto), 21 September 2017
Davide – occupied area (Trento), 20 September 2017
Maria – private flat (Trento), 20 September 2017
Baskim – private flat (Trento), 21 September 2017

References

Bonetti, P., Simoni, A., & Vitale, T. eds (2011). *La Condizione Giuridica dei rom e dei Sinti in Italia. Atti del Convegno Internazionale. Università degli Studi di Milano – Bicocca 16–18 Giugno 2010.* Milano: Giuffrè Editore.

Furlan, F. (2011). Rom e sinti nelle legislazioni regionali. In P. Bonetti, A. Simoni, & T. Vitale, eds, *La Condizione Giuridica dei Rom e dei Sinti in Italia.* Milano: Giuffrè Editore.

Il Sole 24 Ore (2019). Qualità della vita 2019. https://lab24.ilsole24ore.com/qualita-della-vita/classifiche-complete.php.

Italia Oggi (2019, November 19). Qualità della vita: Trento la migliore d'Italia. www.italiaoggi.it/news/qualita-della-vita-trento-la-migliore-d-italia-201911171115217909.

Marinaro, I. C., & Sigona, N. (2011). Introduction. Anti-Gypsyism and the politics of exclusion: Roma and Sinti in contemporary Italy. *Journal of Modern Italian Studies, 16*(*5*), 583–589. https://doi.org/10.1080/1354571X.2011.622467.

Piasere, L. (2004). *I rom d'Europa. Una storia moderna.* Bari and Roma: Laterza.

Misure per favorire l'integrazione dei gruppi sinti e rom residenti in provincia di Trento, n. Legge Provinciale n.12 (2009).

Norme per l'Inclusione Sociale di Rom e Sinti, n. Legge Regionale n. 15 (2015).

Setti, F. (2015). The implications of "naming" on Roma and Sinti right to education and social inclusion: An ethnography of education among a Sinti family network. *Intercultural Education, 26*(*2*), 114–130. https://doi.org/10.1080/14675986.2015.1023011.

Sigona, N. (2002). *Figli del ghetto. Gli italiani, i campi nomadi e l'invenzione degli zingari.* Civezzano: Nonluoghi Libere Edizioni.

Tosi Cambini, S. (2013). Accesso all'abitazione e problemi di salute delle popolazioni rom e sinti. In C. Saraceno, N. Sartor, & G. Sciortino, eds, *Stranieri e disuguali Le disuguaglianze nei diritti e nelle condizioni di vita degli immigrati* (pp. 225–250). Bologna: Il Mulino.

Trevisan, P. (2018). The persecution of Rom and Sinti in Fascist Italy. *Trauma and Memory, 6*(*3*), 48–55. https://doi.org/10.12869/TM2018-3-02.

5 From adequate housing to home

the home-making approach

The empirical work presented in the previous chapters investigated how the provision of "adequate housing" is translated in the design and implementation of policies for the inclusion of Roma as a group in the housing sector, and what are the implications and factors to be considered in this process. The analysis highlighted how the importance of the house for the individual – beyond being a physical repair and the variety of factors affecting housing needs – critically hinders the outcomes of initiatives aimed at providing housing alternatives that simply respect basic adequacy standards. Indeed, the qualitative work conducted here revealed the universe of different emotional, social and economic factors affecting the well-being of the individual in the house, which cannot be fully grasped within quantitative assessments of housing adequacy. In this last chapter, I collect and analyse the main findings of this work with three primary aims: to highlight once more the importance of considering all aspects affecting housing choices; to list a series of insights for future initiatives aimed at the inclusion of Roma in the housing sector; and to propose a reflection for a new understanding of housing rights and policies, based on the concept of home-making.

The house beyond a roof over the head: significance and implications

The analysis of the interviews conducted with the beneficiaries of the initiatives considered here highlighted how the vast majority of them was not completely satisfied with the housing solution provided, despite the initial intentions of the projects to offer alternatives meeting the needs of the group. For instance, the majority of the interviewees living in the Romani village of Coltano in Pisa declared that they would have preferred another housing solution: some complained for the distance from the rest of the city and expressed the desire to live "like everyone else" in apartments; others expressed the preference for solutions that would have allowed them to live solely with their extended family. In Trento, the solution of the apartment represented a source of distress for many Sinti individuals, who would have preferred a micro-area to combine privacy and control of the space with a life in the "open-air". In Messina, the transfer

DOI: 10.4324/9781003184539-6

from the camp to apartments in integrated settings did not always represent an improvement in life conditions, as it limited the possibility of keeping informal economic activities that ensured an income within the camp.

The unsatisfactory results of the projects, therefore, seemed to lie in the failure to provide solutions able to meet the different housing needs. Indeed, the most evident finding of the empirical research was the universe of different stories and perspectives that affected the needs and choices of the individuals. The failure to properly recognise all these differences has raised a series of issues that had an important impact on the results of the initiatives. The first issue is surely connected with the economic sustainability of the solution provided, which always played a critical role for its sustainability. This emerged especially in Pisa, where most of the families that had been provided with apartments found within the regular market have then been evicted later on because they could not afford the housing expenses. Similar issues emerged in Messina when Caritas stopped paying the rent of the families accommodated in apartments found in the market, and the same problem could have arisen for those who took part in the self-build, if they had been asked to pay a lease and to cover the housing expenses. This was indeed the main concern for the president of the local Romani association who emphasised that, without a job and stable income, they could not feel secure. In Trento, this issue was less pressing because of the improved system of social support, which ensured a good coverage of publicly owned housing for those who wanted it. Nevertheless, the problem emerged here as well in reference to those families who, for different reasons, lost the right to public housing and could not afford to pay the rent.

In some cases, the economic difficulties were worsened by other aspects, such as the impossibility of running economic activities carried out within the nomad camp in the new accommodation. This issue emerged especially in Messina, where Roma were used to collecting and selling scrap metal, or to running small informal businesses, within the camp of San Ranieri. These activities could not be maintained after the transfer because of the lack of space to store the scrap metal and of the costs and difficulties of opening a small business outside the camp. In Trento, as well, many Sinti practised scrap metal collection for a living, but here the main problem was the poor profit earned from it. Indeed, the scrap metal collection was practised through a cooperative, but the high costs and the reduction of the profits did not allow Sinti families to cover all the expenses.

Another issue connected to the economic sustainability and raised by the social workers in Messina were the costs connected to the necessity of providing large spaces to host extended families. This issue also emerged for those included in the project because the spaces provided were often insufficient to host all the family's members. Similar observations were raised by Mennucci in Pisa, who highlighted how large families, or the practice of living in extended families in some cases, clashed with the reduced spaces of an apartment and its costs. In Trento, this problem emerged regarding relationships with the neighbours. Here, Bezzi noticed how the high number of children and the habit of living closely with the extended family triggered complaints from the neighbours because of the noise or because of the presence of relatives visiting often.

Finally, all the cases highlighted more or less another aspect that had to be taken into account, namely the presence of different housing needs or different understandings of living in the house. Regarding the first, according to the interviewees, the most common necessity was associated to a life in the community and was, therefore, related to the need of spaces to preserve a community life. This aspect emerged in Messina, where both the social workers and Romani representatives emphasised that the Romani families missed a space to celebrate their festivities and maintain the community life that existed within the camp. In Trento this necessity was also emphasised by Bezzi, who explained that, in many cases, Sinti families living well in apartments had space outside where they could meet with the extended family without raising issues with neighbours. This "life in the community" also emerged in Pisa. Here, it was presented as part of what some interpreted as a different "sense/meaning of the house", which in some cases would have hampered the inclusion within a "regular house".

Minghi and Mennucci talked extensively about this issue because it was presented as one of the main difficulties emerging in the relocation into flats found in the housing market. According to the two social workers, some families were damaging the housing structures to change the organisation of the spaces, resulting in important increments in the costs, while others even abandoned the flats, because they were not used to this kind of structure. In this regard, they noticed that even families that had the economic means to sustain the expenses of a rent had decided to go back to the camp, because they were not used to living in apartments:

> Because anyway I remind a family that lives in Oratorio [unauthorised camp still existing] [...] they always managed to have a job, also with an income that, well, they could afford to pay rent, and some singularly even tried to take an apartment independently, but then ... and not because of the costs, because of the separation from the extended family, of the change of lifestyle, that is what they were telling us.

Also, Bontempelli and Dibran recognised that leaving the environment of the camp, with its community life, proved to be a stressful experience for some families and, in some cases, resulted in the abandonment of the provided flats. Nevertheless, according to Dibran, the community "way of life" belonged to the past, and new generations aspired rather to a life together with the rest of society.

Considerations on different ways of living and perceiving the house were raised also in relation to the families living in the village of Coltano:

MENNUCCI: There are some families that see the house as their kingdom, so you enter inside and it is something ... like a villa! Others still tend to see it as something transitory.

Transitory towards?

MENNUCCI: I mean they do not feel the house as something stable and permanent, therefore it is lived differently.

But, according to you, is this because they want to go back to their home country or?

MINGHI: To go back to their country I do not think so at all. The families I think Elisa is talking about are families that … are the Bosnians no? Families that do not have the sense of the house as others have.

Needless to say, similar issues were addressed in Trento, where Sinti families themselves declared their aversion to life in a flat and rather expressed a preference for solutions that allowed them to maintain a community life in the outside. Nevertheless, in none of these contexts were these differences interpreted in solely cultural terms. While living in extended families, preferring a community life and expressing different understandings of the house are often associated with "culture" and "traditions", in Pisa, all the interviewees rather associated these differences with years spent within nomad camps, which, nevertheless, were not seen as the only cause. For instance, Minghi highlighted the fact that some of the families that encountered more difficulties to adapt to the housing structures provided had already lived in environments similar to camps before arriving to Italy and, because of that, had a different idea of the house. Furthermore, Mennucci highlighted the presence of strong differences in living and managing the house between families, also within the same group:

> it depends from family to family: there is a Bosnian family that lives in this way, so you enter their house and you find only a bed, a table, the essentials. Maybe they also live without electricity for a while, then they reactivate it … then there is another family, kin to the previous one, that has a very well-kept house, they care a lot, the garden is very beautiful, with a care for details. It is really variable.

Also, in the case of Trento, all the interviewees recognised a great diversity in housing needs and preferences, which could not be interpreted solely in cultural terms: although a good part still preferred not to live in an apartment, or to have a space outside to balance the need for a better accommodation with the one of preserving some habits connected to a life outside, others aspired to abandon completely the life of the camps. This diversity, after all, is in line with what has already highlighted by other authors: although culture and society surely affect individual housing needs, personal experiences play a major role in defining housing choices (Blunt & Dowling, 2006; Massey, 1995; Richardson, 2019). In Trento, this was evident in the account of Teresa, who, despite the fact that she had lived all her life within a caravan, aimed exclusively to live in a brick house and did not wish at all to live in a micro-area as she preferred to abandon what she perceived as the "Sinti way of life".

The broad consequences of housing segregation and forced evictions

This study has also shown how the failure to consider all aspects connected with house – social, economic, cultural, etc. – risks of worsening even further the conditions of the beneficiaries of the initiatives. Indeed, another important finding of the interviews with Roma and Sinti is the variety and seriousness of the consequences of policies that did not take into account the risks of further evictions and the impact of spatial segregation. They have both proved to be a serious obstacle to the inclusion of the individual not just in the short term, as they leave a mark that will limit the possibility of feeling included, welcome and safe – of feeling at home – for an undefined period of time. In this context, the concept of home-making gains relevance, as it identifies a multi-sensory and emotional process through which the person creates a sense of home. It concerns not only the house itself, but also the surrounding environment and, therefore, the capacity of the individual to feel part of a place or community (Boccagni & Brighenti, 2017; Brun, 2015; Brun & Fábos, 2015; Cancellieri, 2017). Many of the people who took part in this study have been prevented from engaging in home-making because they either lived in nomad camps disconnected from the rest of the urban fabric or because they were frequently evicted from the places where they settled. Their experiences bring an example of how the impossibility of feeling at home hinders socio-economic inclusion within the surrounding context.

The interviews conducted in the Romani village of Coltano, for instance, call attention to the dramatic consequences of living in a segregated space. It is, indeed, significant that Caterina, although she had resided in Pisa for almost 20 years, still felt a "guest" in Italy, giving the impression of living in a sort of "limbo" between the "real home" of her childhood and the "dreamed home" of a life outside of Coltano. The interview with her showed how the distance from the rest of the urban fabric and the impossibility of socialising with Italian people represented serious obstacles to integration. This was even more evident in the interview with Chiara and Daniela: they were born and raised in Italy, they went to school and spoke Italian perfectly, but did not feel Italian. Their only "real home" was the bubble represented by the village of Coltano, where they could feel free to speak their language and maintain practices and traditions that connected them with the country of origin of their parents, Macedonia. It was also telling that they still considered Macedonia their home country, although they had never visited it. On this regard, Dibran, whose family was still living in the village, while he managed to reach higher levels of education and exit the segregation of the camp, argued:

> I am against the cohabitation of Roma in community, because, independently if it is a camp, an illegal or legal settlement, or a village like the one

> in Coltano, it is, in any case, an oppressive and grievous reality. … I am saying oppressive because it closes a strong diversity within its borders. I mean: what is here in the camp, cannot be out of the camp, and this creates a strong separation from the gadjé, namely the non-Roma. … I do not think that it is a context that favours integration, but that limits it, it creates an internal unit which moves independently, completely independent from the rest of hosting society. If you think that very few children here [Coltano village] have a life outside the camp. This prevents the child from facing what is outside of it. He lives in a state of alienation from what is the school reality because it is external to the camp, it is something belonging to the world of the gadjé, and we have to go there as an obligation. But, apart from that, life is inside the camp. Therefore, it becomes natural the automatic claim of our dispositions: "No, I have to get married … this thing I cannot do because it is a 'gadjé thing'". It means to limit ourselves in the possibilities and perspectives for the future, and this is a consequence of the dynamics created within the camps.

Nevertheless, the issue of integration vs. segregation proved to be more complex than it may have appeared at first sight in Pisa, as many factors have to be considered. Indeed, living outside a Romani/nomad camp/village does not forcibly result in an improvement of the level of inclusion and quality of life. This is the case of Messina, where the results of the closure of the nomad camp of San Ranieri were highly contested: while some officers, such as Carmelo Lembo, claimed that the project had a positive impact on the integration of Roma and on the deconstruction of the prejudices, according to the activists from ARCI and Pistorino from Caritas, integration did not improve and, in some regards, even worsened. Similar different opinions emerged in the interviews with the former inhabitants of the camp who did not agree on the results of the transfer to desegregated settings.

If we look to the two different contexts, the main difference between the Romani village of Coltano and the nomad camp of San Ranieri was their position: while the first was located far away from the urban structure and badly connected to the rest of the area, the camp of Messina was in a central area of the city and therefore had an exchange with the rest of the municipality. Furthermore, the neighbourhoods where the inhabitants of the camp of San Ranieri have been moved were generally marginal and exposed to deviance. For this reason, not everyone considered the transfer an improvement. Nevertheless, it was also confirmed that the children could easily integrate with the new non-Romani neighbours and benefited from living in a place not precarious and stigmatised such as the nomad camp.

In addition, along with the separation from the rest of society, the system of the nomad camps may hinder home-making by preventing the individual from feeling in control of the inhabited space. This because the camp is an area managed and controlled by the local authorities, who decide who has the right to stay and where. Furthermore, the separation between one house and the other is rarely clearly marked, and the families end up sharing common spaces, whose maintenance should be ensured by an external entity. One of the main aspects of feeling at home is the sense of responsibility and care produced towards the place. As highlighted also in the works of Catherine Brun (2015) and Adriano Cancellieri (2017), this sense cannot be produced without a minimum level of control of the area, while the provision of a certain level of security and control (i.e. security of tenure and privacy) proved to significantly boost processes of home-making and inclusion.

Especially the interviews conducted in Trento with Sinti living in the nomad camps highlighted the impossibility of feeling in control of the space in which they were living. With this in mind, they were hoping for the micro-areas where they could live alone with the members of their families, controlling and managing their own space. This aspect was also stressed in the interview conducted in Pisa with Agnese and Luigi, who lived in a micro-area. They evidently felt more in control of the space as they proudly talked about the work done in it, while expressing satisfaction with this solution. Furthermore, when speaking about her childhood house, Agnese explicitly emphasised the difference between that house, the micro-area and the camp: while in the latter they were obliged to live with other "stranger Roma", in the micro-area, like in the house of her childhood, she lived only with her family.

Apart from this, home-making can be hindered, or even violently halted, by forced evictions. As well as preventing individuals from continuing living and engaging in a process of inclusion within the area where they are living, the experience of multiple evictions can produce a sense of insecurity that hinders the ability of the individual to feel at home in other places. This aspect emerged in the interview with Emma: although she was at that time living in an apartment with a regular contract, she had the continuous fear of losing it and going back to live in camps. The fact that she had experienced multiple evictions in her past life represented a trauma: this was the first aspect she started talking about with evident anger and distress, and it prevented her from relaxing and doing projects for the future in the new accommodation. Indeed, when asked about the new house and how she would have liked to improve it, she answered that for her "a roof was enough", as long as she did not go back to live in a camp. Also, the impression that I had entering her house, which was not particularly personalised, was that she was not completely settled in and she did not feel safe in investing in it. Similar impressions were the one left by the interview conducted in Pisa with Vincenzo, who, after being evicted and living in a caravan without a safe space to park, was just asking for a "roof over the head".

Finally, another example of the consequences of multiple evictions is the account of Teresa in Trento. Before receiving the apartment, she always lived in a caravan, since she had continually refused to move in a nomad camp. As she reported, when she started living alone, she wanted to settle somewhere, but the police did not allow her to park the caravan in one place. Furthermore, she could not apply for residence, and this precarious condition prevented her from finding a job and earning the money necessary to pay for an apartment. Paradoxically, her inclusion process would have been facilitated by moving to the nomad camp, which would have allowed her at least to acquire the registered permanent residential address and to apply, after some years, for public housing. Nevertheless, as has been shown, the nomad camp itself often represents an essential obstacle to integration, as it is highly stigmatised and obliges the individual to adapt to socio-economic conditions which may hinder their inclusion in other contexts.

Consequently, the accounts collected in the interviews present forced evictions and the system of the camps as two sides of the same coin, both hindering the construction of a home and the consequent socio-economic inclusion of the individual. They furthermore appear to profoundly affect the psychology of the person suffering these conditions, hampering the possibility of imagining a better future. They consequently represent a severe form of violence against the individual and an obstacle to the well-being of the entire society, which would continue hosting marginal components unable to become active parts of its development. Notwithstanding, evictions and nomad camps seem to remain one of the main policy measures used to deal with marginalised communities, especially Roma.

Insights for a new strategy for the inclusion of Roma in the housing sector

Although the general objective of this book is not to propose a comprehensive analysis of the EU and Italian strategy for the inclusion of Roma, the empirical work has highlighted some challenges and opportunities for improvements to the current approach. As a consequence, with the intention of contributing to the debate on the revision of the national strategies for the inclusion of Roma and Sinti, I here present some findings of my research work that can help to develop a new approach.

The first issue presented here is the participation of the Romani beneficiaries in policy-planning: although EU institutions have often highlighted the importance of the involvement of the Romani community, this call has rarely been translated in a meaningful participation. The first part of this section does not only analyse the consequences of a lack of participation, but also the practical implications of what "participation" means in this context. I claim that an involvement of the "community" as such may even be counter-productive and it is therefore necessary to plan participatory mechanisms that look at the individual rather than at the group.

The second issue addressed is the impact of anti-Roma prejudices in the implementation of the initiatives: while such prejudices may trigger protests before the transfer of Roma to non-Romani settings, they can be tackled with mutual knowledge. It is, though, important to plan measures that support the implementation of inclusion projects with initiatives aimed at reducing prejudices both among the policy-makers and general society. Connected to the persistence of anti-Roma prejudices is the continuing tendency of designing and implementing "special projects" for Roma instead of planning their inclusion within structural social policies. As I argue, the "special" nature of these initiatives does not only fail to address the structural barriers to inclusion, but also informs the same prejudices and stereotypes at the base of the exclusion of Roma. Finally, in the last part of this section, I argue that a structural change in the way Roma inclusion in the housing sector is understood must go through a broader availability of housing solutions, not as alternatives only for Roma and Sinti, but integrated into the general housing system. In this regard, a serious debate on the feasibility and desirability of micro-areas appears necessary in order to reach out those who aim for this housing solution.

Participation of the beneficiaries: from the community to the individual

The impossibility of meeting individual housing needs, preferences and possibilities proved to also be a result of the failure of the participatory mechanisms used in the development and implementation of the projects. As Dibran in Pisa effectively explained, the most common mistake of all policy-makers in this sector is to provide solutions considered as the "best fit" without consulting the individuals concerned. In order to meet the needs and preferences of the beneficiaries, it is necessary to ensure their participation in project planning and development. For this reason, the issue of the participation of the Roma is particularly relevant.

Both EU and Italian policy documents call for further involvement of Romani beneficiaries in project planning. Nevertheless, the rhetorical weight given to the importance of participation is not balanced by clear recommendations on the actual meaning of this term. Furthermore, when EU documents present "success stories" it becomes evident how the participation of beneficiaries is overshadowed (see Chapter 1). The issue becomes even more critical in consideration of the fact that, as Violeta Vajda emphasises, a tokenistic understanding of participation can be used to further justify and veil relations of power (Vajda, 2015). Within the Italian context, Sigona harshly criticises how participation of Roma is understood and used. He emphasises how such "participation" is most of the time ensured by simply appointing the role of the "representative" to one older inhabitant of the nomad camp. In this way, the decisions taken by non-Romani policymakers are presented as "endorsed" by the Romani community. Furthermore, Sigona highlights how asking Roma to choose between living in a camp or another housing solution cannot be considered real participation: instead of continuing living in an area without electricity and running water, they would probably opt for an alternative, no matter which one (Sigona, 2002).

The "Città Sottili" project foresaw the active participation of Roma, with the idea of providing solutions reflecting as much as possible the necessities of the families. Nevertheless, it is questionable how this participation has been achieved. According to Minghi and Mennucci, the Romani community was involved in the decision process, especially at the beginning of the project planning, with the organisation of informal meetings inside the camps and the appointment of some representatives. In this regard, the appointment of representatives already appears questionable because it remains unclear how one person can properly represent the variety of needs and wishes that arise from a personal and intimate issue such as the choice of a house. Indeed, although Mennucci considered this experience as positive, because it created a relation between Roma and administrators, she also recognised that the appointment of representatives created further conflicts within the community.

Furthermore, the numerous and different problems emerged from the beginning prevented the realisation of the project as planned, including the direct involvement of the beneficiaries. For instance, the self-build and reconversion of public buildings into flats, as well as the self-build of the village of Coltano, have been put aside, because of the complexity of the bureaucratic procedures. Nevertheless, the interviews conducted during the study emphasised the fact that all the beneficiaries have been informed about the evolution of the project and none has been obliged to accept housing solutions totally against their will. The impression was that the actors directly involved in the realisation of the project, and in contact with the families, were well intentioned in responding to the needs and desires of each family. These problems emerged because of the difficulties in coordinating all the actors involved and in respecting the required bureaucratic procedures, within political environment that required "easy", "fast" and, as much as possible, "invisible" solutions.

Messina is a similar case in this sense. Facing the imminent eviction, the Romani community of the San Ranieri camp engaged in negotiations with the local organisations and the administration to propose a solution that met the possibilities and necessities of all (including the financial availability of the administration). Although this initial process was remembered positively by the parties involved, the need to find an agreement between all the families on one solution, respecting the limitations posed by the administration, provoked conflicts. For this reason, the final solution of the self-build was not really the product of a proposal coming from the beneficiaries, but rather an idea of the policy-makers, although accepted by the inhabitants. Furthermore, the recognition of the president of the local Romani association as "representative" of the whole community by the institutions provoked further divisions: when they had to choose the collocation of each family within the housing structures, these divisions could not be reconciled, and they agreed on leaving the choice to the project coordinators.

These examples show how it might not be possible to take decisions on policies that crucially affect the life of each individual, by simply involving the beneficiaries as a "community". This is because one solution can never reconcile the different needs of everyone and one representative will never be able to grasp and mediate between them. Furthermore, the inevitable failure of these experiences might reinforce the prejudices that Roma are not able to represent themselves and to take part in decision-making. It is remarkable, indeed, that the public officer from Pisa, on the failing participation of the

Romani community, pointed to their "inability" to appoint representatives able to represent the interests of all, instead of following their own.

The situation in Trento was different, where policies aimed at providing housing alternatives to all Sinti and Roma at once have not been implemented. As has been shown, the passage from the camp to the "house" usually went through the inclusion within the waiting lists for public housing, which was on a voluntary basis. When an inclusion project was developed, it was usually directed to single families who expressed the need and desire to be supported in finding an apartment. Here, the main emerging issue was whether entering into an apartment responded to a real desire or a lack of alternatives, as the Sinti mediator claimed. For this reason, the application of the law on micro-areas seemed particularly crucial for the Sinti community of Trento-Rovereto.

This law was also the product of a dialogue between Sinti and the community, since, as Bezzi explained, it was proposed by a Council member who drafted it in close cooperation with Sinti living in camps and occupied areas. Surely, the law on micro-areas did not reflect the needs and desires of all Roma and Sinti, and it had not been written in agreement with all the community. Nevertheless, it was not meant to produce a policy addressing all Roma and Sinti, but rather to provide the possibility of choosing between one solution or another, as explicitly specified in the legal text. More perplexities were raised by the composition of the body meant to implement the law. It indeed required the presence of three Romani and Sinti representatives, one for each community, but Rovereto sent a non-Romani person, president of a local organisation. The choice, apparently made by Sinti themselves, was interpreted by Boglioni, from the cooperative Gruppo 78, as a consequence of the "incapacity of the Sinti community of Rovereto of appointing leaders".

The impact of anti-Roma prejudices on policy planning and implementation

As evident also in the previous section, many of the issues emerged in the planning and implementation of the policies analysed here are connected to the persistence of anti-Roma prejudices both among the general population and the policy-makers. Indeed, it is still a common idea that Roma cannot represent themselves and be meaningfully part of decision-making. This prejudice forcibly hinders the possibility of carrying out sincere consultations with the beneficiaries of the initiatives, essential for the success of the projects. Furthermore, if the initiatives do not achieve the expected results, anti-Roma prejudices might reinforce the idea that Roma are the one to blame, because "they do not want to integrate" (Marushiakova & Popov, 2015). Finally, as it is further argued in the following section, these prejudices and the tendency of treating Roma as a "special case" moves policy-makers to design and implement "special projects" for Roma instead of addressing the structural obstacle to their full inclusion.

In addition to this, anti-Roma prejudices emerged as an issue every time Roma and Sinti were relocated into non-Romani neighbourhoods. In all the three cases, indeed, the non-Romani neighbours protested against the relocation, even forcing Roma and Sinti out, as in the case of Lorenzo in Trento, or manipulating the idea that Roma creates problems to claim for damages, as Minghi noticed in Pisa. Nevertheless, the most evident actions were the protests organised before and during the relocations. In Pisa, in an article of 2006, Bontempelli reported how in the neighbourhoods where it was planned to move Roma, the local population organised loud protests against their arrival. These protests moved the local administration to adopt a different approach, limiting the action, with the evident fear of losing consensus (Bontempelli, 2006). Nevertheless, it is interesting to note that Minghi and Mennucci, when interviewed in 2016, did not present these protests as one of the main problems, because they mostly faded away after the transfer was finalised. Very similar was the situation encountered in Messina: the protests of the neighbours and the supposed vandalisation of the structures where Roma had to be moved convinced the administration to keep the operation secret, carrying out the transfer during the night and starting the reconstruction works only later. Despite this, here also the initial harsh protests have been followed by reconciliation, which occurred once the two parties – Roma and non-Roma – saw and recognised each other.

It is therefore possible to suppose that a large part of anti-Roma prejudices is not the product of negative personal experiences, but rather of the persistence of stereotypes against Roma fed by media and public discourses. It is also possible to assume that these prejudices would – at least partially – fade away with time and mutual knowledge. Nevertheless, the indirect consequences of these protests are still serious. Both in Pisa and Messina, anti-Roma manifestations moved the local administrations to revise the planned initiatives in order to limit their extent and visibility. The revisions adopted in this sense seriously hindered the effectiveness and sustainability of the results, contributing substantially to their failure: in Pisa the administration decided to limit the project only to those Romani individuals present in Pisa during the census, failing to achieve the objective of dismantling completely the policy of the nomad camps; in Messina, the fear of the protests moved the administration to carry out the transfer during the night when the housing solutions were still not ready. As a result, most of the families here lived in structures completely unfit for habitation for a long period of time.

As a consequence, a change of approach appears essential, one that is able to support the implementation of similar initiatives with the adoption of measures aimed at addressing anti-Roma prejudices both among the general society and the policy-makers. As highlighted by many other recent works on the issue, anti-gypsyism, whose anti-Roma prejudices represent only one aspect, remains the main obstacle to the inclusion of this group and a strategy that really aims to address the inequalities suffered by Roma has to first tackle this issue (Cortés Gomez & End, 2019; Iusmen, 2018; Matache, 2017; McGarry, 2017; Rostas, 2019).

Special projects vs. structural change

Another aspect that emerged both in Pisa and Messina was the reiterated "exceptional" and "special" nature of the projects concerned. In Messina, Caroniti explained that when he proposed the project to the Major, following the decision of the local Court to suspend the eviction, he had to ensure that the project would have represented an "exceptional" and "unique" case. This was due to the fact that implementing inclusion projects towards Roma was considered an unpopular choice that may cause a sudden drop in the approval of the administration. Also in Pisa, at the beginning of the implementation of "Città Sottili", a series of popular protests led the administration to ensure that the initiative would have been limited in time and extent (the number of beneficiaries). This approach, generally, raises a series of issues: on one side, presenting the provision of alternative adequate accommodation to evicted Roma as an "exception" or "special case" prevents their transformation into structural policies, which would be necessary to fully overcome the system of the nomad camps; on the other side, it risks reinforcing the idea that such policies do not represent an obligation but rather an act of "good will". In other words, this narrative dangerously overlooks the fact that these actions are the due consequence of policies that have persistently violated the rights of Romani individuals and hampered their integration.

As happened in both Pisa and Messina, considering the projects as "exceptions" might cause divisions between those who are included in the project and those who remain excluded. The consequence is an inevitable rise of conflicts within the group and the reinforcement of the widespread prejudice that Roma are a "problem to be contained", namely that one single municipality cannot take care of too many Roma. Furthermore, excluding someone inevitably fails the goal of avoiding the creation of new camps.

Another critical aspect of the "special" nature of these projects is the fact that, when they are considered as "acts of good will" rather than "due actions", the policy-makers may deem legitimate to ask for "something more" from the beneficiaries. This was evident from the interview with the municipal officer of Pisa, who, talking about the "code of conduct" applied to the village of Coltano, explained that: "since this is a special initiative (the project), the administration can ask something more from its inhabitants". This "code of conduct" is very common in inclusion projects regarding Roma and it consists in a list of additional rules that Roma have to follow in order to benefit from the project. It conditions the provision of a house, in this case, with the respect of certain rules and/or the engagement to take part in schooling/job training, etc.

As is evident, the application of this "code of conduct" is generally based on the stereotype that Roma do not respect the rules and, for this reason, need further monitoring and disincentives to illegality. It is furthermore based on the idea that the individuals belonging to this group lack the willingness to participate in education and in the job market, and, for this reason, need further incentives to take part in training activities. Another example of this policy practice is the law on micro-areas in Trento. Indeed, the text in Art. 4.4 required that:

> every family, at the moment of the concession, commits to participate at the management of the expenses according to the criteria established by the Province Council. It also commits to participate in projects of educational, schooling and formative support, and of employment integration, including paths towards community service.
>
> (Legge Provinciale nr. 12 del 29/10/2009. Misure per favorire l'integrazione dei gruppi sinti e rom residenti in provincia di Trento, *n.d.*, p. 4.4.)

Finally, as also Tosi Cambini highlights in *Wor(l)ds which Excludes*, the tendency of conditioning the assignment of house/job on participation in training reveals the persistent stereotype that Roma, in order to be included, need to be "educated", since they would be socially and culturally a "deficient" group (Piasere et al., 2014).

In Pisa, the violation of this code has been used to evict one family from the village of Coltano, following a criminal case that particularly caught the attention of the local media. Even before the Court expressed its opinion on the case, the family, with five children, was evicted. Cases like this are evidence of the "special treatment" reserved for Roma, because in no other context, neither for publicly owned housings, would the indictment of one member result in the eviction of the entire family. For this reason, according to Bontempelli this "code of conduct" was one of the most negative aspects of the "Città Sottili" project. Completely different was the opinion expressed by the municipal officer, who declared that the main difficulty in implementing the project was the failure of the Romani beneficiaries to respect the rules.

Finally, because of the "special" status of these projects, where there are shortcomings Roma risk being blamed for not being "willing to integrate" and for being "ungrateful". Indeed, when projects are understood and presented as "acts of good will", rather than "due obligations", beneficiaries are supposed to demonstrate gratefulness and availability to accept any kind of accommodation and to respect the rules imposed. If this does not happen, it may easily be interpreted as a consequence of the incapacity of Roma to cooperate, rather than as a failure of the project to provide solutions that effectively respond to the needs of the beneficiaries. Evidently, the development of projects based on stereotypes that do not fully consider the role of the institutions in maintaining Roma and Sinti in marginal positions results in a vicious circle made of prejudices – special initiatives unable to effectively change the situation – the reinforcement of those prejudices affecting Roma first.

Like in the case of the other issues described above, the implementation of "special projects for Roma" is a clear manifestation of anti-gypsyism, as it is based on the idea that Roma are "different" and need to go through a specific process before being able to be considered as "equal". As already stated, the inclusion of the individuals identified as "Roma" has to go through the deconstruction of all the stereotypes that affect the design and implementation of policies towards this group. With this aim, "special projects" have to become structural policies integrated into the social system, aimed at improving the quality of life of a group of individuals that have been systematically excluded and marginalised by the institutions. This means that these policies should not be limited in time and extent and should not involve "special measures" exclusively for Roma.

Somehow, this is what has been partially done in Trento both with Roma and Sinti. Here, Roma who arrived in the 90s during the wars in the Balkans have not been treated as "nomad", but as regular refugees. Therefore, they have been included within the regular reception system, which allowed them to integrate and become completely independent in a few years. Similarly, the housing issue of Sinti living in the nomad camps was not addressed with special projects, but rather with inclusion in the lists of public housing for those who applied. This approach was leading toward a progressive closure of the remaining nomad camps. Here, nevertheless, the issue of the micro-areas remained unsolved, which, although they were the product of a request of the Sinti community, still presented some potential issues: they were a measure planned exclusively for Roma and Sinti and, according to the provincial law, their concession was conditional on respect for certain special norms.

Diversified solutions for diversified housing needs and the solution of the micro-areas

The transformation of special projects designed exclusively for Roma into structural policies able to facilitate the access to housing solutions that better fit the conditions and needs of each family has to go through a diversification of the alternatives offered in the public and private market. As highlighted many times in this work, the respect of adequacy standards does not necessarily correspond to an improvement of the quality of life and of the level of inclusion. Furthermore, a housing solution that is adequate for some, may be not for others, and this is because of many different possible reasons. As a consequence, it appears necessary to revise the traditional measures adopted to address housing poverty, in order to offer diversified solutions for an increasingly diversified society. This change of approach has probably also to go through a revision of the existing legislation in order to facilitate the access to "non-traditional abodes" and the practice of self-build and self- renovation.

In this book, this issue emerged especially in relation to micro-areas, which are not accessible according to Italian legislation because of the regulations on the use of agricultural lands. As highlighted, the issue did not only emerge in Trento, but also in Pisa and Messina. In Pisa, Minghi, Mennucci and Bontempelli reported that many families explicitly asked for this kind of solution and some adopted it independently. Minghi brought the example of a group of five to six related families that bought a piece of land, constructed there their houses and, according to him, lived very well, keeping excellent care of the space. The problem in their case, as in many others, was the impossibility of legalising the structure, because they built on land meant for agricultural use. They, therefore, considered it desirable to launch a discussion on whether and how to respond to the needs of those living in micro-areas.

A discussion on this topic is also necessary in view of a change of approach towards Roma in general. As mentioned before, one of the main characteristics of the paternalistic approach adopted towards this group is the tendency to treat its members as "children" who cannot decide for themselves and need to be directed towards "the good solution for them" by others. In the housing sector, this approach is usually translated into the forced relocation of Romani families into housing units deemed adequate by the policymaker without consulting the persons concerned. Many of the social workers interviewed in this study agree, as well, on the fact that this approach, other than being incorrect with regard to the individuals concerned, finally results in the failure of the initiative. For this reason, a reflection on the feasibility of the micro-areas is necessary for the sake of those who opt for this solution.

Nevertheless, the creation of micro-areas still attracts a series of criticisms that have to be taken seriously. For instance, Bontempelli, although he considered a debate on the matter necessary, expressed the concern that the institutionalisation of this housing solution may again bind Roma to an inferior kind of accommodation. Furthermore, Berisa feared that micro-areas may become a new form of segregation and, for this reason, completely rejected this solution. These concerns are justified by the fact that nomad camps are the product of policies that were aimed, to some extent, at "meeting the needs of Roma and Sinti". Consequently, the risk that micro-areas become new forms of "nomad camps" is concrete and needs to be seriously considered. According to the law adopted in Trento, these areas did not have to be located in isolated places, but should have been connected with all the necessary public services and should have hosted a maximum of two families. Most of all, the management and control of the area did not have to be under public administration, as for nomad camps, but become the responsibility of the families occupying the area with a regular lease.

This law, though, also presented some issues. First of all, the access to micro-areas remained solely a Roma policy, reinforcing the risk of associating a specific housing solution with a certain group of individuals, with all its consequences. It might have informed the stereotypes that represent Roma as a defined ethno-cultural group different from the rest of the society. Second, it did not facilitate the independent acquisition of a micro-area by the individual or its legalisation, but rather it required the direct intervention of the public authority in order to select the areas and to give their concession to the identified families. It obliged the families who preferred this solution to go through the public administration and the social services. Because of these issues, micro-areas, as conceived in the provincial law of Trento, might have continued to be negatively associated with Roma as a group and with marginality and social problems.

In order to avoid these risks, it seems necessary to devise other mechanisms to facilitate the access to this solution, not only for Roma and not only as a form of "social assistance". With this aim, the adoption of new regulations for the legalisation of this solution looks recommendable, under certain circumstances and in some areas – in order to avoid building speculation. The region Emilia Romagna started moving in this direction with the regional law of 2015 (*Norme per l'Inclusione Sociale di Rom e Sinti*, 2015), and an analysis of its results can surely inform further reflections on this matter. It is important, furthermore, to connect the adoption of these new regulations to a broader process of change in the protection of housing rights. Namely, it is essential to include these regulations within structural policies, in order to make of it a "norm" for everyone and not the "exception" for Roma. After all, the increasing diversification (social, economic and cultural) of present-day societies, together with the increasing levels of housing poverty, call for a revision of the classical means protecting housing rights and providing adequate housing. Therefore, it is in general necessary to rethink those mechanisms that regulate the access to different housing solutions.

A right to home-making? Insights for future reflections

The qualitative work presented in this book aimed to propose a new approach to housing adequacy able to recognise the broad implications of the shelter beyond being a physical repair. By doing so, it highlighted, on the one hand, the universe of factors that intervene in the definition of housing needs and their deeply personal nature, encompassing cultural, social and economic aspects, and, on the other hand, the incapacity of top-down housing policies to recognise and respond to such variety in individual housing demands. The failure to recognise all the factors that direct housing choices and their importance for the well-being and the inclusion of the individual does not only hinder the direct outcomes of the projects, but it may also hinder processes of home-making that are not immediately recognised by the policy-makers. Indeed, home-making is a process that does not exclusively concern the structure of the house, as it involves all those spheres that contribute to achieving a feeling of home: the relationship with the neighbours, the inclusion within the surrounding socio-economic system, the feeling of belonging, etc. For this reason, the transfer of an individual to a new housing unit that better responds to adequacy standards does not forcibly favour home-making if all other aspects are not considered.

In addition, this work has shown how housing rights and policies that do not take into account all factors intervening in the definition of housing needs might reinforce forms of symbolic violence, by identifying as "inadequate" housing choices that do not respond to a certain supposed "norm". Overlooking this risk means, on one side, to propose solutions that do not fit the needs of the individuals concerned and, on the other side, to boost their exclusion from decision-making processes and, consequently, their marginalisation. For this reason, it is necessary to look for a new approach to housing, one able to empower the individual and to increase their autonomy of choice in this sector.

In this regard, the interviews conducted during this study can provide some useful insights. Indeed, not all the interviewees have expressed dissatisfaction with the housing solution provided and this happened especially when the transfer responded to the explicit request of the person concerned. These are the cases of Teresa in Trento and Emma in Pisa. The first received a flat from a local organisation and after a few years became economically independent. This provision was explicitly intended to respond to her desire to abandon the nomadic way of life and the impossibility of her accessing state-owned flats. Emma was also provided with an apartment through an *ad-hoc* initiative aimed at supporting her in the search for a house after she had lived in nomad camps and suffered a series of evictions. In both cases, the beneficiaries were not provided with solutions meant for an entire community. They were instead supported in their search for a house that responded to their individual needs and desires. The success of the two initiatives is not only proved by their satisfaction with the current accommodation, but also by their improved inclusion within the surrounding society.

Indeed, as already highlighted, the feeling of safety and security ensured by a "home" has the potential to boost processes of inclusion, essentially because it pushes the individual to engage with the rest of society in order to take care of the new shelter. This sense of care and responsibility produced by the home was mentioned in the renowned essay of Martin Heidegger, *Building, Dwelling, Thinking* (1971), which inspired numerous other works celebrating "home" and its construction (Bachelard, 1969; Casey, 2001; Relph, 1976; Sack, 1997; Tuan, 2001). These have been later criticised for reproducing an idealised idea of home, based on physical stability and on the division of gender roles, as explained in the first chapter. Nevertheless, as Iris Marion Young also recognised (2005), the reflection of Heidegger can still provide some useful insights, especially for its celebration of the importance of "producing home" and its connection with the other aspects affecting the life of the individual. According to Young, the well-founded criticisms to the argument of Heidegger and his followers should not overshadow the numerous meanings and the importance that "home" has for all.

The qualitative work here presented supports the argument of Young, as it shows the centrality of the construction of a home for the inclusion and well-being of the individual and the importance of the house as a first step in the production of a home. Nevertheless, as Cancellieri also rightly points out (2017), the critical role played by home-making in inclusion processes should not lead to its blind celebration. As he notices, the production of a home – namely of a space where to feel welcome and identify – can reinforce or reproduce the oppression of certain individuals within the same household. An example of this risk can be found in the account of Agnese and Luigi, who engaged in a process of home-making within a micro-area in line with their life-project, but did not fully took into account the impact of their choice on their kids, who may have suffered for living in a shelter that did not offer the same material comforts of an apartment.

This last example shows once more how the construction of a home involves an undefined series of factors and does not culminate in a linear process: home is dynamic, fluid and ambivalent. For this reason, home can be defined as an emotional process through which the person negotiates and manifests their self. In line with these reflections, it seems therefore not possible to identify a series of well-defined characteristics composing "home" and, consequently, to provide an entire group of individuals with housing structures that automatically become a home. Here, the direct engagement of the individual is essential. The examples of Teresa and Emma, among others, support this assumption, as they show how supporting the individual efforts in looking for a home can be more effective than proposing/imposing a "home" to an entire group.

This reflection affects, as well, the definition and protection of housing rights, especially the right to home. Indeed, as analysed in the first chapter, the definition of the meaning and the limits of this right strictly depends on the answer given to the question: what is home? As highlighted here, it is impossible to provide an answer to this question, identifying clear parameters that characterise a home. For this reason, the protection of the right to home by international and European mechanisms is quite poor when individuals expressing an idea of home that does not reflect the "norm" are concerned. Furthermore, the analysis of the protection of this right in comparison with the right to housing has shown how the division of the two rights fails to recognise their complementarity and might produce conflicts between the two. For instance, rigid interpretations of the adequacy parameters may induce the public authorities to intervene with the forced relocations of entire families, overlooking the emotional side of the home. On the other side, the protection of the right to home, considered negative, disregards the conditions that the public authorities have to ensure in order for the individual to enjoy the home.

The jurisprudence of the European Court of Human Rights provides a significant example in this sense. In the case *Chapman v. the United Kingdom,* the Court stated that the violation of the planning regulations was not justified by the lack of halting sites, because "Article 8 does not go so far as to allow individuals' preferences as to their place of residence" (*Chapman vs the United Kingdom*, 2001, par. 81–82). The argument that the right to home does not oblige the State to provide the individual with an "ideal home" has been repeated often and is legitimate in consideration of the impossibility to grasp and satisfy everyone's needs and preferences. Nevertheless, in this case, the Court failed to acknowledge that the lack of halting sites does not concern the provision of a home, but the basic conditions necessary to engage in home-making. Namely, it failed to recognise that the prohibition to camp on public spaces represents an evident interference of the State in the possibility for the concerned individuals to enjoy the home.

It may be argued that the recognition of the complementarity of the two rights is manifested in the requirement of providing adequate housing alternatives to the individuals whose right to home has been violated with a forced eviction. Nevertheless, as the example just mentioned shows, the provision of a shelter that respects a certain list of adequacy standards may not be acceptable to everyone, as it may not reflect their personal idea of the home. The question that rises, consequently, is: how to protect housing rights without denigrating individual choices, but by empowering the person in their process of home-making? I propose here a switch of perspective that brings together the two rights into a new one, aimed at recognising both the negative and positive side of their protection – a right to home-making. The turning point is represented by the replacement of the questions that define and limit the two rights – what is "adequate housing"? and what is home? – with: how to ensure home-making? What are the conditions necessary to allow the individual to engage in home-making?

The first main difference from the previous interpretation is the recognition that the protection of the right to housing cannot neglect the protection of the home, and vice versa. As a consequence, the sole provision of a house respecting adequacy parameters cannot be considered a means to protect home-making, while forced relocations would be considered as violations of the right on a par with forced evictions. At the same time, the intervention of the state is always considered necessary to give access to the material and legal conditions to engage in home-making. In this framework, the lack of halting sites for those living in caravans would be considered as a violation of the right to home-making as it would indubitably represent an obstacle to its realisation. The second main difference between a right to home-making and the right to home/housing is the fact that the first places the individual at the centre of its protection: it is the individual who is engaged in the process of home-making; the state is just supposed to support this process, but not to interfere with their choices – in the limits of the protection of other rights.

In this perspective, the two sides of the right to home-making – the right to housing and the right to home – would not enter into conflict as the first would be considered a necessary condition of the second. Indeed, the home requires a certain level of comfort and safety to be realised and the State should, therefore, allow the individual to have access to those services and resources necessary for its enjoyment. At the same time, the State should allow the access to all those basic conditions necessary for the individual to engage in home-making, without prioritising one specific idea of the home over others. But, with this aim, what are the basic conditions to engage in home-making? Useful insights for answering to this question can be found in the already-mentioned reflection of Iris Marion Young on home, which, as she argues, is today considered a "privilege", while it should be treated as a critical value. In view of a democratisation of home, the author identifies four normative values that should be ensured to everyone: safety; privacy; individuation; and preservation. While the first two are easily identifiable with adequacy standards already largely recognised, the other two normative values refer rather to the emotional side of the home. Individuation refers to the necessity for the individual to have a home that reflects their identity as a material mirror; preservation identifies the act of construction and reconstruction of the self through the sense of care towards the home.

The reflection of Iris Marion Young has the undeniable merit of going beyond an empty idealisation of a home blind to diversity and oppression and of proposing a recognition of the home as a universal and empowering value. Nevertheless, the author does not develop further on the meaning and on the practical implications of the four normative values but opens the way to other analyses. For instance, Catherine Brun uses the four normative values to analyse the housing policies implemented in Georgia for the inclusion of internally displaced persons, highlighting the importance of having a space that ensures a certain level of safety, privacy and personalisation to trigger processes of inclusion. This assumption can be confirmed by the findings of this work and by the results of the interviews, although I would argue that the meaning and implications of the normative value of "individuation" are underestimated by both Brun and Young.

Into the specific, the two authors do not recognise and address the issue that regular housing structures offered in the market may not allow "individuation" for everyone. With this term, indeed, the two authors identify the practice of personalising existing space with objects that mirror the identity of the person, not the possibility of having access to the housing solutions that better fit the personal idea of home. In doing so, the two authors do not fully acknowledge that housing structures are not blank canvases where everyone can freely express themselves but already reflect a certain idea of the home. Neglecting this aspect, as highlighted in this book, represents a form of symbolic violence. It is therefore necessary to recognise the different forms that home can take and to support the individual in their search for a housing structure that better fit their personal idea of the home.

Finally, the development of an approach to housing policies and rights based on the concept of home-making raises a final question, which cannot be answered by this book: what are its limitations in front of other economic and environmental challenges? Indeed, although the identification of the basic conditions necessary for home-making will require further reflections, a discussion in this direction can ground on the findings of this and other works on the creation of home: these conditions can be identified in the provision of the minimum resources, services and legal means that allow each individual to engage in their own home-making process; they require an analysis of the obstacles hindering this process in view of adapting the legislative framework according to the changing and emerging housing needs. On the other hand, how these conditions interact with and impact the available economic and environmental resources represents probably the main challenge for future academic reflections on the topic. While an approach to housing rights based on home-making can favour processes of legalisation, self-build and self-renovation which would improve the access to home-making to those groups living in conditions of housing insecurity, the lack of economic resources, together with pressing environmental issues such as land consumption, cannot be easily solved and appear critical to ensuring equal access to this right. Nevertheless, the answer to these questions and the aim to build an inclusive and just society cannot overlook the importance of ensuring to everyone the right to create and enjoy a home.

References

Bachelard, G. (1969). *The Poetics of Space*. Boston: Beacon Press.

Blunt, A., & Dowling, R. (2006). *Home*. Abingdon: Routledge.

Boccagni, P., & Brighenti, A. M. (2017). Immigrants and home in the making: Thresholds of domesticity, commonality and publicness. *Journal of Housing and the Built Environment, 32(1)*, 1–11. https://doi.org/10.1007/s10901-015–9487-9.

Bontempelli, S. (2006). Vite di Scarto. Marginalita' abitativa degli stranieri a Pisa. *La Nuova Città, 11*.

Brun, C. (2015). Home as a critical value: From shelter to home in Georgia. *Refuge, 31(1)*, 43–54.

Brun, C., & Fábos, A. (2015). Making homes in limbo? A conceptual framework. *Refuge, 31(1)*, 5–17.

Cancellieri, A. (2017). Towards a progressive home-making: The ambivalence of migrants' experience in a multicultural condominium. *Journal of Housing and the Built Environment, 32(1)*, 49–61. https://doi.org/10.1007/s10901-015–9489-7.

Casey, E. (2001). Body, self and landscape. In P. C. Adams, S. Hoelscher, & K. E. Till, eds, *Texture of Places. Exploring Humanist Geographies* (pp. 403–425). Minneapolis: Minnesota University Press.

Cortés Gomez, I., & End, M. (2019). *Dimensions of Antigypsyism in Europe*. Brussels: European Network Against Racism and Central Council of German Sinti and Roma 2019.

Decreto del Presidente della Provincia 12 dicembre 2011, n. 17–75/Leg. Regolamento in materia di edilizia abitativa pubblica (legge provinciale 7 novembre 2005, n. 15 "Disposizioni in materia di politica provinciale della casa e modificazioni della legge, (2011) (Provincia Autonoma di Trento).

European Court of Human Rights (2001). *Chapman vs the United Kingdom. 27238/95.*

Heidegger, M. (1971). Building, dwelling, thinking. In *Poetry, Language, Thought*. New York: Harper & Row.

Iusmen, I. (2018). "Non multa, sed multum": EU Roma policy and the challenges of Roma inclusion. *Journal of European Integration, 6337*, 1–15. https://doi.org/10.1080/07036337.2018.1462803.

Legge Provinciale nr. 12 del 29/10/2009. Misure per favorire l'integrazione dei gruppi sinti e rom residenti in provincia di Trento (Provincia Autonoma di Trento).

Marushiakova, E., & Popov, V. (2015). European policies for social inclusion of Roma: Catch 22? *Social Inclusion, 3(5)*, 2183–2803. https://doi.org/10.17645/si.v3i5.241.

Massey, D. ed. (1995). *A Place in the World: Places, Cultures and Globalisation*. Oxford: Oxford University Press.

Matache, M. (2017). Biased elites, unfit policies: Reflections on the lacunae of Roma integration strategies. *European Review, 25(4)*, 588–607.

McGarry, A. (2017). *Romaphobia. The Last Acceptable Form of Racism*. London: Zed Books.

Piasere, L., Solimano, N., & Tosi Cambini, S. eds (2014). *Wor(l)ds which Exclude. The Housing Issue of Roma, Gypsies and Travellers in the Language of the Acts and the Administrative Documents in Europe*. Fiesole: Fondazione Michelucci Press.

Norme per l'Inclusione Sociale di Rom e Sinti, n. Legge Regionale n. 15 (2015) (Regione Emilia-Romagna).

Relph, E. (1976). *Place and Placelessness*. London: Pion Limited.

Richardson, J. (2019). *Place and Identity. The Performance of Home*. Abingdon: Routledge. https://doi.org/10.4324/9781315816852.

Rostas, I. (2019). *A Task for Sisyphus. Why Europe's Roma Policies Fail*. Budapest: CEU Press.

Sack, R. D. (1997). *Homo Geographicus*. The Johns Hopkins University Press.

Sigona, N. (2002). *Figli del ghetto. Gli italiani, i campi nomadi e l'invenzione degli zingari*. Civezzano: Nonluoghi Libere Edizioni.

Tuan, Y.-F. (2001). Cosmos versus hearth. In P. C. Adams, S. Hoelscher, & K. E. Till, eds, *Texture of Places. Exploring Humanist Geographies* (pp. 319–325). Minneapolis: Minnesota University Press.

Vajda, V. (2015). Towards "critical whiteness" in Romani studies. *Roma Rights, 2* (Special Issue: Nothing About Us Without Us? Roma Participation in Policy Making and Knowledge Production).

Young, I. M. (2005). House and home: Feminist variations on a theme. In *On Female Body Experience: "Throwing like a Girl" and Other Essays* (pp. 123–154). Oxford University Press. https://doi.org/10.1093/0195161920.003.0008.

Index

For Product Safety Concerns and Information please contact our EU representative GPSR@taylorandfrancis.com
Taylor & Francis Verlag GmbH, Kaufingerstraße 24, 80331 München, Germany

www.ingramcontent.com/pod-product-compliance
Lightning Source LLC
LaVergne TN
LVHW021036011026
849160LV00009BA/671
9781032026718